W9-BAS-269

DATE DUE

Date Loaned

J

WITHDRAWN
NDSU

THE LANGUAGES OF THE WORLD

ANCIENT AND MODERN

THE LANGUAGES OF THE WORLD

ANCIENT AND MODERN

The Alphabets, Ideographs, and Other Written Characters of the Languages of the World, in Sound and Symbol

By

Stanley Wemyss

PHILADELPHIA
STANLEY WEMYSS
1950

93934

Copyright, 1950
by
Stanley Wemyss

FIRST PRINTING
May, 1950

P
213
W4

Lithographed in U.S.A. by
Philadelphia Colortype Corporation

411
W47l

To
RUTH LOMAZOVA

PREFACE

Wonderful and curious to the eye are the symbols and letters with which men record their thoughts; strange to our ears are the sounds of tongues of other lands—the glottal stops, the tones, the explosives, the clicks of the Hottentots. The tongues and dialects of the world are many and the characters in which they are written are diverse. It has been estimated that more than 700 languages are spoken by natives of Africa alone. The tongues of the South Pacific language groups might account for another several hundred tongues, and perhaps many more. The Indian post office lists 177 languages and dialects, etc., spoken in all-India. The American Bible Society's publication *The Book of a Thousand Tongues* (1938) exhibits specimens of 1,018 languages and dialects in which the Holy Scriptures, in whole or in part, have been published. According to estimates made by officers of the French Academy, more than 2,800 languages and dialects are spoken in the world today.

There is abundant literature in English, German and other languages on the subject of alphabets and the history of written characters, so that it would seem that another publication on these subjects is not an imperative need. In some respects this is true, but not entirely so. There has been no attempt here to add anything to the work of Canon Isaac Taylor, whose *The Alphabet* (1883) was long considered the best work in the English language on the letters, but now a bit antiquated because of new discoveries of hitherto unknown and undeciphered scripts; however, much of this slack has been taken up by Hans Jensen in *Die Schrift in Vergangenheit und Gegenwart*, and David Diringer in *The Alphabet: A Key to the History of Mankind* (1947).

Study of the alphabet is not the chief purpose of this volume—only insofar as knowledge of these letters is necessary for our needs—namely, identification of the chief languages of the world, their relations one to another, together with native characters in which they are written, so that these tongues may be transliterated into sounds intelligible to English readers. This volume exhibits about 300 alphabets, syllabaries, ideographs and other characters commonly employed in writing most of the languages of the world, ancient and modern. References are made to the languages and dialects which make use of these characters, and this amounts to about 1,000 languages in all.

The book is divided into two sections, each section differing somewhat from the other in treatment. Part I relates to the languages of Europe, chiefly those tongues usually written in the Roman alphabet, several

Slavonic tongues written in Cyrillic letters, German written in *fraktur*, and Greek. In Part I the languages of Europe are transliterated into two alphabets, etc.: 1. Sounds as used in simple English words—*dog, cat, hat.* 1. The *R.G.S.* (Royal Geographical Society) *II System* (intended for British official use). This may seem like redundancy, but in practice that is not entirely true. Each system has useful features not always shared by the other. The first has simplicity; the second has uniformity—a single phonetic alphabet applicable to all of the languages of Europe. Sounds as shown by simple words are pronounced as they are spoken in the United States; *R.G.S. II* sounds are those pronounced in the British Isles.

Part II relates to non-European languages, most of which are written in their own alphabets or syllabaries. Here the phonetic systems employed are the *Standard Alphabet* (modified) of Lepsius and others. But in this as in all phonetic alphabets, a word of caution must be inserted: Sounds given are only approximately correct. It is not possible to convey true sounds of many languages in writing. The study of language presents difficulties. The vocal organs of Bobangi- and Swahili-speaking peoples are by practice caused to function differently than those of English speaking persons. Peculiar vowel sounds are assigned to certain consonants in Sanskrit and other languages of India; and the guttural sounds in Arabic must be heard to be properly understood. In Chinese, tones are of greatest importance, since a wrong tone imparted to a monosyllable might alter the meaning of the expression entirely.

Genealogical order of classification of languages has been adopted. Each tongue is briefly described and presented with the character or alphabet in which it is usually written, together with reference to dialects, if any. An index of the native characters in which most of the languages of the world are written, a list of variant names of languages and dialects, and an alphabetical index of languages are provided, so that any language, any alphabet, may be turned to immediately. An additional feature is the list of 500 tongues commonly written in the Roman characters, which is by no means all inclusive.

An outline sketch of the origin and evolution of the Roman alphabet predicated upon the Phoenician origin theory and notes on the history of the Arabic numerals are included. The literature on these subjects is extensive, and persons seeking more information may resort to more definitive sources.

In a volume of this sort there was much that could not be included. Considering economy and the average reader's limited interest, extensive lists of ligatures sometimes employed in writing Asiatic languages are not generally shown. Eastern languages like Thai (Siamese) are often characterized by a great deal of complexity (native grammars sometimes devote ten to fifteen pages to the "alphabet" alone); care is taken to show coalescent consonants with added vowels in every conceivable combination; yet, for the average person's need, knowledge of only the consonants, vowel points and diacritics are needed in order to form many of these necessary combinations. Much the same might be said of Burmese, Tamil and Malayalam, to mention only a few.

The list of Chinese radical characters ought never be considered an "alphabet." Chinese dictionaries sometimes exhibit as many as 1,000 characters whose functions are phonetic alone, yet in this regard there are about as many exceptions as there are rules. So too, extensive lists of characters or at least the so-called 300 basic elements must be shown in addition to the radicals, else the study of the cursive scripts is very difficult. The radicals in Chinese, as in Japanese, are used to determine in a very general way a character's class and are an "alphabetical" aid for listing the characters in native dictionaries. Aside from various styles of *kana*, a Japanese alphabet would probably consist of about 1,000 Chinese characters arranged under about 300 sounds.

Some obsolete or long forgotten scripts of no great historical interest or practical importance have not been included since employed by relatively few people with no appreciable literature; however, reference is made to many of these tongues or characters in the text. Scripts such as Bukvitsa (an adaptation of Glagolitic and Cyrillic), Elbasan, Buthakükye, Argyrokastron or Veso Bei's script (old Albanian alphabets), Pamphylian and Lydian (Asianic languages), Tagbanua, Mangyan, Iloco, Pangasinan, Pampangan and Buhil (Philippine Islands), Passipa and Uighur of Mongolia, the latter a transitional alphabet derived from Nestorian, Sogdian (Eastern Turkestan) and Balti (Tibet) have not been included. Several native African scripts are mentioned in the section on the languages of Africa, but are not discussed at length—Vai, Mende, Bamum, Nsibidi, since none of them are of great importance to the average reader.

The objective set out for when this project was first entertained several years ago seemed to become increasingly more difficult to attain as the work progressed. The subject embraced is vast and access had to be had to a great number of books on letters and language. Sources and authorities are sometimes in disagreement one with another. In many tongues like Tibetan and Mongolian, to which the author had brought little or nothing in the way of previous knowledge for guidance, he has had to accept a great deal in faith. Acknowledgment is made for many references and sources, a partial list of which follows. Thanks are due to Miss Ruth Lomazova, who made all the drawings which appear in this book. The author also wishes to acknowledge his indebtedness to the following persons for their criticism, advice and aid:

Patrick Darcy (Celtic, Romance and other languages), several members of the University of Pennsylvania faculty and of the University Museum, for indicating errors in several archaic languages, the Free Library of Philadelphia for numerous excellent reference books on language, correspondents who have offered suggestions and criticism, and to numerous native speakers who have read some of these proofs.

Further acknowledgments are given to Milton F. Wells and the staff of the Philadelphia Colortype Corporation for composition of this book with its thousands of foreign characters and diacritical marks—a difficult project indeed.

Language specimens are from: John 3:16; Genesis 1:1-5; Matthew 6:9-13; etc. A number of types were taken from native publications and old German textbooks on language. Diacritical marks have been inserted by hand since many were unobtainable otherwise. Often, assertions as to the origins of letters of certain ancient languages are predicated upon commonly accepted theory of the origins of these letters. Some ancient tongues remain undeciphered and phonetic values shown are conjectural values only.

For errors of omission or of commission the reader's indulgence is asked. Always, attempt has been made to correct these as they appeared, but perhaps some may have escaped notice. And so to conclude with an excerpt from *Colloques ou Dialogues avec un Dictionaire en Six Langues* (Antwerp, 1576), ". . . .Belouyde reder receaue this boke gladly, trough the wyche, in case you rede it wythe onderstandinge and diligence, you shall fynde that it shall not only be profytable for you, but also verry nedefull."

S. W.

Philadelphia, August 1, 1949

REFERENCES

Faulmann, Karl: *Das Buch der Schrift Enthaltend die Schriftzeichen und Alphabete Aller Zeiten und Aller Volker des Erdkreises*, Vienna, 1880; Astle, T.: *The Origin and Progress of Writing*, London, 1876; Frey, E.: *Pantagraphia*, London, 1799; Sayce, A. H.: *Introduction to the Science of Languages*, London, 1880; Birt, T.: *Das Antike Buchwesen*, Berlin, 1882; Skinner, F. N.: *Story of the Letters and Figures*, Chicago, 1906; Strange, E. F.: *Alphabets*, London, 1907; Mason, W. A.: *A History of the Art of Writing*, N. Y., 1920; Meillet, A., and Cohen, M.: *Les Langues du Monde*, Paris, 1923; Bodmer, F.: *The Loom of Language*, London, 1943; Moorhouse, A. C.: *Writing and the Alphabet*, London, 1946; Von Ostermann, G. F., and Giegengack, A. E.: *Foreign Languages, etc.*, Washington, 1935; Diringer, David: *The Alphabet, A Key to the History of Mankind*, New York, 1947.

Wutke: *Geschichte der Schrift;* John C. C. Clark: *The Origin and Varieties of the Semitic Alphabet*, Chicago, 1884; Faulmann: *Illustrirte Geschichte der Schrift*, Vienna, 1880; Jensen, Hans: *Die Schrift in Vergangenheit und Gegenwart*, Hamburg, 1935; Clodd: *The Alphabet;* Hilprecht, H. V.: *Old Babylonian Inscriptions*, 1890; Hopkins, L. C.: *The Six Scripts*, 1881; Premare, P.: *Notitia Linguae Sinicae;* Buhler: *Indische Palaeographie*, 1920; Taylor, Isaac: *The Alphabet*, London, 1883; Morley, S.: *A Primer of Maya Hieroglyphs;* Callery: *Systema Phoneticum Scripturae Sinicae*, 1841; Chalfent: *Early Chinese Writing*, 1906; Ball, J. C.: *Chinese and Sumerian*, Oxford, 1913.

Lange: *Einfuhring in die Japanische Schrift*, Stuttgart, 1896; Chamberlain: *An Introduction to the Japanese Written Language;* Pilling: *Bibliography of the Algonquin Languages;* Lenormant: *Essai sur la Propogation de l'Alphabet Phenicien;* Sethe: *Der Ursprung des Alphabets*, 1916; Sprengling, M.: *The Alphabet, etc., from the Sinai Inscriptions*, Chicago, 1921; Lidzbarski: *Handbuch der Nordsemit*, 1856; Littmann, E.: *Syriac Inscriptions*, 1934; Major-General Lord Edward Gleichen and John Reynolds: *Foreign Languages Transcribed into English* (R.G.S.H.), London, 1921; U. S. Government Printing Office *Style Manual*, Washington, 1945; Moritz: *Arabic Palaeography*, Cairo, 1905; Berger: *Histoire de l'Ecriture dans l'Antiquite*, 1891; Hess, J. J.: *Die Entzifferung der Thamudischen Inschriften*, Paris, 1911; Grimme, H.: *Die Sudsemitische Buch Schrift*, 1930; Evans: *Scriptoa Minoa;* Steinhal: *Die Entwicklung der Schrift*, 1832; *Kanyó Sōsho Jiten; Penji Tsukejo Jiten.*

Danzel: *Die Anfange der Schrift*, Leipsic, 1920; Erman: *Die Hiero-*

glyphen, 1912; Spiegelberg, W.: *Demotische Grammatik*, 1925; Moller, G.: *Die Buchschrift der Alten Aegypter*, 1919; Sundwall: *Die Kretische Linear-schrift*, 1915; Migeord: *The Languages of West Africa*, 1913; Shamasastry: *The Origin of the Devanagari Alphabet*, 1906; Pelliot: *Les Systemes d'Ecriture en Usage chez les Anciens Mongols*, 1925; Thompson, E. M.: *Handbook of Greek and Latin Palaeography*, London, 1906; Ceitler: *Die Albanesischen und Slavischen Schriften*, Vienna, 1883; Diehl, E.: *Inscriptiones Latinae*, 1912; Luft, W.: *Studien zu den Altesten Germanischen Alphabeten*, 1898; North, Eric M.: *The Book of a Thousand Tongues*, New York, 1938; Lepsius, C. R.: *The Standard Alphabet*, London, 1863; Sylvestre: *Paleographie Universelle*; Humphreys, H. M.: *A History of the Art of Printing*, London, 1868; Rose-Innes, Arthur: *Beginner's Dictionary of Chinese-Japanese Characters*, Tokyo, 1927; Lyall, A.: *A Guide to the Languages of Europe*, London, 1940; Johnson, J.: *Typographia*, London, 1824.

ERRATA

Page 9, line 31–R.G.S. II.
Page 20, line 14–Cypriote, line 19–century.
Page 42 (German) 3rd line from bottom–ÄU (not AU).
Page 43 (Danish) line 1–*Himmelen*, last line page 44–ÖI-ÖÜ.
Page 50 (Irish) "Phonetic Equivalents," lines 1-17. These are anglicized letters without reference to Irish orthography. For sounds based upon Irish spelling see "Sounds in Irish" (p. 51).
Page 53 (Welsh)–*tragwyddol.*
Page 59 (Latin) line 11–U vowel.
Page 61 (Italian) line 2–*sopra.*
Page 62 (Spanish) line 26–CH (not C,H)...as in English. C before E, I-TH.
Page 63 (Portuguese) line 5–*luz e as trevas.* Page 64, line 6–the vowel has an I or U sound combined with it. Line 7–ÃE, ÃO, ÕE, OU. Line 20–when final O-OO. Ã–ÃE.
Page 66 (French) -E, or neutral E in *je.* Â–long A, OIN–more nearly WA-ng.
Page 67 (Walloon) line 9–or
Page 87 (Russian) line 5– Д –D as shown elsewhere.
Page 91 (Croatian) line 18 ǵ–dž.
Page 92 (Czech)–*ņezahynul.* Line 4–A.
Page 93 (Polish) Ź–hard Z: Ż–ZH.
Page 94 (Slovak) line 11 Ť–Ť.
Page 95 (Wend) line 2–Sorbian.
Page 96 (Basque)–*maite.*
Page 112 (Egyptian)–was retained, not was known. Line 7–Herodotus (5th century B.C.).
Page 120 (Hausa) line 25–Y not used as a vowel.
Page 122 (Yoruba) line 12–E-*let.*
Page 133 (Ladino) *Thav*–T (Palestine), elsewhere–S.
Page 163 (Kashmiri)–India.
Page 166 (Tamil) line 16 is correct. No letter is omitted in blank space.
Page 176 (Chinese) 攴 –a man with a flail.
Page 198 (Japanese) line 12 N–NG, NK (medial) before G, K. Page 200–E and YE are reversed. See page 195 for correct order.
Page 205 (Malay)–*Wasl* serves as a bridge between consecutive letters.
Page 208–Guadalcanar, also Guadalcanal.
Page 210 (Maori)–*te tangata.*
Page 213, line 13–Greenland.
Page 220 (Cree)–Swampy, Moose.

MODERN LITHUANIAN (John 3:16)

16. Taipo Dievas mylėjo svietą,
kad savo viengimusįjį sunų davė,
jeib visi į jį tikintieji ne prapultų,
bet amžinąją gyvatą turėtų.

CONTENTS

PART I
THE LANGUAGES OF EUROPE

PART II
NON-EUROPEAN LANGUAGES

PART I

THE ROMAN ALPHABET, ARABIC NUMERALS, PHONETIC TABLES, THE LANGUAGES OF EUROPE

THE ROMAN ALPHABET

Max Müller, an English philologist and Orientalist of German birth (1823-1900), estimated that 24 letters formed in every possible combination might produce every word used in every language of the world, and 24 letters formed in every possible combination might produce 620,448,401,733,239,439,360,000 words.

The Roman alphabet, employed in most of the modern languages of Europe, is used by many millions of people; moreover, the Roman letters have been adopted for the writing of hundreds of primitive languages with no characters of their own. Further, the Roman letters are, more or less, used or understood by millions of people in addition to their own alphabets and other native characters.

The Roman alphabet is derived through Greek from the Phoenician alphabet, the parent of most of the alphabets of the western world. The word alphabet is from two Greek words, *alpha* and *beta*, the names of the first two letters in the Greek alphabet. These were called *alef* and *beth* in Phoenician and Hebrew, and were written A and B by the Romans. The Phoenician letters (22) were probably borrowed in part from the peoples in the region of the eastern Mediterranean, northern Arabia or Egypt. Some of the Phoenician letters show close resemblance to characters in the Sinaitic inscriptions, and a few characters show some evidence of Egyptian origin.

The Phoenicians were the earliest people of antiquity to possess a true alphabet, with characters or letters denoting sounds instead of ideographs and pictographs. About 1500 B.C. Sidon and Tyre, two great Phoenician cities, were centers of what was then a world wide maritime trade. Phoenician traders, with their celebrated Tyrolean purple and glass, visited the British Isles as early as the first millennium B.C. Their navigators had sailed around the continent of Africa and early Phoenician colonies were established at Carthage (870 B.C.), Utica, and Gadez or Cadiz in Spain, which latter city is believed to be the oldest city in western Europe.

In this chapter on the origin and evolution of the Roman alphabet Phoenician sources alone are noted. This is not the time and place for discussion of Rawlinson's doubts that the Phoenician characters may or may not be modifications of Egyptian, Hittite or Cypriote. Arthur J. Evans has cited a number of instances where it is believed the Cretan syllabary was derived from the Egyptian. He further states the Cretan contention of

THE EVOLUTION OF THE ROMAN ALPHABET

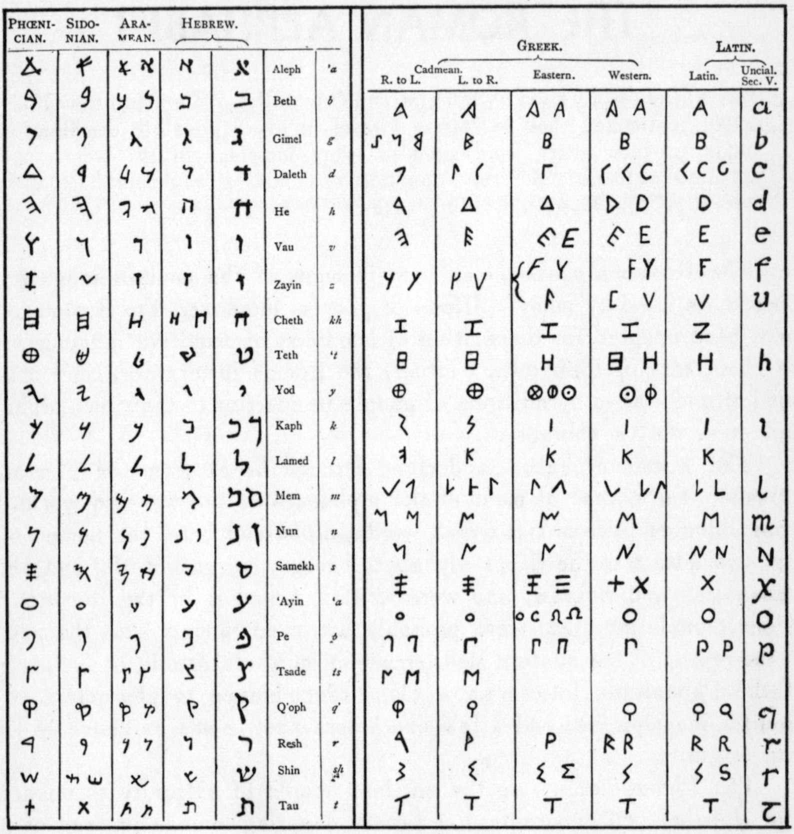

Hebrew	Name	Value
א	Aleph	'a
ב	Beth	b
ג	Gimel	g
ד	Daleth	d
ה	He	h
ו	Vau	v
ז	Zayin	z
ח	Cheth	kh
ט	Teth	't
י	Yod	y
כ ך	Kaph	k
ל	Lamed	l
מ ם	Mem	m
נ ן	Nun	n
ס	Samekh	s
ע	'Ayin	'a
פ	Pe	p
צ	Tsade	ts
ק	Q'oph	q'
ר	Resh	r
ש	Shin	sh
ת	Tau	t

Greek: Cadmean R. to L.	Greek: Cadmean L. to R.	Greek: Eastern	Greek: Western	Latin: Latin	Latin: Uncial Sec. V.
A	A	A A	A A	A	a
	B	B	B	B	b
Γ	Γ	Γ	C C	C G	c
Δ	Δ	Δ	D D	D	d
E	E	E E	E E	E	e
Y Y	Y V	F Y	F Y	F	f
		F	C V	V	u
I	I	I	I	Z	
B	B	H	B H	H	h
⊕	⊕	⊗ ⊕ ⊙	⊙ Φ		
		I	I	I	ı
	K	K	K	K	
Λ	Λ	Λ Λ	V Λ	L L	l
M M	M	M	M	M	m
N	N	N	N	N N	N
≡	≡	Ξ ≡	+ X	X	x
o	o	o C Ω Ω	O	O	o
Π Π	Γ	Π Π	Γ	P P	p
M M	M				
Φ	Ϙ		Ϙ	Q Q	q
P	P	P	R R	R R	r
Σ	Σ	Σ Σ	S	S S	s
T	T	T	T	T	t

ROMAN CURSIVE

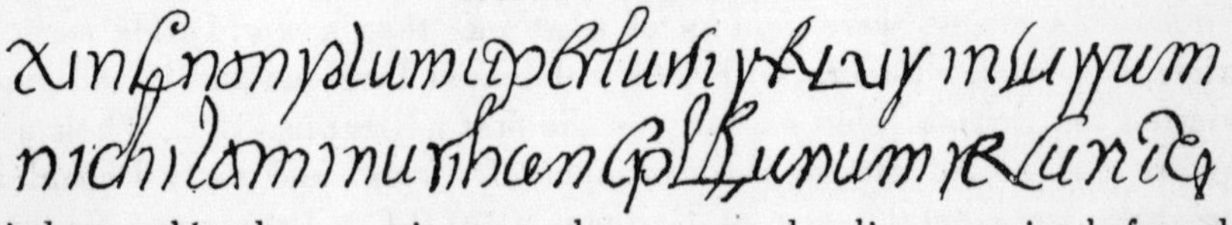

Diodorus, that these ancient people possessed a linear script before the introduction of the Phoenician, that the Phoenicians had not invented the written characters, but had simply altered them for their own purposes.

The ancient Phoenician language, like other Semitic languages, was written from right to left. The first letter A or *alef* of the Phoenician alphabet was an ox head ( ) evidently borrowed from ( ) in the Sinaitic inscriptions. The letter *alef* was usually tilted in early Phoenician writing, but in course of time *alef* was turned upside down ( ) to become the Greek *alpha*. B-*beth* ( ), a house. In Egyptian hieroglyphics, house was written ( ) which closely resembled hieratic and the same character in the Sinaitic inscriptions. C is of Roman origin. It is a form of the Greek *gamma* or the Phoenician *gimel* (7–>). D-*daleth* (Δ), a door. This letter became the Greek *delta*. The Roman D is the Greek *delta* with rounded edges. G-*gimel* (7), a camel. *Gimel* became the Greek *gamma*. E-heh ( ), a window, became Greek *epsilon*. Because of the late Greek practice of writing from left to right, the letter attained a position opposite that which it held when written from right to left.

F or V-*vav* ( ), a hook or nail. The Roman letter F resembles the obsolete Greek *digamma* ( ) inverted. F was written ( ) in Teutonic Runes. H-*cheth* ( ), a fence. In Phoenician, as in Greek, the E vowel might be either aspirated or unaspirated. The E vowel was written (✱) in Minoan characters. T-*teth* (⊕), a basket or bale. This letter with the power of TH became the Greek (Θ) *theta*. Z-*zayin* ( ), a dagger. This letter was the Greek *zeta*. I (J), (Y)-*yod* ( ), a hand with thumb pointed forward. In the Roman alphabet I had in addition to its vowel value, the consonantal power of Y as initial; Y was later supplanted by the improvised J consonant.

K-*kaph* ( ), the palm of the hand. This letter was stood on end to form the *kappa* of the Greeks and the Letter K of the Romans. L-*lamedh* ( ), a whip. *Lamedh* was the ancestor of the Greek *lambda* (Λ) and the Roman L. M-*mem* ( ), water. This letter is similar in most early Semitic languages. The word water was written ( ) in Egyptian hieroglyphics. N-*nun* ( ), the eye or head of a fish.

O-*ayin* (O), the eye. This letter is similar in the Sinaitic inscriptions. P-*pi* (7), the lips or portion of the mouth. TS-*tsadi* ( ), a scythe—Arabic (ص) *tsad*, Greek (Ψ) *psi* but with sound of PS. Q-*koph* (φ), the head. The letter Q was invented by the Romans. R-*resh* ( ), the back of the head. S-*sin* or *shin* (W), the teeth or a branch—Arabic (س) *sin*. The Phoenician *sin* or *shin* was stood on end to form the Greek (Σ) *sigma*. In Roman usage the letter was turned around, the lower line was dropped and the corners were rounded (Σ-Ʒ) to form the Roman S.

T-*tau* (+), a cross or a mark. This letter is similar in a number of early Semitic languages. X or hard S-*samech* ( ), a foundation.

According to early Greek legend, Cadmus of Thebes brought 15 of the Phoenician letters to Greece about 1493 B. C. The letters were:

ΑΒΓΔΙΚΛΜΝΟΠΡΣΤΥ

About 1125 B.C. Palamedes of Argos invented the double characters Θ, Χ, Φ, Ξ, and Simonides added Ζ, Ψ, Η, Ω, about 500 B.C. The letter E was added perhaps about the same time. This alphabet of the Greeks was in use until about 400 B.C., at the time of the introduction of the Ionic alphabet of 24 letters into Greece. As early as the first Olympiad (776 B.C.) the Greeks had begun to write from left to right, which accounts for the "backwards" appearance of many letters taken from the Phoenician alphabet. Hitherto the Greeks wrote sometimes from right to left, or in lines alternatively right to left and left to right in *boustropheidon* because such writing resembled the course taken by oxen plowing a field. Then only capital letters were used. The small Greek letters were invented long after the decline of ancient Greece. The Greeks, however, had much earlier added vowels to their alphabet which were probably borrowed from the Minoan or Cretan or Mycenaean and Cyprote characters used many centuries before.

The earliest Italic letters, like those of the archaic Greek period, were sometimes written from right to left. In the Italian peninsula several alphabets, all derived from the Greek alphabet, were developed about or before the seventh or eighth millennium B.C. Among the early Italic scripts might be mentioned: Etruscan, Faliscan, Oscan, Umbrian and Latin or Roman which later became the adopted character of most of the alphabets used in western Europe today. The Romans borrowed 18 letters from the Greeks and added several letters of their own.

EARLY ROMAN ALPHABET

A B C D E F H I K L M N O P Q R S T V (X Y Z)

Note: The Latin alphabet, which is derived from the Greek, is essentially identical with its Hellenic ancestor. Seven letters, C, D, L, P, R, S, X, differ in form; three letters, C, H, V, differ in values; F-from *digamma*, and Q-from *koppa*—letters which had become obsolete in Greek—were retained in the Latin alphabet.

In ancient Rome the letter C was first used for both C and K. Later, a bar was added to C, converting the letter to G. The Romans had Q, which was not used by the Greeks. The letter R was formed by adding a stroke to the Greek letter (P). The letter H retained its consonantal value. The letter J was not used in early Rome. This letter was a later form of I, used both as vowel and consonant. K was rarely used by the Romans, but the power of K was usually written by C. The letters Y and Z, although used in early Latin writings, had become obsolete but were reintroduced into the Roman alphabet at a later period.

Roman scripts were sometimes written with serifs or finishing strokes, and this contributed to the development of minuscule letters which differed in form from the early capital letters or majuscules. The cursive Rustic, a slightly compressed character employed in common texts, was adapted from prevailing majuscule letters and cursive majuscules. The round Uncials and semi-uncials are of later date.

Some common scripts developed during the Middle Ages were: 1. Insular of Ireland and the British Isles. Uncials, half-uncials and pointed letters. 2. Visigothic or *Littera Toletana* of Spain. 3. North Italian, Beneventan scripts (10th century). 4. Merovingian of France, a cursive style. 5. Carolingian, a script partly uncial and partly cursive. 6. Gothic, adapted from Carolingian i. *Textura*, the formal script, usually employed in writing Latin. ii. *Bastarda*, a mixed script of the vernaculars. iii. *Rotunda* of Italy, a round script. The early English printers—Caxton, Wynkyn de Worde and Pynson—employed *black letter* types, derived from *textura* and *bastarda*. 7. Humanistic hand of the Italian Renaissance, a simplified script under Carolingian influence. 8. Italic of Aldus Manutius (c. 1501).

LATIN MS: 15th-16th Centuries

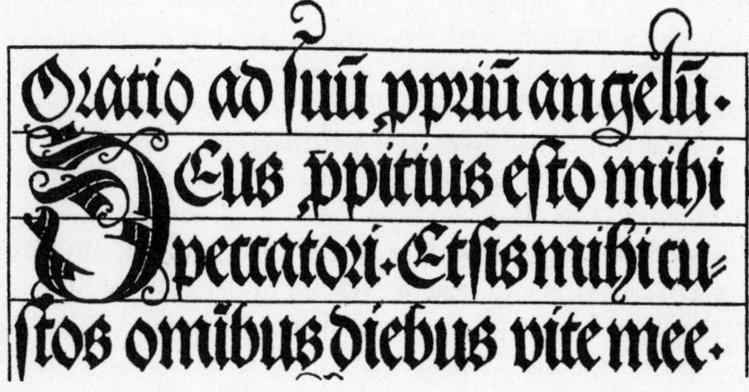

Oratio ad suũ ppriũ angelũ·
Deus ppitius esto mihi
peccatori·Etsis mihi cu=
stos omibus diebus vite mee·

THE ARABIC NUMERALS

Since earliest recorded time man has made use of some system of counting, else he would not have been able to distinguish one from two. To primitive man one definitely meant one, but two or more might mean more or many. Larger sums like forty or fifty, therefore, might mean as we might describe it—infinity. Perhaps the earliest, most commonly used medium employed by man for counting were his natural digits, namely—his fingers or toes. Aristotle in *Problemata* asserted that since man has always these natural counters or tallies, it seems natural that he should employ them in counting all things. However adequate for his needs this method seemed, it had but temporary value; and once the count had been made, the record was lost save that which might have been retained in memory.

The next step in computation was taken when man began to keep his recordings of number, whether the medium by which this was done was the accumulation of tally sticks or piles of pebbles. In early Madagascar heaps of pebbles were employed to indicate the number of men in an army. When each soldier passed a given spot a pebble was dropped and the accumulated pile of pebbles was then counted; thus, a more or less primitive system of permanent recording of number was supplied. The Peruvian Indians made use of the *quipu*—a system of knotted strings of various colors which resembled the ancient *chieh-sheng* or notched strings of the ancient Chinese. Both of these primitive systems were adequate within prescribed limitations of function.

But the number concept, or the comprehension of more than a few numbers of early man like our own powers of visual apperception, is limited. In tallies and game scores, etc., we write I, II, III, IIII, respectively, for 1, 2, 3, 4, but we employ ~~IIII~~ for 5, because additional strokes or lines might appear to us, at first sight, confusing. This, then, is a quinary (5 base) system of groupings. Imagine our tedious task in consulting our records, if we were required to recount each line or bar one by one. This, then, will indicate the necessity for what we are pleased to style a system of limitations or groupings in numeration.

As suggested before, Aristotle stated that the system most widely used in counting is the decimal system (10 base) for the reason that man has but ten fingers and/or ten toes, whence it comes that we count in unit groupings of tens and multiples of tens instead of twos or threes, sixes or sevens. As far as concerns our daily traffic in mathematics and commerce, etc., this, the decimal system, seems quite satisfactory—in fact the only system of numeration. But however prevalent is the use of the decimal system among the nations of the world today, it is but one of many.

The Mayas of Yucatan and Central America used the vigesimal (20 base) system for counting, perhaps for the same reasons as stated above; but with additional considerations, man had had in all twenty tallies, that is—ten fingers and ten toes. Higher orders of numbers used by the Maya were: 20 x 20, and 20 x 20 x 20. The early Babylonians employed the sexagesimal system of numbers. In the Babylonian sexagesimal count, perhaps the earliest known principle of number position was used; and an abstract character, probably equivalent to zero, was known. The Babylonians possessed a remarkable calendar based upon the year of 360 days, derived from a rather profound study of solar and lunar calculations, etc. In the circle of 360 degrees and its aliquot parts and in modern chronology—60 seconds to the minute, 60 minutes to the hour—we see remnants of the sexagesimal system.

Another commonly used system in numbers was the duodecimal (12 base) system. The Romans used the decimal system for simple numbers, or integers, but fractions of numbers were duodecimal: the *uncia* (or ounce—a numismatic term) was 1/12th of the *libra, aes* or Roman pound. In England, the duodecimal system of numeration is retained in some currency terms—twelve pence to the shilling. The words *dozen, gross,* and the old English *hundred* (120), called by the Normans *Anglicus Numerus,* are duodecimal units.

The quinary (5 base) system or ½ the decimal system was probably suggested by fingers of one hand. It has been asserted that the Roman V (5) was derived from a pictograph portraying the opened hand, ( ) but in course of time several "fingers" were omitted in the interests of more rapid writing. This, then, is a step towards what may be styled conventionalization of symbol. Accepting (or rejecting) this hypothesis, then we may believe further the theory that the Roman V is simply the upper half of the numeral X (10).

In order to retain a permanent record of any number of things, symbols are necessary. The practice, which seemed almost universal among early peoples, was the employment of lines, strokes or bars even as we use them today. In this system, one stroke, of course, meant one; additional strokes, lines, or bars were added to indicate higher numbers. The Egyptians employed 1-9 strokes or bars to represent the numerals 1-9 respectively. (Note: In the table of ancient alphabets, variant forms of Egyptian numerals (5-9) are shown, but the customary practice in Egypt was the additive system—an additional bar for each subsequent letter—1-9.) The

Maya used a system of dots and bars (in the short count). Thus, 1-4 dots might represent the numerals 1-4, but the numeral 5 was indicated by a bar and 6 was shown by a dot added to the bar. In Chinese and Japanese the first three numerals—1, 2, 3—are represented by 1, 2, 3 simple lines respectively. The Babylonians and Assyrians employed cuneiform or wedge shape characters in similar manner.

EGYPTIAN NUMERALS

			1
			2
			3
			4
			5
			6
			7
			8
			9
			10

Many of the people of antiquity employed letters of their alphabets for numerals. Thus, *alpha, beta, gamma* in post-Herodian numeration meant 1, 2, 3 to the Greeks. The Hebrews and other semitic peoples counted with the letters of their alphabets as *alef, beth, gimel.* In the Greek system the first nine letters stood for the first nine numerals, but subsequent letters represented higher order in numeration such as units of tens, twenties, etc. But since the alphabet had only 24 letters, several obsolete letters were employed for higher numbers. Sometimes a stroke or bar was added to a letter to increase its order or value.

The Romans employed symbols or letters for numerals—I, II, III, V, X, etc. This additive system was very cumbrous, hence the use of certain quinary numerals—V, L, D, and the subtractive principle—V less I (IIII)—IV; X less I (VIIII)—IX. Nevertheless, even with these shortenings and economies, Roman numerals seem awkward and entirely unsuited for mathematics. Consider this problem: CCCLXVI × IX + VIII.

Now of symbols representing numerals and how they came to us, there are several theories, however ill-founded in fact. The following cut will illustrate one theoretical origin of our numerals. It is interesting to note here that each primitive "numeral" contains by count the number of lines equivalent to each digit's numerical power.

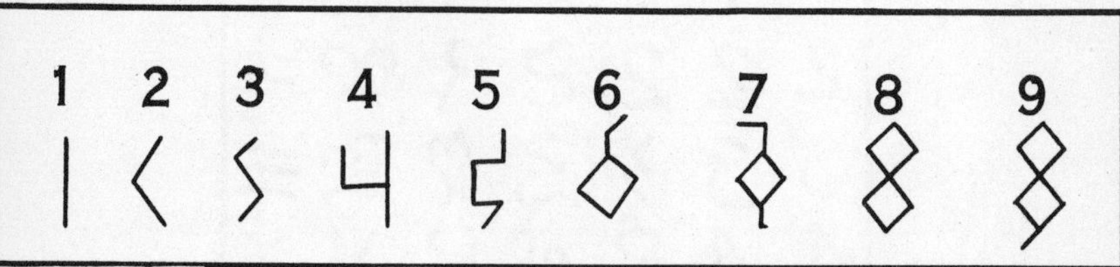

The greatest advance in numerical systems and mathematics was made by introduction of the Arabic numerals into Europe. The Arabic, or more properly, Hindu numerals, were borrowed from India by the Arabs about 773 A. D., and introduced into Europe through Spain about the twelfth century. Arabic numerals were employed in the science of *algorism* (arithmetic), a corrupted form of the name of Al Khuwarisimi of Abu Ja'far Ibn Musa who published *Al Jabr w'al Mogabala*—a treatise on the decimal system of notation with a method of calculation.

ARABIC NUMERALS

Eastern	١ ٢ ٣ ٤ ٥ ٦ ٧ ٨ ٩ ١٠
Western	1 2 3 4 5 6 7 8 9 10

Early European writers on numerals were Maximus Planudes and Leonardo of Pisa of the thirteenth century, in whose *Liber Abaci* the term zero or *zephyro* was employed. The use of the numerals in India may be traced back to the *Nana Ghat* inscriptions of the early third century B. C. There were two distinctive styles of the Hindu numerals known to the Arabs: 1. Eastern. 2. Western (*Ghobar* or "dust" numerals).

The Hindu numerical system was based upon a principle of assigning a definite symbol to each of the first nine numerals. Later the symbol zero (0) was added, and with this the system of orders or position was established. Thus the first nine letters belonged to the first order or posi-

EUROPEAN GOBAR INDIAN

tion; but eleven or the first letter of the second count or second order, pushed the one back and added zero to indicate second order. Groups of tens, etc., then fell into the second order; groups of hundreds, indicated by two zeros (00), fell into the third order. Therefore, according to this system almost any amount might be designated with economy—in groups and in periods, as units, thousands, millions, etc. Thus the problem given above in Roman numerals is restated in Arabic numerals: 366 × 9 + 8. Here was the beginning of a system of notation that was workable in calculation, mathematics, and, subsequently, science.

INDIAN NUMERALS

१	२	३	४	५	६	७	८	९	०
1	2	3	4	5	6	7	8	9	0

Hitherto, in Europe, calculations were done on the abacus, which seems to have been in general use from about the tenth century. But this device was no new discovery; Boethius, in the *Geometria*, alludes to its use with ciphers in the fifth century A. D. Herodotus states that the use of the abacus was common practice in Egypt. The Chinese *swanpan*, consisting of a wire frame with beads as counters is still in general use, and the *sangi* or square sticks for solving problems in algebra may still be seen in the Orient. In Europe during the Middle Ages, calculations

COMPARATIVE TABLE OF NUMERALS

	1	2	3	4	5	6	7	8	9	0
Hieratic	[illegible]	[illegible]	[illegible]	[illegible]	[illegible]	[illegible]	[illegible]	[illegible]	[illegible]	
Gupta	[illegible]	[illegible]	[illegible]	[illegible]	[illegible]	[illegible]	[illegible]	[illegible]	[illegible]	
Maledive	[illegible]	[illegible]	[illegible]	[illegible]	[illegible]	[illegible]	[illegible]	[illegible]	[illegible]	
Lepcha	᱁	᱂	᱃	᱄	᱅	᱆	᱇	᱈	᱉	᱀
Tibetan	༡	༢	༣	༤	༥	༦	༧	༨	༩	༠
Nepali	[illegible]	[illegible]	[illegible]	[illegible]	[illegible]	[illegible]	[illegible]	[illegible]	[illegible]	[illegible]
Devanagari	१	२	३	४	५	६	७	८	९	०
Kashmiri	[illegible]	[illegible]	[illegible]	[illegible]	[illegible]	[illegible]	[illegible]	[illegible]	[illegible]	[illegible]
Bengali	১	২	৩	৪	৫	৬	৭	৮	৯	০
Assamese	১	২	৩	৪	৫	৬	৭	৮	৯	০
Telugu	౧	౨	౩	౪	౫	౬	౭	౮	౯	౦
Tamil	௧	௨	௩	௪	௫	௬	௭	௮	௯	[illegible]
Malabar	൧	൨	൩	൪	൫	൬	൭	൮	൯	൦
Sinhalese	[illegible]	[illegible]	[illegible]	[illegible]	[illegible]	[illegible]	[illegible]	[illegible]	[illegible]	[illegible]
Burmese	၁	၂	၃	၄	၅	၆	၇	၈	၉	၀
Siamese	๑	๒	๓	๔	๕	๖	๗	๘	๙	๐
Cambodian	១	២	៣	៤	៥	៦	៧	៨	៩	០
,, (simplified)	[illegible]	[illegible]	[illegible]	[illegible]	[illegible]	[illegible]	[illegible]	[illegible]	[illegible]	[illegible]
Javanese	꧑	꧒	꧓	꧔	꧕	꧖	꧗	꧘	꧙	꧐

were made upon the reckoning board, which was similar to a chessboard, hence the word *exchecquer,* since these boards were used by bankers and money changers. It is interesting to note that the records of the British exchecquer were kept on notched willow tally sticks for a thousand years and that the consumption of these by fire in 1834 caused a conflagration in Lords and Commons.

The Arabic numerals are in almost universal use among the nations of the world today. Even those countries that have distinctive numerals of their own employ as a secondary system of numerical notation the numbers of the Arabs. All of this is due to one simple truth—the Arabic numerals are one of the great heritages that have come to us from the East. It is a system that *works.* All other numerical systems are forgotten, limited in use, or relegated to the interest of antiquarians. The Arabic numerals have stood the test of time.

Man has learned slowly but surely. It has been a long journey in time from the finger counting of neolithic man to the complex machinery of today that computes with superhuman speed and mechanical precision the most complex mathematical problems, using only nine simple Arabic letters, 1, 2, 3, 4, 5, 6, 7, 8, 9, and *zero.*

CAXTON'S TYPES

For as it ſemed it was forto done
To enden in ſom vertuous ſentence
And forto yeue hym place and audience
And bad to our oſt he ſholde to hym ſey
That alle we to telle his tale hym preye
Our oſte hadde the wordis for vs alle
Sir preeſt quod he now fair moot you befalle
Saith what ye liſt and we ſhul gladly here

PHONETIC TABLES

THE R.G.S. II. SYSTEM OF PHONETICS

From Rules for the spelling of Geographical Names for British Official Use. Table of phonetic sounds devised by the Permanent Committee on Geographical Names, of the Royal Geographical Society, London.

Generally, vowels are pronounced as in Italian and consonants are pronounced as in English. Every letter is pronounced and no redundant letters are used. Accents and diacritical marks shall be retained.

The neutral vowel is the sound of the vowel I in stir or the letter E in French je. The neutral vowel may be represented by E or A italicized.

An inverted comma (‘) denotes the Arabic sound of ‘*ain* or the Hebrew sound of ‘*ayin*, used in Semitic languages, etc. The apostrophe (’) in foreign words indicates a liquid sound as in d’you, shown thus d’. The hyphen is not used except to indicate pronunciation of adjoining words. The accute accent is used generally to indicate or emphasize stress. Neither vowels or consonants are doubled except when the sounds are to be repeated.

Liquid or palatalized sounds when pertaining to D, L, N, R, T, etc, as in new, *d’you, lure, onion,* are indicated by the consonant Y inserted after the above letters, except when the letter is final or when not practicable to use Y because of a following consonant. In such instances liquid or palatalised sounds are indicated by the apostrophe, as follows: D’, L’, N’, R’, T’.

The neutral or indeterminate vowel–about like E in *often* or in *hasten,* I in *stir,* IO in *nation, station,* O in *connect,* etc., may be shown by Italic A or E.

Special Characters:

German: Ä, Ö, Ü – Ä, Ö, Ü

Danish: Ä, Æ, Ö, Ø,–Ä, E, Ö

Norwegian: Ä, Å, Ö, Ø – Ä, Ö, Ö

Swedish: Ä, Å, Ö – Ä, O, Ö

French: É, È, Ê – E, Ä, Ä; Ç – S

Spanish: CH, LL, Ñ, RR – CH, LY, L’, NY, N’, RR

Portuguese: Ã, ÃE, ÃO, Ç, LH, NH, ÕE, – AI, A, IN (Fr.),
AN+ON (Fr.), S, LY, L’, NY, N’, ON (Fr.)

	Dutch	German	Danish	Norwegian	Swedish	French	Italian	Spanish	Portuguese
A	A	A	A, Ä	A	A	A	A	A	A, AI
B	B, P	B	B, P	B, P	B	B	B	B,V	B
C	S, K	TS, K	S, TS, K	S, K	S, K	S, K	CH, K	S, K, TH	S, K
D	D, T	D	D, DH	–, D	–, D	D	D	D, DH	D
E	E, *E*	E	E	E, Ä, E	E	*E*	E	E	I, E
F	F	F	F	F	F	F	F	F	F
G	KH	G, KH	G, GH, KH	K, G, Y	G, Y	G, ZH	J, G	G, KH	G, ZH
H	H	H	H, –	H, –	H	mute	mute	mute	mute
I	I	I	I	I	I	I	I	I	I
J	Y	Y	Y, –	Y	Y	ZH	I, Y	H, KH	ZH, Y, HY
K	K	K	K	K, KY	K, CH	(K)	(K)	(K)	(K)
L	L	L	L	L	L	L	L	L	L
M	M	M	M	M	M	M	M	M	M, –
N	N	N	N	N	N	N	N	N	N, –
O	O	O	O	O, AW	O, U	O	O, AW	O	O, U, W
P	P	P	P	P	P	P	P	P	P
Q	K	K	K	K, KV	K	K	K	K	K
R	R	R	R	R	R	R	R	R	R
S	S	Z, S	S	S	S	S, Z, –	S, Z	S, Z, TH	S, Z, SH, Z
T	T	T	T	T	T	T, –	T	T	T
U	*U*, Ü, Ö	U	U	U	–, ÜW	Ü	U	U	U, –
V	F	F	V	V	V	V	V	V	V
W	V, W	V	V	V	V	(W)			
X	X	X	X	X	X	X, S, –		X, SH	SH, Z, S, X
Y	AI, EI	I, Y	Ü	Ü	Ü	Y, I		Y, I	I, Y
Z	Z	TS	S	Z	S	Z, –	TS, DZ, Z	TH, Z	ZH, Z

THE STANDARD ALPHABET OF LEPSIUS
(Outline)

ROMAN GREEK LETTERS, ETC., OF THE ALPHABET

a, ā, ă, ã, ā̃, å, ḁ, ʾa, ʿa; b, b̔, b́, b̄; č́, č̄, č', ċ; d, d̔, d', ḍ, ḍ̔, ḍ̄, ḏ, d̦, d̦; δ, δ̱; e, ē, ĕ, ẽ, ē̃, ḙ, ē̱, ĕ̱, ẹ, ˙ē̩, e̩, e̥, ẽ̥; f, f́; g, g̔, ǵ, g̔, ḡ, ġ; γ, γ́, γ̇; h, h̔; i, ī, ĭ, ĩ, ī̃, i̩, ī̩, i̥, ï; j, ǰ, ǰ, j̃; k, k̔, ḱ, k̔, k', ḱ', ḵ, k̇, k̇'; χ, χ́, χ̇; l, l̄, ĺ, ḷ, ł, l̥, l̥̄; m, m̔, ḿ, m̥; n, n̔, ń, ṅ, n̔, ń, ṇ, ṇ̇, n̈, n̥; o, ō, ŏ, õ, ō̃, o̱, ō̱, ŏ̱, ọ, ọ̄, o̤, ō̤; p, p̔, ṕ, p'; q, q'; r, r̔, ŕ, ṙ, ṛ, ř, r̄, r̥, r̥̄; s, ś, s̱, š, ṣ̌, š, s̀; t, t̔, t́, ṭ, ṭ̔, ṯ, t', ț, ț̄, .ț', ț́, ț; θ; u, ū, ŭ, ũ, ū̃, u̥, ụ, ů, ṳ, ṳ̄; v, v̔, v́; w, w̔, w̱; y, ỹ; z, ź, ẕ, ž, ž, z̀,; ˟, ꞉; ˈ, ˮ, !, ˊ; -ˈ, -ꜜ, -ˋ, -ꜝ, -ˏ, -ꜟ, -ˎ, -ꜜ, -ᵀ.

PHONETIC VALUES

Vowels.

ā engl. *father*, fr. *âme*.
ă ger. *Mann*, ital. *ballo*.
ḗ fr. *mère*, ger. *Bär*.
ḗ̆ engl. *head*, ger. *fett*.
ẹ̄ engl. *cane*, *vein*, fr. *donné*.
ī engl. *see*, fr. *lit*.
ĭ engl. *sin*, fr. *fil*.
ō̱ engl. *all*, ital. *però*.
ŏ̱ engl. *hot*, *not*.
ọ̄ engl. *no*, fr. *faux*.
ū engl. *rule*, fr. *nous*.
ŭ engl. *foot*, fr. *ours*.
ō̤ fr. *beurre*, *coeur*.
ŏ̤ engl. *cunning*, *but*.
ọ̤̄ ger. *König*, fr. *feu*.
ṳ̄ fr. *fûmes*, ger. *Güte*.
ṳ̆ fr. *but*, ger. *Glück*.
ai engl. *mine*, ger. *Kaiser*.
au engl. *house*, ger. *Haus*.
aṳ ger. *Häuser*, *heute*.
ei span. *reina*.
oi engl. *join*.
ã fr. *an*, *en*.
ẽ fr. *examen*, *Inde*.
õ fr. *on*.
õ̤ fr. *un*.
e̥ engl. *nation*, ger. *Verstand*.
r̥˙ sanskr. ऋ.

Consonants.

A. Explosive. *a.* Fortes.

ʿ arab. ع (*ʿaïn*).
k engl. *cool*, fr. *cause*.
k̔ old sanskr. च.
č modern sanskr. च, engl. *ch*.
ṭ sanskr. ट.
t engl. *town*, fr. *ton*.
p engl. *pine*, fr. *peu*.

b. Lenes.

’ arab. ء, hebr. א, gr. spir. len. ’.

q arab. ق *(qaf)*.

g engl. *gold*, fr. *gauche*.

ǵ old sanskr. ज.

ǰ modern sanskr. ज, engl. *j*.

ḍ sanskr. ड.

ḏ(ṯ) arab. ط (see below).

d engl. *dear*.

b engl. *by*.

c. Nasales.

ṅ engl. *singing*, ger. *enge*.

ń sanskr. ञ, ital. *gnudo*, fr. *regner*.

ṇ sanskr. ण.

n engl. *no*.

m engl. *me*.

B. Fricativae. *a.* Fortes.

ḱ arab. ح *(ḱa)*.

h engl. *hand*.

χ ger. *Buch*, *ach*; pol. *chata*.

š engl. *show*, fr. *chat*, ger. *schon*.

χ́ ger. *ich*, *recht*.

ṣ̌ old sanskr. ष.

ś mod. ind. श, pol. *świt*.

ṣ arab. ص *(ṣād)*.

s engl. *sense*, fr. *savoir*.

θ engl. *thin*, mod. gr. *θεός*.

f engl. *fine*.

b. Lenes.

γ arab. غ *(γaïn)*.

ž fr. *jeune*, pol. *bażant*.

γ́ mod. gr. *γέφυρα*.

ź pol. *później*.

z fr. *zèle*, engl. *zeal*.

δ engl. *thy*, mod. gr. *δίψα*.

δ̣ arab. ظ *(δ̣a)*.

ẕ arab. ض *(ẕa)* (see below).

c. Semivocales.

y engl. *year*, fr. *Bayonne*, ger. *ja*.

w engl. *we*.

C. Liquidae.

ṙ germ. and fr. dialects.

ṛ sanskr. र.

r engl. *very*, ital. *rabbia*.

l′ ital. *gli*, fr. *mouillé*.

ḷ sanskr. ळ.

l engl. *low*.

OTHER PHONETIC ALPHABETS

Pitman

VOWELS.

Guttural.

A	a	*as in*	am, fast, far
Ꭺ	ɐ	,,	*a*lms, f*a*ther
E	e	,,	*e*ll, h*ea*d, *a*ny
Ɛ	ɛ	,,	*a*le, *ai*r, b*ea*r
I	i	,,	*i*ll, pit*y*, fil*i*al
Ꙇ	ı	,,	*ee*l, *ea*t, m*e*re

CONSONANTS.

Mutes.

P	p	*as in*	ro*p*e, *p*ost
B	b	,,	ro*b*e, *b*oast
T	t	,,	fa*t*e, *t*ip
D	d	,,	fa*d*e, *d*ip
Ͼ	ç	,,	e*tch*, *ch*ump
J	j	,,	e*dg*e, *j*ump
K	k	,,	lee*k*, *c*ane
G	g	,,	lea*g*ue, *g*ain

Labial.

Ɔ ɔ *as in* on, not, nor
Ω ω „ all, l*aw*, *ough*t

Ɣ ɣ „ *up*, son, j*our*nal
Ơ ơ „ ope, co*a*t, p*ou*r

U u „ f*u*ll, f*oo*t, co*u*ld
Ɯ ɯ „ *do*, food, t*ou*r

DIPHTHONGS.

Ɨ ɨ *as in* b*y*, k*i*nd, n*igh*
Ч ч „ n*ew*, d*ue*, *u*nit
OU ou „ n*ow*, p*ou*nd
OI oi „ b*oy*, v*oi*ce

FOREIGN SOUNDS.

Œ œ as in je*û*ne (French)
Ʋ ʋ „ d*u* (French)
Ɯ ɯ „ d*û* (French)
И ŋ „ *un* (French)
X x „ i*ch* (German)
Ψ ч „ Sie*g* (German)

Continuants.

F f *as in* sa*f*e, *f*at
V v „ sa*v*e, *v*at
Ƕ ƫ „ wrea*th*, *th*igh
Ƌ đ „ wrea*the*, *th*y
S s „ hi*ss*, *s*eal
Z z „ hi*s*, *z*eal
Σ ʃ „ vi*ci*ous, *sh*e
Ʒ ʒ „ vi*s*ion, plea*s*ure

Nasals.

M m *as in* see*m*, *m*et
N n „ see*n*, *n*et
Ŋ ŋ „ si*ng*, lo*ng*

Liquids.

L l *as in* fa*ll*, *l*ight
R r „ mo*r*e, *r*ight

Coalescents.

W w *as in* *w*et, q*u*it
Y y „ *y*et, *y*oung

Aspirate.

H h *as in* *h*e, *h*ope

I.P.A. PHONETICS WITH SCRIPT

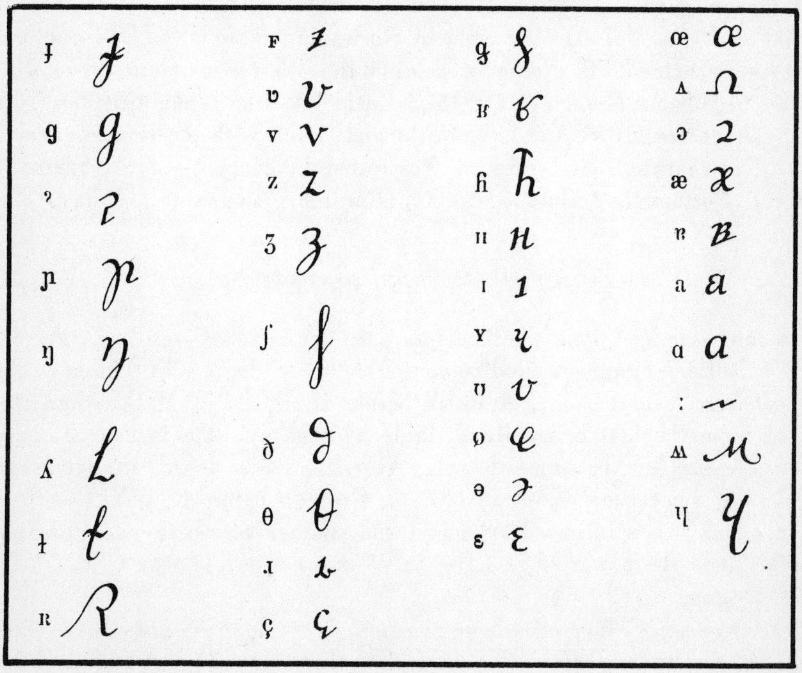

ɟ	ɸ	ɠ	œ
g	ʋ	ʁ	ʌ
ʔ	v	ɦ	ɔ
ɲ	z	ʜ	æ
ŋ	ʒ	ɪ	ɐ
ʎ	ʃ	ʏ	a
ɫ	ð	ʊ	ɑ
ʀ	θ	ɷ	ː
	ɹ	ə	ɯ
	ç	ɛ	ɥ

TEUTONIC LANGUAGES

ENGLISH

A B C D E F G H I J K L M N O P Q R S T U V W X Y Z
a b c d e f g h i j k l m n o p q r s t u v w x y z

Teutonic: Low German. Roman alphabet. Spoken by more than 250,000, 000 people in the British Isles, the Dominion of Canada, Newfoundland and Labrador, the Commonwealths of Australia and New Zealand, the Union of South Africa and the United States of America and its possessions.

The English language is derived from Anglo-Saxon, a Germanic tongue, with considerable additions from Latin and other languages of the European continent, but English is basically Germanic in structure. Modern English is an amalgam of language growth in the British Isles with contributions from the following major sources: 1. Celtic (before 43 B.C.). 2. Latin or "early Latin" of the Roman occupation (43 B.C.–410 A.D.). 3. Anglo-Saxon, of the Angles, Saxons and Jutes—Northumbrian, Mercian and Kentish (450 A.D.–1066 A.D.). 4. Latin, or "Ecclesiastical Latin" or "Church Latin" brought by Christian missionaries into England from the continent. 5. Norse or Danish, the Viking invaders (about 780 A.D.). 6. Norman French or the third Latin invasion brought by the Norman conquerors (1066 A.D.). 7. Latin and Greek with the Renascence or revival of learning. 8. Borrowed from other languages:—Greek, Spanish, Italian, Portuguese, Dutch, Arabic, Persian, Hindustani, Malay, etc.

MODERN ENGLISH PHONETICS

A long—*state;* A long modified—*preface;* A circumflex—*parent;* A short—*hat;* A Italian—*father;* A middle—*dance;* A broad—*law;* A like short O as in *wonder;* A short—*many;* A Italic before D, F, L, N, P, O, when the vowel is in the last or middle syllable and the syllable is unaccented—*infant;* AI—*aisle;* AI—*main;* AI—*said;* AU—*because* or as AU in *sauerkraut.*

B—*bat,* sometimes silent as in *debt;* C—*cent;* before E, I, Y; C—SH or as in *ocean,* when followed by E or I and another vowel; C—*cut.* In a few words C has the power of Z; CH—*church* or as in *machine* or CH as K in *echo;* D—*dog.*

E long—*me;* E long modified—*creation;* E as long A—*obey;* E short—*error;* E circumflex before R—*where;* E before R when not followed by

ENGLISH COURTHAND

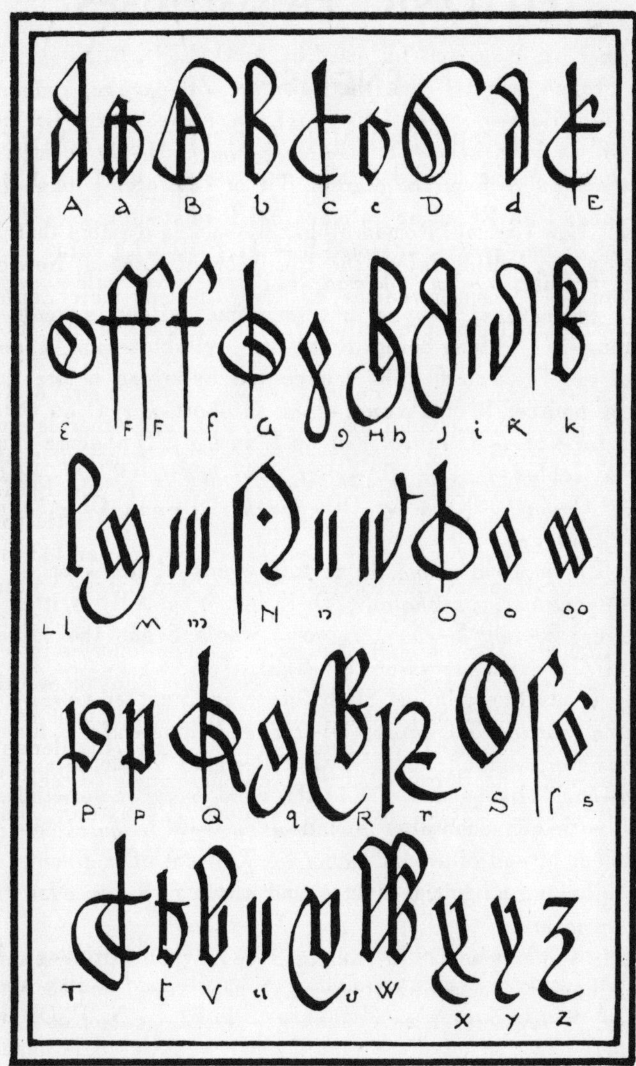

another R in the following syllable—*fern, berth;* E Italic before N or L—*novelty;* E silent at end of word (usually after long vowels and a preceding syllable)—*write;* E—usually pronounced short U in the word *the* (thu); E long as U in *new;* EA—*steak;* EA—*breathe;* EA—*breath;* EA—*swear;* EA—*meat;* EE—*meet;* EE—*queer;* E in *mere;* EI—*height;* EI—*vein;* EI—*their;*

EO–*leopard;* E–consonantal U or as YU in *feud;* EW–long U–*blew;* EW–consonantal Y or YU in *ewe;* EY–*prey;* EY–*key;* F–*fat;* F has the value of V in a few words–*of.*

G before E, I, Y–*gem;* G followed by A, O, L, U, R, S–*gun.* In certain words of French origin G has the power of ZH–*garage, rouge.* In some words G is silent–*foreign;* GH–*ghost.* In some words GH is silent–*through;* GH as F in some words–*laugh, cough;* H–*hat.* Sometimes H is silent but serves to form the digraph TH or CH, etc. I long–*ice;* I long modified–*idea;* I as EE or as in *machine;* I short–*pin;* I–*bird;* I as consonant Y in *onion, genius;* IE–*pie;* IE–*chief;* IU with value of U or YU.

J–*jam;* K–*kite;* L–*law;* M–*man,* but sometimes silent as initial in words like *mnemonics;* N–*noon,* but sometimes silent in words like *condemn;* O long–*old;* O long before R in some syllables–*port, horse;* O long modified–*obey;* O circumflex in unaccented syllables before R, but not followed by another R or a vowel–*lord;* O short–*not;* O as OO in *prove* or as U in *love* or as U in *worm* or as U in *wolf*; O obscure sound in unaccented syllables–*reckon;* OA–*goat;* OA–*board;* OI, OY–*boil, oyster;* OO–*boot;* OO–*food;* OO–*door;* OU–*dough;* OU–*out;* OU–*thought;* OU–*enough;* OU–*through.*

P–*pet;* PH as F in *phone.* In certain words of Greek origin initial P is silent–*pneumatic, psychology;* Q–K but is usually written with U–*quick;* R–*run;* S–*sun;* S–*easy.* In some words S has the value of SH–*sugar,* or of ZH–*usual, decision;* SH–*shut.*

T–*ton;* T has the value of SH before I and another vowel in the syllable–*nation, partial;* TH–*thick;* TH–*these;* U long–*rule;* U long modified after N–*numeral;* U long modified after R–*rude;* U short–*full;* U–*urn;* U very short–*but;* U like sound of I in the word *busy;* U sometimes silent–*tongue;* U with consonantal Y sound–*use;* U–W in *quick;* V–*vest;* W–*word.* W silent at end of a word–*window;* W silent at beginning of a word –*who;* W following an initial H in sound although W precedes the initial letter–*when, where.*

X–*extra;* X about as GS in *examine;* X–Z when initial–*xylophone;* Y vowel as I long–*my* or as I short–*hymn.* Y as a vowel has the same value as I; Y–*my;* Y–*mystery;* Y as consonant–*yet;* Z–*zest* or as ZH in some words–*azure.*

FIVE PERIODS OF ENGLISH LANGUAGE GROWTH

1. Old English or Anglo-Saxon (450-1100).

2. Early English–the period of bilingualism in England–Norman-French and Anglo-Saxon (1100-1250).

3. Middle English—the period of blending the new elements—the new and old elements of the language. The English of Chaucer, (1250-1485).

4. Tudor English. The age of Shakespeare (1485-1603).

5. Modern English (1603-).

MODERN ENGLISH DIALECTS

SCOTLAND

1. Shetland and Orkney. 2. Caithness. 3. Aberdeen, Banff, Elgin. 4. Forfar, Kincardine. 5. Perth, Fife, Stirling. 6. Ayrshire, Dumfries, Kircudbright. 7. Argyle, Renfrew, Lanark. 8. Kinross, Clackmannan, Linlithgow, Berwick, Peebles, Edinburgh, Haddington. 9. Selkirk, Roxburgh. Braid Scots.

IRELAND

Ulster, Dublin and Wexford.

ENGLAND AND WALES

1. *Northern:* Northumberland, Durham, Cumberland, Westmorland, Lancashire, Yorkshire. 2. *Midland:* Lincolnshire, Cheshire, Derby, Staffordshire, Denbigh, Nottingham, Shropshire, Warwickshire, Leicestershire. 3. *Eastern:* Cambridge, Rutland, Northampton, Essex, Hertford, Huntingdon, Bedford, Norfolk, Suffolk, Buckingham, Middlesex. 4. *Western:* Shropshire, Hereford, Radnor, Brecknock. 5. *Southern:* Pembroke, Glamorgan, Dorset, Wiltshire, Somerset, Gloucester, Devon, Hampshire, Berkshire, Surrey, Worcester, Warwick, Isle of Wight, Oxford, Kent, Cornwall.

ANGLO-SAXON

Teutonic: Low German. Roman alphabet with special Anglo-Saxon letters. Anglo-Saxon, the ancestor of the English language, was spoken in England from about the sixth to the twelfth centuries. It is a highly inflected language and many of its complex grammatical forms, verbal changes, etc., persisted although greatly modified in old and early middle English. Chief Saxon dialects of England were: Northern Saxon-Northumbrian and Mercian or Midland dialects, Southern Saxon-Kentish and West Saxon dialects. The Anglo-Saxon letters *thorn* and *sithan* soon became obsolete and were replaced by the digraph—TH.

ANGLO-SAXON

BRYTENE ıᵹlanꝺ ıꞅ ehꞇa hunꝺ mıla lanᵹ. ⁊ ꞇƿa hunꝺ mıla bꞃáꝺ. Anꝺ heꞃ ꞅẏnꝺon on þam ıᵹlanꝺe ꝼıꝼ ᵹeðeoꝺu. Ænᵹlıꞅc. ⁊ Bꞃẏꞇ-ƿẏlıꞅc. ⁊ Scẏꞇꞇıꞅc. ⁊ Pẏhꞇıꞅc. ⁊ Boclæꝺen.

Anglo-Saxon Form.			Modern Form.		Anglo-Saxon Form.			Modern Form.	
Ā	A	a	A	a		N	n	N	n
	B	b	B	b		O	o	O	o
L	C	c	C	c		P	p	P	p
	D	ꝺ	D	d		R	ꞃ	R	r
E	Є	e	E	e	Ꞅ	S	ꞅ	S	s
	F	ꝼ	F	f		T	ꞇ	T	t
Ᵹ	G	ᵹ	G	g	Ð	Þ	ðþ	Th	th
H	Ꮒ	h	H	h		U	u	U	u
	I	ı	I	i	Ɯ	Ƿ	ƿ	W	w
	K	k	K	k		X		X	x
	L	l	L	l		Y	ẏ	Y	y
M	ᗰ	m	M	m		Z	z	Z	z

Æ | æ | Æ | æ

Vowels are: A, E, I, O, U, Y, AE. Long vowels are sometimes indicated Â, Ê, etc., or Ā, Ē. Diphthongs: EA, ĒA, EO, ĒO, IE, ĪE, IO, ĪO, OE.

B, D, K, L, M, N, P, R, T, W, X, are pronounced about as in English.

A—*ask;* Ā—*father;* AE—*man;* ĀE—*there;* C—K; E—*men;* Ē—*they;* F—V; G—*get;* H—H, CH and occasionally WH; I, IE, Y—*fin;* Ī, ĪE, Ȳ—*brief;* O—*not;* Ō—*note;* S—*sister,* but Z between vowels; U—*full;* Ū—*rule;* EA—Ĕ—ĂH; ĒA—AI—ĂH; EO—Ĕ—O; ĒO—AI—O. Special characters: *Thorn* (þ) TH, *eth* (ð), *wen* (ƿ) W.

John 3:16

16. God lufode middaneard swā þæt hē sealde his *āncennedan* Sunu, þæt nān ne forwurðe þe on hine gelȳfð, ac hæbbe þæt ēce līf.

DUTCH

In den beginne schiep God den hemel en de aarde. De aarde nu was woest en ledig, en duisternis was op den afgrond; en de Geest Gods zweefde op de wateren En God zeide: Daar zij licht! en daar werd licht. En God zag het licht, dat het goed was; en God maakte scheiding tusschen het licht en tusschen de duisternis. En God noemde het licht dag, en de duisternis noemde Hij nacht. Toen was het avond geweest, en het was morgen geweest, de eerste dag.—Genesis 1:1-5

A B C D E F G H I J K L M N O P Q R S T U V W X Y Z
a b c d e f g h i j k l m n o p q r s t u v w x y z

Teutonic: Low German. Roman alphabet. Spoken by about 16,000,000 people in the Netherlands, Dutch East Indies, Dutch West Indies and Dutch Guiana. Cape Dutch or Afrikaans, a mixture of Dutch with English and Bantu words, is spoken by the Dutch settlers in South Africa. Dutch Creole is spoken by negroes in the Danish West Indies and Georgetown, British Guiana.

The Dutch alphabet is the same as English, but C (except in CH, SCH), Q, X, and Y, occur only in words of foreign origin. The diphthong IJ is sometimes written Y. A double vowel is equivalent in value to a single long vowel. The diaeresis (¨), over the second of two vowels, indictates that each vowel is pronounced separately. Common contractions are: 'S, an abbreviation of DES (the genitive of the definite article) before a name, and 'T, an abbreviation of HET (the definite neuter article). The stress usually falls on the first syllable.

F, H, K, L, M, N, P, R, S, T, Z, are pronounced as in English.

A—*father;* B—*bit* but almost P when final; C—*cent* before E, I, or Y, otherwise K in *kite;* D—*do,* but as T in *ton* when final; E long—A in *fate;* E short—*bed;* but German E as final; G—KH but German GH when final; I long—*machine;* I short—*bit;* J—Y in *year;* J—French J or ZH in loan words; N—*never,* but often silent when final; O—*low* or *oven;* Q—K in foreign words; S—*sister;* U—almost like U in *sure* or German Ü or as EE in *reel;* U short—*jug;* V—F in *fan;* W (initial)—V in *vine,* otherwise as W or V; X—*tax* in foreign words; Y—I in *machine.*

CH—Scotch *loch;* NG—*singer*—not as in *finger;* SJ—SH in *shut;* TH—T in *tin;* SCH (initial)—S+Dutch CH, otherwise as SS in *hiss;* IE—*brief;* EU—UR in *fur;* OE—OO in *boot;* OU—OW in *how;* UI—OY in *toy;* EI, IJ—Y in *my,* but IJ when final before K is often like I in *tic;* AAI—AH+EE;

OOI–O+EE; EEUW–AY+OO; IEUW–EE+OO; AI, AAI–*aisle;* AU, AAU–*house;* EI–*aisle;* IEU–EE+U; OA–O; EE–AY in *day;* LJ–LI; GN–NY.

FLEMISH

Want alzoo heeft God de wereld bemind, dat Hij zijn eeniggeboren Zoon heeft gegeven, op dat al wie in Hem gelooft niet verga, maar het eeuwige leven hebbe.

Jn. 3: 16.

A B C D E F G H I J K L M N O P Q R S T U V W X Y Z
a b c d e f g h i j k l m n o p q r s t u v w x y z

Teutonic: Low German. Roman alphabet. Spoken by about 3,500,000 people in Belgium, particularly in Flanders. Flemish is closely related to Dutch, and Flemish letters are pronounced as in Dutch except where noted below. The Dutch diphthong IJ is usually written Y in Flemish and pronounced as Y in *try*. Initial SCH is like SK; G–*get;* V–*vine;* H initial is almost mute.

B, F, H, K, L, M, N, P, Q, R, T, V, W, X, Z, are pronounced as in English.

A–*father;* AA, AE–long A; C–*cut;* CH–German CH; D–D or German D, DT; E–*pet;* EU–French EU; EE–A in *day* or E in *me;* I–*pin;* IE–I in *pin;* IEU–AY+OO; J–Y in *year*; O–*note*; O short–*not;* OE, OO–O long or as WA in *was;* OEI, OEY–O+E; S–*sister;* U–German U short; UU, UE–U; Y–I in *machine* or as Y in *try;* AEI, AEY, AI, AY–AI in *said;* OEU–German Ö; OI, OY–WA in *was;* OIN–W followed by nasal sound.

FRISIAN

Hwent sa ljeaf hat God de wrâld hawn, dat Er syn ienichstberne Soan jown hat, dat in elts dy't yn him leaut, net fordjerre, mar it ivige libben hawwe mei.

Jn. 3: 16.

A B C D E F G H I J K L M N O P Q R S T U V W X Y Z
a b c d e f g h i j k l m n o p q r s t u v w x y z

Teutonic: Low German. Roman alphabet. Spoken in the province of Friesland in the Netherlands. Frisian is closely related to Flemish and

Dutch. Frisian, of all languages spoken on the European continent, stands nearest to English. The following couplet is both English and Frisian:

> Good butter and good cheese
> Is good English and good Fries.

GERMAN

Am Anfang ſchuf Gott Himmel und Erde. Und die Erde war wüſte und leer, und es war finſter auf der Tiefe; und der Geiſt Gottes ſchwebte auf dem Waſſer. Und Gott ſprach: Es werde Licht. Und es ward Licht. Und Gott ſah, daß das Licht gut war. Da ſchied Gott das Licht von der Finſternis; und nannte das Licht Tag und die Finſternis Nacht. Da ward aus Abend und Morgen der erſte Tag.—Genesis 1: 1–5.

Printed	Script	Printed	Script
A a	A a	N n	N n
B b	B b	O o	O o
C c	C c	P p	P p
D d	D d	Q q	Q q
E e	E e	R r	R r
F f	F f	S ſ s	S ſ s
G g	G g	T t	T t
H h	H h	U u	U u
I i	I i	V v	V v
J j	J j	W w	W w
K k	K k	X x	X x
L l	L l	Y y	Y y
M m	M m	Z z	Z z

Teutonic: High German. German Gothic alphabet (fraktur) or Roman alphabet. German is spoken by about 78,000,000 people in Germany, Austria and other parts of central Europe. The German Gothic alphabet is commonly used in writing German. Simple vowels are: A, E, I, O, U, Y, and the modified letters: Ä, Ö, Ü. Double vowels are: AA, EE, OO. Diphthongs are: AI, AU, EI, EY, EU, ÄU. Compound consonants are: CH, SCH, PF, PH, QU, SP, ST, TH, CHS, CK, NG, SZ, TZ. The *umlaut* sign (¨) over A, O, U, alters the sounds of these letters but the diaeresis (¨) over E or I, indicates that these letters do not form a diphthong with an adjoining vowel. Capitals Ä, Ö, Ü, are often written Ae, Oe, Ue. Some German dialects are: Bern and Zurich (Switzerland); Erzgebirish, Low German or *Plattdeutsch,* Transylvanian (Rumania). "Pennsylvania Dutch," spoken in eastern Pennsylvania is a dialect of German (not Holland Dutch). Yiddish, spoken by the Jews of western Europe, is basically a German dialect with admixtures of words from other languages. Yiddish is usually written in rabbinical characters.

B, D, F, K, L, M, N, P, Q, T, are pronounced about as in English.

A – *father;* Ä – *share* but when short like E in *sell;* B – P when final or immediately preceding a final consonant; C – *cut* before A, O, U, and consonants and as final; C – TS in *sets* before Ä, E, I, Ö, Ü: CC – K + TS before E and I, otherwise CC – CK in *pack;* CH – guttural sound like CH in Scotch *loch,* after A, O, U, AU; CH – H in *hew,* after Ä, E, I, EU, EI, ÄU, Ö, Ü; CH – K followed by a radical S; D – nearly T when final; E – A in *ale;* E short – E in *end;* G – *get* at the beginnings of syllables or words; G – K in *kite* after a long vowel, after a short vowel + R, L, or before another consonant; NG–*sing;* H–*hat* as initial in a word or a syllable, otherwise silent but indicates that the preceding vowel is long; I – *machine;* I short – *sin;* J – Y in *year;* O–*note*; O short – nearly O in *not;* Ö – about as UR in *fur;* PH – F (in words of Greek origin); QU – more nearly KV, not like QU in *quick;* R – *run* but strongly sounded; S – *sister* (Austria and South German); S – *cease* (North German); S – *sun* when final. Generally S before vowels – Z in *zest,* but about like SH in *shut* as initial before T and P; SCH – SH in *shut;* SS – S in *sun;* SP and ST are pronounced about as in English; SZ – *sharp;* S in *sun;* T – TS in the syllables *-tion, tient,* otherwise as T in *tent;* U – *blue;* Ü – I pronounced with pursed lips, almost as EE in *eel;* V – F in *far;* W – V in *vine;* X – *tax;* Y vowel – *lyric;* Z, TZ – TS in *sits.* TH – T in *ten.*

AA – *father;* AI – I in *high;* AU – OW in *cow;* EE – A in *date:* EI – I in *high;* EU – OY in *toy;* OO – long O; IE – *brief;* ÄU – OY in *toy.* Stress generally falls on the first or second syllables, but simple words always have one accent on the root syllable.

DANISH

In Begyndelsen skabte Gud Himmelsen og Jorden. Og Jorden var øde og tom, og der var mørkt oven over Afgrunden, og Guds Aand svaevede oven over Vandene. Og Gud sagde: vorde Lys; og der blev Lys. Og Gud saae, at Lyset var godt, og Gud gjorde Skilsmisse imellem Lyset og Mørket. Og Gud kaldte Lyset Dag, og Mørket kaldte han Nat; og der blev Aften, og der blev Morgen, første Dag. –Genesis 1: 1-5.

A AA B C D E F G H I J K L M N O P Q R S T U V W X Y Z Æ Ö Ø
a aa b c d e f g h i j k l m n o p q r s t u v w x y z æ ö ø

Teutonic: Scandinavian. Roman alphabet or German Gothic alphabet (Modern Danish is rarely written in German Gothic characters). Spoken by about 3,000,000 people in Denmark, the language is considerably clipped or short and jerky. The alphabet is the same as English with the addition of the letters Æ and Ö– sometimes written Ø, Ö, or Œ. The letters C, Q, and W, occur only in words of foreign origin. Danish J is being abolished, except in place-names where it is often silent unless when initial or beginning of a word. Danish DET is pronounced DEH and OG is pronounced OH. Danish is closely related to Norwegian.

B, C, F, H, K, L, M, N, O, P, T, and V, are pronounced as in English.

A–*father* or A short–*hat;* Æ, E–long A as in *date* or short as E in *red;* C–*cut* before A, O, U, or consonants, otherwise C–*cent;* CH-SH or CH in *chorus;* D–*dog* but usually silent after L, N, R, or before S or T; E-A in *mate;* E short–*bed;* G–*get*–*Y* as in *yet* before E, I, or Y; G as final or between vowels is often silent; H–*hat* but silent before J or V; I long–*machine;* I short–*sit;* J-Y in *year;* O–*globe;* O short–*pot;* Q (U)–– is usually written KV; R–*run* but strongly sounded; S–*sister;* U–*true;* U short–*pull;* W-V in *vine;* X-KHS or as X in *tax;* Y–German Ü or nearly EE in *eel;* Z–*zest* or as S in *sin;* SJ-SH; SK-SK.

Æ– German Ä, about as A in *share;* Ø-UR in *fur* or about as U in *rug;* Ö-UR in *fur;* AA-AW in *law;* AJ-AI or I in *high;* AU-UW in *hour;* EG-I in *high;* EJ-I in *high;* IR-EER or as in *mere;* ØJ-EI in *grey;* GJ-Y in *yet;* YR-ÜR; Final T in the word DET and final G in the word OG is silent. Final T in ET (the) is usually pronounced as TH in *this.* Stress usually falls on the first syllable.

NORWEGIAN

I Begyndelsen skabte Gud Himmelen og Jorden. Og Jorden var øde og tom, og der var Mørke over Afgrunden; og Guds Aand svaevede over Vandene. Da sagde Gud: Der blive Lys! Og der blev Lys. Og Gud saa, at Lyset var godt, og Gud skilte mellem Lyset og Mørket. Og Gud kaldte Lyset Dag, og Mørket kaldte han Nat. Og der blev Aften, og der blev Morgen, første Dag. –Genesis 1: 1-5.

A B C D E F G H I J K L M N O P Q R S T U V W X Y Z Æ Ø Ö Å
a b c d e f g h i j k l m n o p q r s t u v w x y z ae ø ö å

Teutonic: Scandinavian. Roman alphabet or German Gothic alphabet (Modern Norwegian is usually written in Roman letters). Spoken by about 3,000,000 people in Norway. There are two Norwegian dialects: Riksmaal or Dano-Norwegian, but with orthography and pronunciation differing from modern Danish in some words. Landsmaal, a language made up from modern dialects. Landsmaal terms are often used in names of places. But Riksmaal is the chief spoken language. The Norwegian alphabet is the same as English with addition of the letters Æ and Ö or Ø. The letters C, Q, W, X, Z, occur only in words of foreign origin. Norwegian X is usually written KS in native names. Vowels are short before a double consonant or two consonants. Short vowels are indicated by doubling consonants, formerly written singly in old Norwegian. The stress usually falls on the first syllable.

B, C, D, F, H, K, L, M, N, O, P, T, V, are pronounced as in English. I, E, Æ, HJ, J, HV, R, S, Ø are generally pronounced as in Danish. AU, SK, SJ, SKJ are generally pronounced as in Swedish.

A–*father;* A short–*hat;* C–*cut* before A, O, U or consonants, otherwise C–*cent;* D is often silent before S or T or when final; E-A in *mate;* E short–*bed;* G–*get* but G-Y in *year* before I, Y. Final G is silent after I. H–*hat* but silent before J or V; I–*machine;* I short–*sit;* J-Y in *yet;* L is silent before J in some words; O–*globe;* O short–*pot;* QU is usually written KV; R–*run* but strongly sounded; S–*sister;* U–*rule;* U short–*pull;* V– *vest* but silent after L when final; W-W, V; Y-Ü; Z-S in *sister;* X–X.

AE–A in *care;* Ø–German Ö or nearly UR in *fur;* Å–nearly AW in *law;* AA–AW in *law*; AI–*aisle*; EI–*aisle;* EER–about as *air*; OI–OI in *toil;* ØI–French OEI or UR+EE; GJ-Y in *year;* AU-OW in *cow;* SJ, SKJ-SH in *shut;* SK-SK but SH before a soft vowel. OEU-OU in *house;* OI–E in *grey.*

SWEDISH

In begynnelsen skapade Gud Himmel och Jord. Och jorden war öde och tom, och mörker war på djupet, och Guds Ande swäfde öfwer wattnet. Och Gud sade: Warde Ljus; och det wardt Ljus. Och Gud såg ljuset, att det war godt. Då skilde Gud ljuset ifrå mörkret; och kallade ljuset Dag, och mörkret Natt. Och wardt af afton och morgon den förste dagen. —Genesis 1: 1-5.

A B C D E F G H I J K L M N O P Q R S T U V W X Y Z Å Ä Ö
a b c d e f g h i j k l m n o p q r s t u v w x y z å ä ö

Teutonic: Scandinavian. Roman alphabet or German Gothic alphabet (Modern Swedish is usually written in the Roman alphabet). Spoken by about 6,000,000 people in Sweden the alphabet is the same as English with addition of the letters Å, Ä, Ö. The letters C (except in CK), Q, W, and Z, are used in words of foreign origin. Recent changes in Swedish orthography and spelling: Ä is now written for Ē; K and S substitute for hard and soft C; K is used for Q before V as in KV; K and T are used instead of G and D before T; V takes the place of W; T is used for TH except in adjoining syllables; V is used for F (when pronounced like V) as medial or final when not followed by S or T; F and H are omitted before V; letters now doubled were formerly written singly. Stress usually is on the first syllable.

B, D, F, L, M, N, P, R, T, V, are pronounced as in English.

A—*father* or as U in *rug;* C—*cent* before soft vowels and some foreign words, otherwise C—*cut;* D is silent before J; E-A in *mate;* E short—*bed;* F—V at end of a word; G—Y in *yet* before soft vowels in stressed root syllables and after L and R in the same root syllable, otherwise G—*get;* G is silent before J; J—Y; K—*kite* but as CH in *church* before soft vowels in stressed root syllables; K is never silent before N (as in English); L is silent before J; N—NG before K; O—*solo* or as OO in *broom;* Q—K; RR—almost RR in *hurry;* S—*sister;* U—*rule;* U short—*put;* W—V in *vest;* X—KHS or as in *tax;* Y—German Ü; Z—S in *son;* Å—AW in *law;* Ä—about as A in *share*; Ö—about as UR in *fur*; AU—OW in *cow*; CH—K in *kite*; EU—OY in *toy*; NG—*singer*, not as in *finger*; DJ, HJ, LJ—Y in *year*; SCH, SKJ, SJ, STJ, SK—SH in *shut*; TJ—CH in *church*; OR—about as OO in *food;* SK before A, O, U and consonants—SC in *scold;* H—H but silent before J.

ICELANDIC

A Á Æ B D E É F G H I Í J K L M N O Ó Ö P R S T U Ú V X Y Ý Z Ð Þ
a á æ b d e é f g h i í j k l m n o ó ö p r s t u ú v x y ý z ð þ

Teutonic: Scandinavian. Roman alphabet or German Gothic alphabet. Icelandic is spoken by about 100,000 people in Iceland. The language is a direct descendant of old Icelandic, spoken by colonists from the Scandinavian mainland of Europe. Modern Icelandic differs considerably from the old language in which the classical sagas were written. Icelandic has special characters for DH and TH, and Æ and Ö. The values of other vowels including Y, may be altered by the accute accent. Consonants when doubled, are pronounced twice. The letter W is not used, and the letters, C, Q, Z, are usually omitted in writing Icelandic. A, E, I, O, Ö, U, before NG, NK, are pronounced like Á, EI, Í, Ó, AU, Ú, respectively.

B, D, G, H, K, L, M, N, P, R, S, T, V, X, are pronounced about as in English.

A—nearly A in *father;* Á—OW in *cow;* Ð—TH in *these;* E long about as A in *day* or as E in *bet* (short); F—*far* but like V in *vest* between vowels or as final; G—*get,* not as in *gem;* I—*sin;* Í—*machine;* J—Y in *year*; O—*not*; Ó—*note;* R—pronounced strongly; S—*sister,* not as in *easy;* U—about like French U; Ú—OO in *moon*; Y—I in *sin;* Ý—I in *machine;* Z—S in *sister;* Æ—Y in *try*; Ö—German Ö; Ð—TH in *these;* Þ—TH in *thin.* Accent usually is on the first syllable.

FAROESE

Teutonic: Scandinavian. Roman alphabet or German Gothic alphabet. Faroese is spoken in the Faroe Islands, north of the British Isles. It is a dialect of Icelandic but with considerable differences of pronounciation. Faroese orthography is uncertain; the language has been written only since the middle of the nineteenth century. Faroese makes use of the Icelandic alphabet. The letter (Þ) is not used.

RUNES

Ancient runes used by peoples of northern Europe are believed to have been derived from various sources—Latin, Greek, Phoenician, still their origin is unknown. The name *runic* meant the mystery of alphabets and writing. The letters were usually arranged in an order called *futhork* or *futhark* which takes its name from the sounds of the first six letters.

RUNIC ALPHABETS

	GOTHIC	ANGLIAN	SCANDINAVIAN
f	ᚠ ᚠ	ᚠ ᚡ	ᚠ
u	Λ ᚢ	ᚢ ᚢ	ᚢ
th	D ᚦ ᚦ	ᚦ	ᚦ
a,æ,o	ᚨ ᚨ	ᚩ ᚪ	ᚬ
r	ᚱ ᚱ	ᚱ	ᚱ ᛦ
c,k	ᚲ ᛣ	ᚳ	ᚴ
g	X	X	
v,w	ᚹ	ᚹ	
h	N И H H	ᚻ	ᚼ
n	ᚾ ᚾ	ᚾ	ᚾ ᚿ
i	ᛁ	ᛁ	ᛁ
y,ge,j,a	ᛃ ᛃ ᛃ	Φ	ᛅ ᛆ
ih,i,eo	ᛇ ᛇ	ᛇ	
p	ᛈ	ᛈ ᛈ	K
a,i,k,z	ᛉ	ᛉ	
s	ᛊ	ᛋ	ᛋ
t	ᛏ	ᛏ	ᛏ ᛐ
b	ᛒ	ᛒ	B
e	Π ᛖ	ᛖ	
m	ᛗ	ᛗ	ᛘ ᛘ
l	ᛚ	ᛚ	ᛚ
ng	ᛜ ᛜ	ᛝ	
d	ᛞ ᛞ	ᛞ	
o,oe	ᛟ ᛟ	ᛟ	

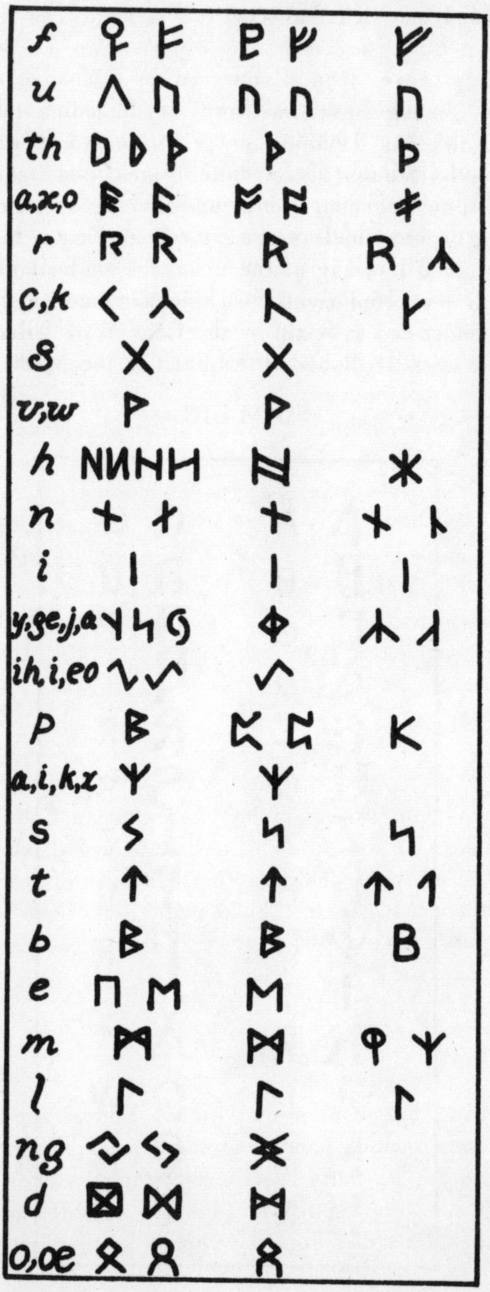

The *futhork* was subdivided into three *aetters*, sometimes called *frey*, *haegel* and *tyr*. Some runes were known as bitter runes, employed by sorcerers. 2. Good runes that averted misfortune. 3. Medical runes with healing power.

Runic writings have been discovered in a number of countries in northern Europe. Among these are: Nordic or Scandinavian runes of Denmark, Norway, Sweden; Teutonic or primitive Norse runes, Haelsinge runes, Manx, Slavic, Stungar rûnic (dotted runes) and Oghams. They were usually inscribed on weapons, stones and bracteates (circular pendants).

Runic writing began to decline about the beginning of the tenth century. They were abolished in many of the countries that adopted Christianity because of their purported mystic significance and pagan origin. Runic writings were condemned in Spain by the Council of Toledo in 1115. The runic characters were abolished in England in the sixth century.

GOTHIC

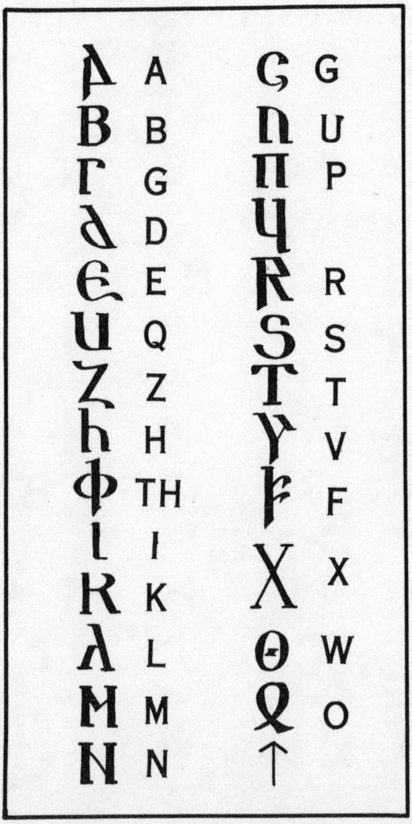

𐌰	A	𐌾	G
𐌱	B	𐌿	U
𐌲	G	𐍀	P
𐌳	D	𐍁	
𐌴	E	𐍂	R
𐌵	Q	𐍃	S
𐌶	Z	𐍄	T
𐌷	H	𐍅	V
𐌸	TH	𐍆	F
𐌹	I	𐍇	X
𐌺	K	𐍈	W
𐌻	L	𐍉	O
𐌼	M	𐍊	
𐌽	N		

CELTIC LANGUAGES

IRISH

Óir is mar so do ġráḋuiġ Dia an doṁan, go dtug sé a'éinġein Ṁheic féin, ionnus gid bé ċreideas añ nac racaḋ sé a múġa, acd go mbeiṫ an beṫa síorruiḋe aige.

A	a	A	G	g	G	O	o	O
B	b	B	H	h	H	P	p	P
C	c	C	I	i	I	R	r	R
D	d	D	L	l	L	S	s	S
E	e	E	M	m	M	T	t	T
F	f	F	N	n	N	U	u	U

Celtic: Goidelic. Irish or Erse alphabet. Irish is an ancient language and is closely related to Gaelic. Irish is the principal language of the Goidelic group of the Celtic language family, and with English it is the official language of the Irish Free State (Eire). The Irish alphabet was introduced into Ireland by Christian missionaries in the fifth-sixth centuries. Irish types and script are identical.

Certain rules in Irish must be noted.—Broad and slender vowels and consonants:

A, O, U are broad. E, I, are slender.

Long vowels are indicated by marks over them—Ó, É.

A consonant is broad when a vowel next to it in the same word is broad. A consonant is slender when the vowel next to it in a word is slender.

PHONETIC EQUIVALENTS

Long Vowel Sounds				*Short Vowel Sounds*			
1.	AA	A in	*half*	7.	A	A in	*hat*
2.	AE	AE "	*Gaelic*	8.	E	E "	*met*
3.	EE	EE "	*see*	9.	I	I "	*hit*
4.	AU	AU "	*taught*	10.	O	O "	*nŏt*
5.	O	O "	*so*	11.	U	U "	*much*
6.	OO	OO "	*tool*	12.	U	U "	*good*

Diphthongs

EI	EI in *sleight*	OI	OI in *toil*
OU	OU " *south*	EW	EW " *few*

Obscure vowel sounds: A, E as in c*ulpable*.

Consonants: B, F, M, P, V, W, Y, as in English. H as in English except in CH, DH, SH, TH. K, L, N, R, as in English. G–*get;* NG–*sing;* DH–TH in *this;* D–*day;* TH–*thick;* T–*tune;* R–*run*; S–*sister;* SH–*shut;* CH–GH; W–W (Connaught); W–V (Munster); V–V (Connaught); V–silent (Munster)

1. No consonant can be flanked by a broad vowel on one side and a slender vowel on the other side. Both vowels must be either broad or slender. 2. *Eclipsis*–This means that certain initial letters are sometimes silenced when other letters are prefixed to them, the sound then of the prefixed letter is heard instead of the eclipsed initial letter. Thus B may be eclipsed by M, C by G, D by N, F by BH, G by NG, P by B, S by T, and T may be eclipsed by D. 3. *Aspiration*: Only consonants may be aspirated. This is shown by a dot over the consonant to be aspirated in the Irish alphabet, or by adding the letter H after the consonant in the Roman alphabet. Thus the letter is softened or silenced. The letters B, C, D, F, G, M, P, S, and T, are aspirated in writing. Sometimes consonants are aspirated for euphonic effect, at other times aspiration is due to grammatical rules.

The letters J, K, Q, V, W, X, Y, Z, are not used in Irish (Roman alphabet) but the sounds of several of these letters are supplied as noted elsewhere. In Irish sometimes a "helping" vowel or indeterminate vowel is pronounced between two consonants, as in CN, LB, LG, LM, RG, GN, RN, pronounced then CAN, LAB, etc., although this indeterminate vowel is not written. In digraphs where one vowel is marked, the marked vowel has a long sound, the other vowel is almost mute. Final short vowels are never silent. In words of two syllables, the accent is usually upon the final syllable.

Sounds in Irish

A long as in *aught*	I short as in *hit*
A short as in *not*	O long as in *note*
E long as in *Gaelic*	O short as in *son*
E short as in *met*	U long as in *rule*
I long as in *machine*	U short as in *put*

Digraphs: AI, EA (A–*hat*); AE, AO (AE–*Gaelic*); AI, EA (AU); EI (E–*met*); OI (E–*met*); EO (YO); IO (I–*hit*); IA (EE–A); IA (EE); IU (EW); OI (U); UA (OO–A); AOI (EE); EOI (EO); IAI (EE–A); IUI (EW); UAI (OO–A).

Consonants: B, F, M, P, G, L, N, R, S (or SH), D (broad)–DH; T (broad)–TH. The letters L, N, also have thick sounds, made by pressing the tongue against the back of the upper teeth. The strong Irish R sound has no English equivalent. The Irish guttural GH sound is nearly similar with the sound of the modern Greek *gamma.* Irish grammarians distinguish differences between broad and slender sounds of some consonants.

Aspirated Consonants

The sounds of certain consonants are altered by adding a dot above the letter in the Irish alphabet, or by adding the letter H in the Roman alphabet, TH–H; SH–H; PH–F; FH is silent; BH, slender, next to E or L–V; BH, MH slender, as final–V, but sometimes silent in Munster; BH, MH slender, as initial–U; BH, MH broad as initial–W. But if either BH or MH is followed by a long vowel, U; CH broad–CH or GH; CH slender–H (Y) but H in Munster; DH, GH slender–Y as initial but are silent when medial or final, however DH, GH, slender lengthen a preceding vowel; DH, GH broad, are silent as medial or final; but they lengthen adjoining short vowels; DH, GH broad,–guttural GH when initial.

The letter D is silent in DL, DN; the letter N is silent in LN; LNG–L or N. In Connaught and Ulster MN–MR and CN–CR.

GAELIC

Oir is ann mar sin a ghradhaich Dia an saoghal, gu'n d'thug e 'aon-ghin Mhic féin, chum as ge b'e neach a chreideas ann, nach sgriosar e, ach gu'm bi a'bheatha shiorruidh aige.

A B C D E F G H I L M N O P R S T U
a b c d e f g h i l m n o p r s t u

Celtic: Goidelic: Roman alphabet. Gaelic is spoken in the highlands of Scotland. Vowels are broad—A, O, U, and slender—E, I. Long vowels are indicated by accent placed above them. Consonants—C, CH, D, DH, G, GH, L, N, R, S, T, have either broad or slender sounds and are always written between vowels of the same class (broad or slender). The consonants L, N, R, are long and are followed by the neutral or indeterminate vowel in LB, LBH, LG, LGH, LM, NBH, NCH, NM, NMH, RB, RBH, RCH, RG, RGH, RM.

Aspiration occurs in words according to grammatical rules and at the beginning of some words and is indicated by adding H to the consonants except L, N, R, and S in SG, SM, SP, ST. The strong stress always falls on the first syllable and final vowels in polysyllables are very short.

Vowels: Broad—A, O, U. Slender—E, I.

		Mutable
Consonants	Plain	G, C; D, T; L, N, R, S
	Aspirated	GH, CH; DH, TH, (LH), (NH), (RH), SH
		Immutable
Consonants	Plain	B, P; F, H, M
	Aspirated	BH, PH; FH, MH

A long—*far*	À,	ÀI,	EÀ,	EÀI	U short—*put*	U,	IU,	UI,	IUI
A short—*sofa*	A,	AI,	EA,	EAI	E long—*there*	È,	ÈA,	ÈI,	ÈU
O long—*lord*	Ò,	ÒI,	EÒ,	EÒI	E short—*yet*	E,	EA,	EI	
O short—*pot*	O,	OO,	OI,	EO,	E long—*they*	É,	ÉI,	ÉU	
	EOI								
O long—*doe*	Ó,	ÓI,	EÓ,	EÓI	E short—*convey*	(E),	EA,	EI	
O short—*piano*	O,	OI,	(EO),	(EOI)	I long—*machine*	Ì,	ÌO		
U long—*bull*	Ù,	ÙI,	IÙ,	IÙI	I short—*pin*	I,	IO,	AI	

AO is always long U as in *furl*. In diminutive suffixes, AG, (EAG) and AN, A has short, open sound—Ă. In the diphthongs IA and UA, both letters are distinctly sounded. AI-AI in *mountain*. Long A and long O before LL and NN are sounded AU, OU. Consonants except B, F, M, P, are mutable, with broad or slender quality, according to their positions with broad or slender vowels. With exceptions of L, M, N, R, S, (liquids and nasals) consonants are said to be voiceless, and the sound of nasals is carried into a succeeding consonant.

F, H, M, P, PH (F) are pronounced as in English.

B—P in *pet;* but B as initial; BH—V but often W or silent when final; C broad (with A, O, U)—hard C; C slender (with E, I)—K; CH broad—*loch;*

CH slender–German *ich;* D broad–T with point of tongue against front lower gum; D slender–T in *tin;* DH–GH broad; DH slender–GH slender; FH–usually silent; G broad–hard C; G slender–K; GH broad–guttural G but almost silent when final; GH slender–Y in *yet;* L–L with point of tongue against front lower gum; L–Italian *gli* or as in *million,* except when initial; L aspirated (LH) broad or back L in *hull;* L–(LH) slender front L in *mill;* MH–V in *vim,* but W or silent as final; N broad–N but as NI in *onion* when aspirated or as medial; R–broad or slender-trilled; S broad–*sun* but silent after T; T broad or slender–T in *ton;* TH–H. TH is silent in Gaelic *thu;* CHD–CHC; N after C, G, or M, is often sounded R; C, P, T, are explodent. Final C and P and T after short vowels take the breathing before them.

WELSH

Canys felly y carodd Duw y byd, fel y rhoddodd efe ei unig-anedig Fab, fel na choller pwy bynnag a gredo ynddo ef, ond caffael o hono fywyd tragywyddol.

A B C CH D DD E F FF G H I J K L LL M N O P PH R RH S T TH U W Y
a b c ch d dd e f ff g h i j k l ll m n o p ph r rh s t th u w y

Celtic: Brythonic. Roman alphabet. Welsh is spoken by about 2,500,000 people in Wales. Long vowels are sometimes marked (^). Initial consonants are subject to changes or mutations according to grammatical rules. Thus, *mawr* (masculine), becomes *fawr* (feminine)–*mynydd mawr* (great mountain), *afon* (avon) *fawr*–great river. Stress is usually on the penultimate syllable, but compounded words retain their proper accents.

B, D, H, M, N, P, R, S, T, are pronounced about as in English.

A–*father;* A short–nearly as in *man;* C–*cut;* CH–Scotch *loch;* DD–TH in *they;* E–A in *date* or short E as in *men;* F–*of* or as V in *vine; FF–afford;* G–*get;* I–*machine* or I short–*tin;* J–IA (in foreign words); L–*law* but with slight liquid sound; LL–LYI or Italian GLI or as about as LLI in *million*–a sound made by pressing the tip of the tongue against the teeth; O–*rose;* O short as in *not;* PH in *phonetic;* R–run but strongly sounded; RH–*arrow* but trilled; TH–*thin;* U–Y in *hymn;* W–OO in *tool;* Y–U in *run;* K–K but rare.

BRETON

A B C C'H D E F G H I J K L M N O P R S T V W Y Z
a b c c'h d e f g h i j k l m n o p r s t v w y z

Celtic: Brythonic. Roman alphabet. Spoken in Brittany in northern France. Breton is not related to the Romance languages. Dialects are: Leon (St. Pol de Leon), Vannes, Treguier, and Cornouaille.

Breton like Welsh is subject to certain consonantal mutations and provections. In the Leon dialect C'H is mutated into J and initial D is assimilated to a preceding N. The definite article becomes *al* before L and *an* before D, N, T, or a vowel; French accents are rarely used except in the Vannes dialect. AN and UN, as in French, are sometimes nasal, but not EN or ON. The letters B and D are explosive and N may have either hard, liquid or nasal sound.

CORNISH

En dallathvaz Dew aveth' wraz neve ha noare. Gen.1.1.

Celtic: Brythonic: Roman alphabet. Formerly spoken in Cornwall, southwest England, but since the beginning of the nineteenth century the language has become practically extinct. Cornish is akin to Breton and Welsh. Old Celtic origins are shown in names of places and people in Cornwall.

MANX

Son lheid y ghraih shen hug Jee da'n theihll, dy dug eh e ynrycan Vac v'er ny gheddyn, nagh jinnagh quoi-erbee chredjagh aynsyn cherraghtyn, agh yn vea ta dy bragh farraghtyn y chosney. Jn. 3. 16.

Geltic: Goidelic: Roman alphabet. Manx is a form of Gaelic spoken in the Isle of Man.

OGHAM SCRIPTS

Ogham scripts were runic characters of Celtic origin, used in Britain before the Roman conquest. The Ogham runic alphabet consisted of 20 letters or lines placed either above, below, or across a line. The letters were divided into 4 groups, each group containing 5 letters.

MANX RUNES

ABCDEF IKLMNORSTTHU

OGHAM

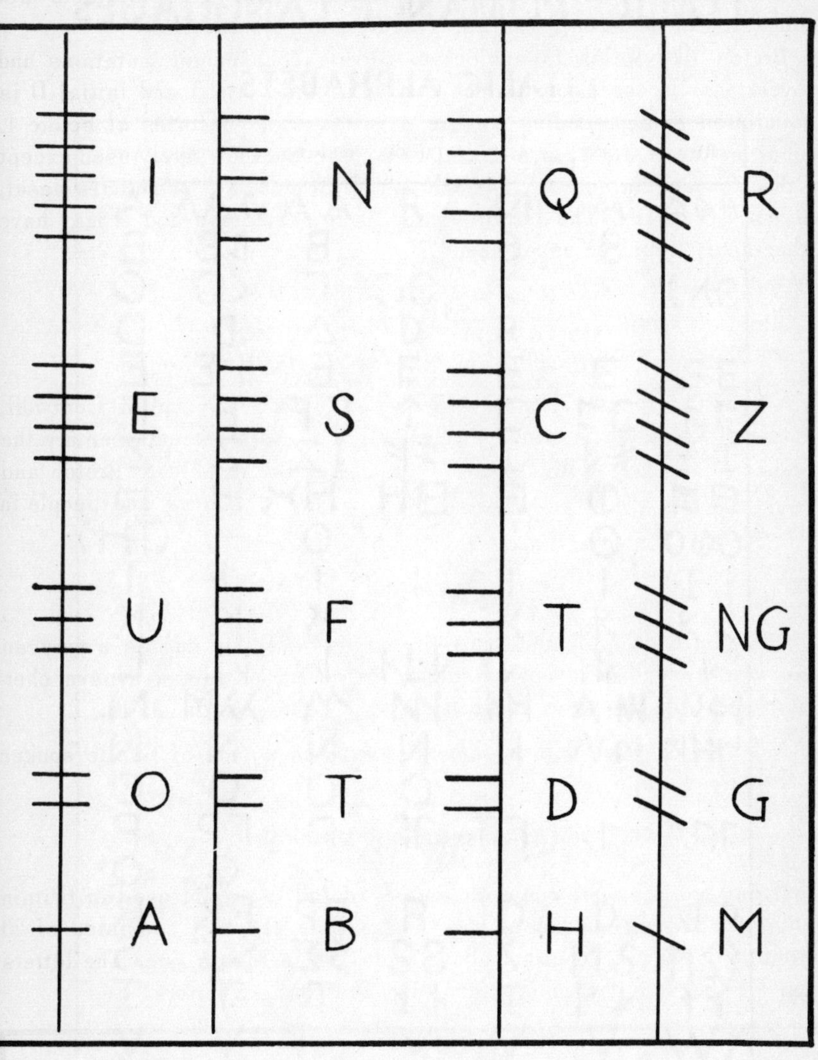

ITALIC, ROMANCE LANGUAGES

ITALIC ALPHABETS

ETRUSCAN	UMBRIAN	OSCAN	FALISCAN	MESSAPIAN	LATIN ARCHAIC	LATIN
AAA	A	◸	Я	A A	ΛAA	A
	8	8		B	BB	B
ƆλƆ		>	ƆC	Γ	<C	C
		Я	ᗡ	Δ	D	D
ƎƎ	Ǝ	Ǝ	Ǝ	E	II E	E
ꟻꟻ	ꟻꟻ	ꟻ	↑	[F	F	F
I ±	≠ ⅃	I	‡F	IZ	Z	Z
⊟ 目	Φ	⊟	⊟H	HX	H	H
O⊕O	⊙			⊙		(TH)
I I	I	I	I	I	I	I
> ꓘ	ꓘ	>I		K	K	K
⅃	⅃	⅃	⅃L⅃	V	VL	L
⋈ M	M Λ	HI	M	M	MM	M
ИHИ	ИV	H	N	N	N	N
			O	O	O	O
⅂ΠΛ	⅂	Π	⅂Γ	Γ	ΓP	P
					Q	Q
ꟼ D	D	D	Я	RP	PR	R
ΣƧM	ƧM	Ƨ	SƧ	≷Σ	≷S	S
ꓕf	ꓕY	T	ꓕY	T	T	T
YVV	V	V	V		V	V
↓			X	X	X	X
Φ ꟻ						(PH)
8CF	8	8				(F)
	d					(RS)
	q	⊢				(IE)

The chief alphabets employed in writing the languages of the Italian peninsula in earliest recorded times were: Etruscan, Oscan, Faliscan, Volscian, Messapian and Latin, all of which were derived from Greek. In the earliest inscriptions, most of the Italic alphabets were written from right to left or in boustrophedon except Latin which was nearly always written from left to right. Mention may be made, too, of Picenian, Siculan and Venetic letters (6th Century B.C.). Still, little is known of these ancient tongues and with the exception of Latin they possess but antiquarian or archaeological interest in the study of modern comparative philology.

The classical Etruscan alphabet dates from about the eighth century B.C. In earliest times, 23 letters were employed.

About 400 B.C., several letters were in disuse and the "classical" Etruscan alphabet employed 20 letters (See table of Italic alphabets).

Etruscan, Oscan and Umbrian had the letter 8 (f) which was not used in Latin. Etruscan omitted B, D, O, Q, but retained M (san) and the aspirated mutes ⊗, Φ, Ψ, not used in Latin. Umbrian retained ⊗, >I(k) but omitted C, O, Q, D, X Φ, Ψ. Oscan omitted ⊗, Φ, Ψ, X, O, Q, but retained C and K. Faliscan retained C, D, O, X, but omitted B, K, Q, ⊗, Φ, Ψ. Etruscan retains the soft mutes, TH, KH, PH, but omits B, G, D, whereas in Latin the rule is reversed. A new letter Ↄ (f) is retained in Etruscan, Oscan and Umbrian, but the letter Q is characteristic of Latin alone. According to some writers, all of the alphabets of the Italian peninsula are derived from the Pelasgic alphabet which was in turn derived from Chalcidian characters or west Greek.

LATIN

> In principio creavit Deus caelum et terram. Terra autem erat inanis et vacua, et tenebrae erant super faciem abyssi: et spiritus Dei ferebatur super aquas. Dixitque Deus: Fiat lux. Et facta est lux. Et vidit Deus lucem quod esset bona: et divisit lucem a tenebris. Appelavitque lucem Diem, et tenebras Noctem: factumque est vespere et mane, dies unus. —Genesis 1: 1-5.

Indo-European: Italic. Latin characters or Roman alphabet. The Latin language was spoken in Latium in the Italian peninsula from about the eighth century B.C. From earliest times the letters were usually written from left to right. Archaic Latin letters were borrowed from Phoenician through Greek or the Chalcidian dialects of west Greek spoken in Italy.

Latin was the language of ancient Rome and the official language of all the provinces of the Roman Empire from about the eighth century B.C. to the downfall of the empire of the West (C. 476 A.D.). Further, Latin was long retained as a cultural lingua franca in Europe until the Renaissance. Classical Latin was the chief literary language of the Middle-Ages, Latin terminology is retained in much of scientific nomenclature and legal phraseology in most of the nations of western Europe and in America, and is still employed as the pontifical language of the Roman Catholic church. Further, Latin is the mother tongue of all the Romance languages and its influence upon most of the languages of Europe has been profound. The most widely used characters are those of the Roman Alphabet employing the Latin characters.

Archaic Latin was written in capital letters: A B C D E F H I L M N O P Q P (R) S T V X. The letters Y and Z were added after the conquest of Greece and subsequent Greek influence upon Roman culture. The letter G was invented about 230 B.C. Before this innovation, the letter C had the power of G. But with addition of a small bar to the letter, C a great distinction was made thus converting the archaic C to our phonetic G (as in get) while retaining C without distinguishing bar which thereafter had the phonetic power of K (the letter K was rarely used by the Romans). The letter Y was introduced into the Roman alphabet about the time of Cicero. The letters Y and Z had become obsolete during the latter years of the late republic and early empire but were reintroduced at a later period. In earliest Latin Ϝ (digamma) was sometimes combined with H to represent the power of F. In some inscriptions P inverted or ꟼ stood for R; M had five strokes and Q had the form of Greek *Koppa.* The letters, J, U, were added later to the alphabet (adaptations of I, V).

Classical Latin so defined as established by more or less uniform grammatical rules with consistent spelling, was the tongue of Virgil, Horace and Plautus. Latin orthography of the first century is commonly used in editions of the classics.

In the classical language the vowels are: A, E, I, O, U, Y. Diphthongs are: AE, AU, EI, EU, OE, and in early Latin: AI, OI, OU, UI. A long–*father;* A short–nearly A in *hat;* E long–A in *day;* E short–E in *met;* I long–*machine;* I short–*sit;* O long–*bone;* O short–about like O in *not* or O in *obey;* U long–*rule;* U short–OO in *foot;* Y vowel between U and I–about like French U or German Ü.

Diphthongs: AE–AI in *aisle;* AU–OW in *cow;* EI–*eight;* EU–*feud;* OE–OY in *boy;* UI–OO+EE.

Consonants are about the same in English with exceptions noted: B—*boy* but was sometimes sounded like P before S or T; C—*come*, never like C in *cent*. In late Latin C sometimes had the power of S or as C in *cent;* G—*get*, never as G in *gem;* I consonant—Y in *year*; (About 300 A.D. I consonant began to take the sound of J in *jam*, but this pronunciation was not uniformly adopted. The improvized I with a small hook or J was added to the alphabet to indicate this sound.) N in NF, NS, might indicate nasalization of a preceding vowel, which was lenghthened; final M in an accented syllable might impart nasalization of a preceding vowel: CH—K; PH—P or more commonly (because of Greek influence) like F or PH in *telephone;* TH—T; S—*sit*, not as in *ease;* V (U consonant)—W in *west;* Z—DZ in *adze*.

Quantity: A vowel preceding H or another vowel is short. A vowel formed by contraction is long. A diphthong is long. A vowel before GN, NF, NS, is long. A vowel before ND, NT, is short. A syllable containing a long vowel or a diphthong is long. A syllable containing a short vowel followed by a mute before L or R, is short, but sometimes long in poetry. A syllable with a short vowel followed by two consonants, except a mute before L or R, or by a double consonant, X, Z, is long, but the vowel is short. A syllable with A, E, O, U, following I consonant, is long. In quantity H is not counted as a consonant, nor is U consonant in GU, QU, SU.

Accent: Words of two syllables—accent on the first syllable. Words of more than two syllables—accent on penult or next to the last syllable if the penult syllable is long; if the penult syllable is short, accent on the antepenult. When an enclitic is joined to a word, accent falls on the last syllable preceding the enclitic.

The Roman Numerals

I	1	XI	11	XXI	21
II	2	XII	12	XXX	30
III	3	XIII	13	XL	40
IV, IIII	4	XIV	14	L	50
V	5	XV	15	LX	60
VI	6	XVI	16	C	100
VII	7	XVII	17	CC	200
VIII	8	XVIII	18	D	500
IX	9	XIX	19	DC	600
X	10	XX	20	M	1000

LATIN SCRIPTS OF THE MIDDLE AGES

1. Early uncials. 2. Insular. 3. C. 9th-10th Cent. 4. C. 10th-11th Cent. 5. C. 11th-12th Cent.

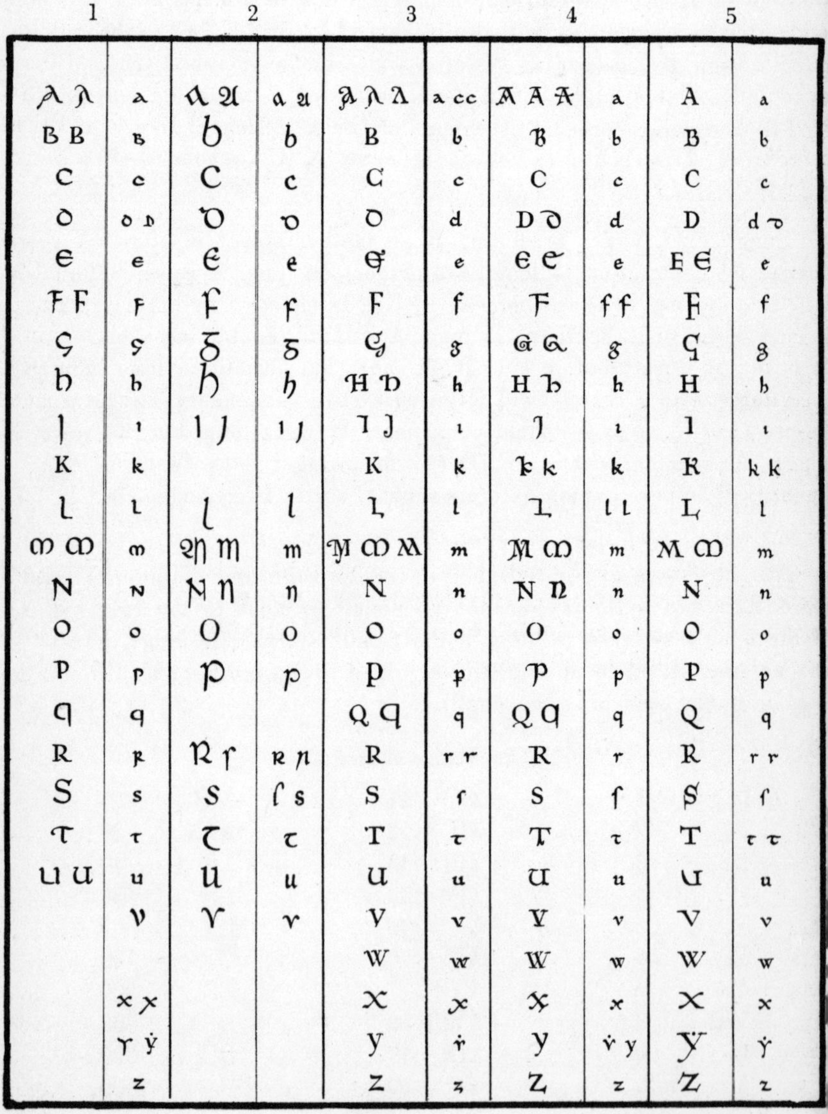

1		2		3		4		5	
A A	a	A A	a a	A A A	a cc	A A A	a	A	a
B B	b	b	b	B	b	B	b	B	b
C	c	C	c	C	c	C	c	C	c
D	d d	D	d	D	d	D D	d	D	d d
E	e	E	e	E	e	E E	e	E E	e
F F	f	F	f	F	f	F	f f	F	f
G	g	G	g	G	g	G G	g	G	g
h	h	h	h	H h	h	H h	h	H	h
I	i	I J	i j	I J	i	J	i	I	i
K	k			K	k	K k	k	K	k k
L	l	l	l	L	l	L	l l	L	l
M M	m	M M	m	M M M	m	M M	m	M M	m
N	N	N N	n	N	n	N N	n	N	n
O	o	O	o	O	o	O	o	O	o
P	p	P	p	P	p	P	p	P	p
q	q			Q q	q	Q q	q	Q	q
R	r	R r	r r	R	r r	R	r	R	r r
S	s	S	ſ s	S	ſ	S	ſ	S	ſ
T	t	T	t	T	t	T	t	T	t t
U U	u	U	u	U	u	U	u	U	u
	v	V	v	V	v	V	v	V	v
				W	w	W	w	W	w
	x x			X	x	X	x	X	x
	y ẏ			y	ẏ	y	ẏ y	Y	ẏ
	z			Z	z	Z	z	Z	z

ITALIAN

Nel principio Iddio creò il cielo e la terra. E la terra era una cosa deserta e vacua; e tenebre errano sopre la faccia dell' abisso; e lo Spirito di Dio si moveva sopra la faccia delle acque. E Iddio disse; Sia la luce. E la luce fu. E Iddio vide che la luce era buona. E Iddio separò la luce dalle tenebre. E Iddio nominò la luce Giorno, e le tenebre Notte. Così fu sera, e poi fu mattina, che fu il primo giorno. –Genesis 1: 1-5.

A B C D E F G H I J (K) L M N O P Q R S T U V (W) (X) (Y) Z
a b c d e f g h i j (k) l m n o p q r s t u v (w) (x) (y) z

Romance. Roman alphabet. Spoken by about 40,000,000 people in Italy, Sicily, etc. Of all Romance languages, Italian is the nearest to Latin. The Florentine or Tuscan dialect is the literary language. Italian differs from other Latin languages in the curious use of the letter I instead of L after C, F, P. There are no true diphthongs in Italian, vowels are pure and phonetic. Consonants with a few exceptions are clearly pronounced and when doubled are prolonged. There is but one accent, the grave(`) placed on the last accented syllable, but when accent is not on the final syllable, the penultimate syllable usually receives the stress. Some Italian dialects are: Abruzzi, Bergamesco, Bolognese, Calabrian, Corsican, Friolan, Genoese, Milanese, Neapolitan, Piedmontese, Romagnuola, Roman, Caliaritan, Venetian, Florentine or Tuscan, Sardinian, Lugudorese Sardinian, Tempiese Sardinian and Sicilian.

B, D, F, L, M, N, P, QU, T, V, are pronounced as in English. A, I, H, O, GN, R, are pronounced generally as in French.

A–*father;* C–CH in *church* before E or I; C–*cut* before A, O, U, or a consonant; E–A in *mate;* G–*get* before A, O, U, or a consonant, but G is like G in *gem* before E or I; H is silent but makes a preceding C or G hard, thus CH is like K and GH is like G–*get;* I–*machine;* J–Y in *year;* K–*kite* used only in words of foreign origin; O–*bone;* O short–about as AW in *law;* R–*run;* S–*sister,* but S between two vowels is pronounced like S in *ease;* U–*rule;* W–*west,* but rarely used; X–X but rarely used except in words of foreign origin; Y–long I used chiefly in foreign words; CH–K in *kite;* CI–CH in *church;* GI–G in *gem* (the letter I is not sounded); GH–G in *get;* GL– about like LI in *pavilion;* SC–SH before E or I, otherwise SK. J is rarely used.

SPANISH

En el principio creó Dios los cielos y la tierra. La tierra empero estaba sin forma y vacía; y yacían tinieblas sobre la haz del abismo; y el Espíritu de Dios cobijaba la haz de las aguas. Y dijo Dios: Haya luz, y hubo luz. Y vió Dios que la luz era buena; y separó Dios la luz de las tinieblas. Y llamó Dios á la luz Día, y á las tinieblas llamó Noche. Y hubo tarde y hubo mañana el día primero. —Genesis 1: 1-5.

A B C CH D E F G H I J (K) L LL M N Ñ O P Q R RR S T U V (W) X Y Z
a b c ch d e f g h i j (k) l ll m n ñ o p q r rr s t u v (w) x y z

Romance. Roman alphabet. Spoken in Spain, Central America, parts of the West Indies and South America, except Brazil. Castilian is the standard tongue and the literary language of Spain. In Mexico LL is usually pronounced like Y in yet, and the letter X may have various sounds—X, H, 'H, Z, SH: X—tax between two vowels; X-Z in *Tlaxcala* (tlazcala); X-H in *Oaxaca* (wahaka); X-'H or slightly guttural CH or KH in *Axayacatl* (achayakatl). The Berber SH is often written X—*Xeres* (shereth), now written *Jerez* ('hereth). Mexico is sometimes written *Mejico* and pronounced me'hiko (nearly).

The letter U in diphthongs when marked with (¨) is pronounced separately. Stress usually is on the last syllable, unless the word ends with a vowel. N or S, when it is on the last but one; otherwise, the acute accent indicates stress is on the syllable over which it is written. Some dialects are: Asturian, Catalan, Gallician or Gallego (similar to Portuguese), and Curaçao.

B, C, H, F, K, L, M, N, P, T, V, are pronounced as in English. K and W are used in foreign words. A, O, R, I, QU, Y, H, are pronounced generally as in French.

A—*father;* B is soft B, about like V; C—*cut* but C before E or I; C—TH as in *thick* (in Spain), but C before E or I—S or as C—*cent* (in Spanish America); D—*dart* when following L or N or as initial, otherwise D is almost like TH in *these* but D as final letter is sometimes lisped or silent; E—A in *mate;* G—*get,* but G is about like H in *hat* before E or I; H is silent; I—*machine;* J—guttural H or KH or about like CH in Scotch *loch,* but J is almost silent when final; LL—LI in *million;* Ñ—NI in *onion;* O—*obey;* R—*run* but strongly pronounced; RR—*hurry* but strongly pronounced or rolled on the tongue. S—*sun;* U—*rule;* Y—I vowel in *machine;*

Y—*yet* when between two vowels or as initial before a vowel; Z—TH in *thin* (in Spain), but Z—S in *sun* (in Spanish America); GU—GU in *guess* but GW before A, O, U; AI—*aisle*.

CATALAN

A B C Ç CH D E F G GU GÜ H I J K L L.L LL M N O P QU QÜ R S T U V X Z
a b c ç ch d e f g gu gü h i j k l l.l ll m n o p qu qü r s t u v x z
NY

Romance. Roman alphabet. Catalan or Catalonian is spoken by about 4,000,000 people in Catalonia, northeastern Spain. Catalan is akin to Provençal.

Catalan pronunciation differs from Castilian Spanish as follows: CH—Spanish CH, final K; G—J before E and I, not as K H;- LL—L, not LI or Y; Ñ is not used, but is replaced by NY; NY before a consonant—N' but not NI.

SARDINIAN

Aici, nau a bosu, incit hat essiri gosu ananti de is angelus de Deus po unu peccadori chi s'est convertiu.
Lk. 15.10 Cagliaritan dialect.

Sardinian is a very ancient Romance language, with many old Latin words unchanged. There are two main dialects: Logudorese spoken in Central Sardinia, Cagliaritan spoken in southern Sardinia, and Sassarese and Tempiese spoken in northern Sardinia.

PORTUGUESE

No príncípio creou Deus os céus e a terra. E a terra era sem fôrma e vazia; e havia trevas sôbre a face do abismo: e o Espírito de Deus se movia sôbre a face das águas. E disse Deus: Haja luz: E viu Deus que era boa a luz: e fez Deus separação entre a luz as trevas. E Deus chamou à luz Dia; e às trevas chamou Noite. E foi a tarde e a manhã, o dia primeiro. Genesis 1:1—5.

A ÃE ÃO B C Ç D E F G H I J (K) L LH M N NH O ÕE P Q R S T U V (W) X Y Z
a ãe ão b c ç d e f g h i j (k) l lh m n nh o õe p q r s t u v (w) x y z

Romance. Roman alphabet. Spoken by about 48,000,000 people in Portugal and Brazil. Portuguese is akin to Spanish but has certain affinities with French–nasal sounds, etc. Some Portuguese dialects are: Galician of Spain, and Indo-Portuguese, formerly spoken in Ceylon. Marks of accent are: Accute (´) to indicate the stressed syllable, Circumflex (^) to indicate that the vowel marked has an I or U sound, or to show that O is pronounced O and not U. Except in AE, AO, OE, OU, noted below, each vowel is sounded distinctly. Except when marked with the accute accent, stress is usually on the penultimate syllable.

B, C, D, F, L, M, N, P, T, V, are pronounced as in English. Ç, CH, G, H, J, R, are generally pronounced as in French.

A stressed–about as in *father;* A unstressed or before M or N–almost ER or about as in *pert;* C–*cent* before E or I, otherwise C–*cut;* Ç–S or as C in *cent* before A, O, U; E (open)–A in *date;* E (closed)–about as E in *met,* but E is sometimes silent when final; G–ZH or as Z in *azure* before E, I or Y, otherwise G–*get;* H is usually silent; I stressed–*machine;* I unstressed–*perish;* J–ZH or as Z in *azure;* K–*kite* but used rarely; LH–LI in *million;* M–*man* but with additional nasal sound or more nearly NG when final; N–*not* but with slight nasal sound, about as NG, when final; NH–NI in *onion;* O (closed)–*pole;* O (open)–*north;* when O–OO or O as in *do;* QU–K before E, I, or Y, but QU–KW before A or O; O; S–*sun* when initial or at beginning of a syllable; S–*tease* when between two vowels; S–SH before a consonant; S–ZH or as Z in *azure* when final; U–*rule* or short U in *put,* but U is silent in GUI, GUE, QUI, QUE; W–V in *vest;* X between E and another vowel–Z in *azure,* otherwise X–SH in *shut;* Y with stress–*machine;* Y unstressed–*pin*; Y–Y in *yet* before a vowel; Z–*zest,* but Z as final–ZH or as Z in *azure.*

ÃE–about as in *fat* with nasal sound or nearly AH–ENG; ÃO–about as A in *mar* with nasal sound or nearly OWNG; AI–*aisle;* EI–*vein;* ÕE–about like AW in *law* with nasal sound or nearly OING; OU–O in *hope.*

FRENCH

Au commencement Dieu créa le ciel et la terre. La terre était informe et vide; les ténèbres couvraient l'abîme, et l'Esprit de Dieu se mouvait au-dessus des eaux. Dieu dit: "Que la lumière soit!" et la lumière fut. Et Dieu vit que la lumière était bonne; et Dieu sépara la lumière et les ténèbres. Dieu appela la lumière Jour, et les ténèbres Nuit. Et il y eut un soir, et il y eut un matin; ce fut le premier jour. –Genesis 1: 1-5.

A B C D E F G H I J K L M N O P Q R S T U V W X Y Z
a b c d e f g h i j k l m n o p q r s t u v w x y z

Romance. Roman alphabet. French is spoken by about 68,000,000 people in France, also in parts of Belgium, Switzerland, Haiti, in the French colonies and possessions in North Africa, Asia, and in the Province of Quebec in the Dominion of Canada. Some French dialects are: Amiens, Auvergne, Bourgogne (Burgundy), Dominica, St. Lucia (Grenada and Trinidad), Franche Comte, Grasse Provençal, Guernsey (Channel Islands), Mauritius Creole (Mauritius, Madagascar), Marseilles Provencal, Saintonge, Toulouse, Vaudois, Limousin, Lyonnais, Dauphine.

French is not a phonetic language. Many letters are silent or absorbed and often sounds of final consonants are continued as initial sounds of following words. Nasal sounds are peculiar to the French language. The nasal sound might be described as if one were about to say *bong* (for *bon*) but with the final *ng* sound almost silent, or as it might be pronounced *bo'* with the mouth kept open. This sound must be heard to be properly understood. Diphthongs with nasal sounds are: 1. AM, AN, AEN, EM, EN, AON. 2. AIM, AIN, EN, EIM, EIN, IM, IN, YM, 3. OM, ON. 4. UM, UN, EUN. These sounds resemble nearly: 1. AR or A in *father*. 2. A or A in *share*. 3. AW in *law*. 4. UR in *fur*. But each combination of letters or each diphthong has the nasal sound described nearly as a final *ng* yet hardly heard. The diphthong OIN is equivalent to the nasal IN preceded by W. Yet these combinations of letters, except when they form definite syllables, do not always possess nasal sounds. In general, a final M or N alters the value of a preceding vowel and imparts the nasal sound.

Liaison, or the joining of words, is another peculiarity of French. Many final consonants although mute or silent, are continued and sounded when the following word has an initial vowel or an initial silent H. Thus, final C is continued with sound of K, final F is continued with sound of V. Final S is continued with sound of Z, final X is continued with sound of Z.

Orthographical signs are: 1. The apostrophe (') which denotes elision of a final vowel. 2. The trema or diaeresis (¨) over E, I, U, when either of these vowels form a dysyllabic with a preceding vowel, except with E which becomes É. 3. The cedilla (¸) under C which gives that letter the value of S before A, O, U. 4. The hyphen (-) is used to join together names, etc. The marks of accents are: Acute (´) over E expecially when followed by another vowel and forming a dysyllable with that vowel. Grave (`) over A or E, especially the latter, when followed by a syllable with a mute vowel. Circumflex (^) over a vowel to indicate contraction or omission of S. Final consonants: Generally consonants at the end of a word are not sounded but a few exceptions may be noted: Final C, F, L, R, are usually sounded but final R in verbs of the first conjugation is silent. Final F is silent in a few words. Final L is silent in *fils* but S is sounded.

B, C, D, F, K, L, M, N, P, S, T, V, X, Z, are pronounced about as in English but see notes below—variant sounds, etc.

A—about as in *ask* but broader; A—*father*, before final *sion, tion*, final S (except when denoting plural), final se, before ILL, RR. C—*cent* before E and I; C—*cut* before A, O, U; Ç (with cedilla)—*cent;* CH—SH in *shut* but—K in some words of Greek origin; É—A in *day;* É—A in *day* immediately preceding D, R, and Z; È—*met* but broader before consonants except D, R, Z; Ê—first E in *there;* unaccented E at end of syllables is silent, but as final followed by another word with initial consonant E, imparts full articulation to the preceding consonant. Es in plurals of nouns is silent. *Es* and *ent* in conjugations are silent. E is pronounced like short A in the word *femme* and in adverbial terminations.

G—*get* before A, O, U but as ZH or Z in *azure* before E and I; GN—NY about as in *onion;* GU—G in *get* before E and I; H is silent; I—*machine* but somewhat shorter; I—*machine;* J—ZH or as Z in *azure;* K—*kite* (generally used only in foreign names); L—*law* but liquid L has nearly the value of Y in the following combinations of letters: AIL, AILLE, EIL, EILLE, EUIL, OUIL, IL, ILLE. Initial ILL does not have the liquid L sound.

M followed by N is silent in a few words; O—*note* before final S, SE, T, TION; O closed—between O in *bone* and AW in *law;* Ô—*note;* P—pull but silent in a few words; Q—K as in *kite* but also like KW in a few words; QU—K as in *kite* but also like KW in a few words; R—*run* but sharply pronounced; R in ER, and ERS, is sometimes silent; S—*sun* but more nearly Z between two vowels; final S is silent.

T—*tent* but like S in final TION, TIAL, TIEL; T final is usually mute or silent; TH—T as in *ton;* U—pronounced with pursed lips about as EE in *eel;* W—V as in *vest;* X in a few words has the value of S, but is generally silent as final; Y vowel like long E; I in *machine;* Y consonant—Y in *yet;* Z is generally silent when final.

AI, AY, EI, EY—A in *day;* AI—A in *day* when initial or final sound; AI, AY, EI, EY—E in *set* but longer; AU, EAU—O in *hope* EU, OEU—U in *but;* EU, OEU before X, S, T,—nearly like UR in *fur* pronounced with rounded lips; OI—WA in *wash;* OU—OO in *room;* Y between two vowels alters the sound of the first vowel if the first vowel is A, E, O—OEI—ÖI; OUI—WEE. Stress is about evenly distributed.

PROVENÇAL

Car Dio ame enaymi lo mont, qu'el dones lo seo filh un engenra, que tot aquel que cre en luy non perissa, mas aia vita eterna.
Jn. 3:16.

Ancient Provençal was developed during the 11th and 12th centuries in southern France when Latin was yielding to vernacular speech. Provençal was the language of the Waldensians and Albigensians.

Old Provençal was no longer used as a literary language after the 15th century, but the spoken language was continued as a patois. Modern Provençal was revived by the Felibrige in the 19th century. It differs considerably from the ancient tongue. Dialects spoken in southern France are Grasse Provençal and Marseilles Provençal. In Provençal the old Latin AU retains its value as a distinctive diphthong—AU. In other Romance languages AU has become O.

VAUDOIS

Car Dieus amet aysi lo mont qu'el sieu engenrat filh dones per el, que totz aquels que crezon en el non periscan, mas aian vida durabla. Jn. 3:16.

Ancient Vaudois was spoken by the Waldensians in the Piedmont region of Italy during the middle ages. Modern Vaudois is spoken in northwestern Italy and southeastern France.

WALLOON

« Quî èst-ce, mi mame? èt wice èst-i m'parintèdje? Et tapant 'ne loukeure so lès cis qu'èstit st-assiou âtoû d'lu, i' dèrit: « Vochal mi mame èt mès parints, ca c'èst l' ci qui fait l' volté dè bon Diu du'èst m'fré, mi soûr, et m'mame. » Mk. 3:33-35.

Romance. Roman alphabet. Spoken in southern Belgium and northeastern France. Walloon is a Latin language and is akin to French but with certain Teutonic elements.

Walloon retains the Teutonic W which is pronounced variously V and F when used in Teutonic words, instead of the French G of GU. The letter W is pronounced in QU as in English, but these letters are sometimes spelled CU or COU in Walloon. CH is pronounced as CH in church. The sound of the letter S is retained before T and other consonants; otherwise Walloon pronunciation is similar to French.

RHAETIC

Perche cha Deis ha tant amâ il muond, ch'el ha dat seis unigenit figl, acio cha scodüin chi craja in el non giaja a perder, ma haja la vita eterna. Lower Engadine dialect. Jn. 3. 16.

Romance. Roman alphabet. Rhaetic, an ancient Romance language, is a descendant of the old "lingua rustica" of the Romans. There are two dialects: Romansch and Ladin. Romansch is spoken by about 46,000 people in Switzerland and is now one of the four official languages of that country.

Dialects or vernaculars of Romansch are: Lower Engadine, spoken in the lower Engadine Valley in Switzerland. Upper Engadine dialect, spoken in the Upper Engadine Valley, eastern Switzerland; Oberland dialect, spoken in the Oberland region of canton Grisons, central Switzerland; Ladin, spoken in parts of south Tirol.

RUMANIAN

Fiindcă atît de mult a iubit Dumnezeu lumea, că a dat pe singurul Lui Fiu, pentruca oricine crede în El, să nu piară, ci să aibă viaţa vecinică.

A Ă Â B C D Ḑ E É Ĕ Ê F G H I Ĭ Î J K L M N O Ó P R S Ş T Ţ U Ŭ V X Y Z
a ă â b c d ḑ e é ĕ ê f g h i ĭ î j k l m n o ó p r s ş t ţ u ŭ v x y z

Romance: Eastern. Roman alphabet. Rumanian or Wallachian is the most easterly member of the Romance language family, but its vocabulary has a large mixture of Slavonic, Magyar, Greek and Turkish words. Rumanian is spoken by about 13,000,000 people in Rumania, parts of Macedonia, Albania and Thessaly. Formerly Rumanian was written in the Cyrillic alphabet or in Greek characters, but modern Rumanian is written in Latin characters with diacritical marks to represent Slavonic sounds. Dialects: Macedonian, Daco Rumanian, Megleno, Aroumanian.

Rumanian spelling has undergone many reforms and sometimes texts written in the old spelling are quite confusing because of the different forms used in spelling the same word. But recently Rumanian orthography has been modified and a number of old diacritical marks have been abolished. There are three classes of diphthongs: Diphthongs ending in I, including AI, ÂI, EI, UI. Diphthongs in which the stress is on the first vowel, and these include AU, ĂU, EU, OU, IO, OA. Diphthongs in which the stress is on the second vowel, and these include: EA, IA, IE, IU.

Even four or more vowels may occur together. The vowel combinations: AIŬ, EIU, UIU are pronounced as a single sound. Stress is irregular but is often on the penultimate syllable.

B, D, F, L, M, N, P, T, V, X, Z, are pronounced as in English. A, J, R, O, Y are pronounced generally as in French. C, CH, G, GH, U, are pronounced generally as in Italian.

A–*father;* Ă–about like in *cigarette;* Â–UR in *fur;* C–CH in *church;* before E, I, otherwise K; E–E in *yet* or more nearly like YAY as initial or when preceding a vowel, otherwise E–A in *mate;* EA–YA in *yard;* G–G in *get*, but as G in *gem* before E or I; H–KH or almost like CH in Scotch *loch;* I–*machine;* I–Y in *yet* before a vowel, but I is almost silent when final; Î–about I in *fir*; J–ZH or as Z in *azure;* O–note; OA–WA in *wad;* R–*run* but pronounced sharply; S–*sister;* Ș–SH in *shut;* T–*ton;* Ţ–TS in *sits;* U–*rule;* Y–Y *vowel;* CH–K in *kite;* GH–G in *get.* The following letters are obsolete or rarely used in modern Rumanian: Ḑ, DI–Z (now written Z); É–EA (now written EA); Ĕ–Ă; Ê–Â; Ĭ–almost silent I; Î–Â (now used only as initial); Ó–OA (now written OA); Ŭ–almost silent U.

LATIN–INCUNABULA TYPES

Pater noſter qui es in celis ſan=
ctificetur nomē tuū. Adueniat regnū
tuū Fiat uolūtas tua: ſicut in celo et
in terra. Panē noſtrū ſupſubſtātialē
da nobis hodie. Et dimitte nobis de=
bita noſtra: ſicut et nos dimittimus
debitoribus noſtris. Et ne nos indu=
cas in temptationē: ſed libera nos a
malo.

BALTIC, FINNO-UGRIAN AND THRACO-ILLYRIAN LANGUAGES

FINNISH

Alussa loi Jumala taivaan ja maan. Ja maa oli autio ja tyhjä, ja pimeys oli syvyyden päällä, ja Jumalan Henki liikkui vetten päällä. Ja Jumala sanoi: „tulkoon valkeus," ja valkeus tuli. Ja Jumala näki valkeuden hyväksi. Niin Jumala eroitti valkeuden pimeydestä. Ja Jumala kutsui valkeuden päiväksi, ja pimeyden kutsui hän yöksi. Ja tuli ehtoosta ja aamusta ensimmäinen päivä.—Genesis 1: 1–5.

A D E G H I J K L M N O P R S T U V Y Ä Ö
a d e g h i j k l m n o p r s t u v y ä ö

Finno-Ugrian. Roman alphabet. Spoken in Finland. Finnish is akin to Hungarian, Estonian, Lapp, etc. The alphabet consists of 21 letters, the letters C, Q, W, X, Z, are not used; B, F, are used only in foreign names. Vowels, including Y are short when single but are made long by doubling them. In diphthongs, both vowels are sounded but as if they formed one syllable. Principal stress falls on the first syllable of each component word; the accented syllable is indicated by (') placed above a letter in the syllable. Dialect-Karelian.

D, H, K, L, M, N, P, T, are pronounced about as in English.

A–about like A in *father* but short; AA–A in *arm;* Ä–*hat;* E–*pen;* EE–about like E in *eh;* G–*get,* used only in combinations with N, and in foreign words; H–*house* but strongly aspirated, nearly German CH in *ich;* I–*sin;* II–*machine;* J–Y in *yet;* O–about O in *not* or O in *log;* OO–AW in *law;* R–*run* but sharply trilled; S–*sister;* U–*bull* or longer as OO in *wood;* UU–OO in *boot;* Y–German Ü; Ö–nearly ER in *herb.*

AI–*aisle;* AU–OW in *cow;* AI–Ä + I; ÄY–Ä + Ü; EI–*eight;* IE–IE in *Vienna;* IU–about like U in *duty;* OI–*toil;* ÖI–French OEI; OU–O in *hope;* ÖY–Ö + Y; UO–U + O or about like WA; YI–Y + I; YÖ–Y + Ö. B, C, D, F, G, Q, X, Z, Å occur in foreign words.

ESTONIAN

A Ä B D E F G H I J K L M N Ö Õ Ô P R S Š T U Ü V W Z Ž
a ä b d e f g h i j k l m n ö õ ô p r s š t u ü v w z ž

Finno–Ugrian. Roman alphabet. Spoken in Estonia. Single vowels are short but are made long by doubling them. The vowels are pronounced about as in Finnish with exceptions noted below. Vowel pairs (18) are: AI, ÄI, AU, ÄU, EA, EI, IU, ÕE, OE, ÖE, ÕI, ÖI, OI, ÕU, OU, UE, ÜI, and UI (U + I). The consonants B, D, G, are not used as initials except in words of foreign origin. Some dialects are: Reval, Dorpat, Setu.

B, D, F, K, L, M, N, P, T, V, are pronounced about as in English.

G–*get;* H–*house* but always aspirated; J–Y in *year;* LI–similar to Italian GLI; NI–nearly like Italian GNI; Õ–between u in *rug* and UR in *fur;* R–*run* but strongly sounded; S–between S in *easy* and S in *sister;* SS–*miss;* Š–SH in *shut,* usually in foreign words: Ž (in foreign words)–ZH or Z in *azure.*

LITHUANIAN

Taipo Dievas mylėjo svietą, kad savo viengimusįįį sunų davė jeib visi į įį tikinetieii ne prapultų, bet amzinąįą gyvatą turetų.

A Ą B C Č D E Ė Ę F G H I Į Y J K L Ł M N O P R S Š T U Ū Ų Ů V W Z Ž Ż
a ą b c č d e ė ę f g h i į y j k l ł m n o p r s š t u ū ų ů v w z ž ż
CH, CZ, SZ

Baltic. Roman alphabet. Spoken by about 1,600,000 people in Lithuania and East Prussia. Pronunciation of Lithuanian letters is similar to Polish pronunciation. Four nasal vowels are generally used in inflection. Stress is irregular. Dialect–Samogit.

B, D, K, L, M, N, O, P, R, S, T, V, Z, are pronounced as in English.

A–*father;* Ą–nasal A; C–TS in *sets;* Č–CH in *church;* E–open E, nearly EH or AH as initial, or nearly YA in *yard* when stressed after a consonant, often marked with tilde–Ẽ; Ę–nasal E about like French En; Ė–AI; F–*far* in foreign words; G–*get;* H–*hat* in foreign words; I–about as in *hit;* Į–nasal I as in French *In;* Y–*machine;* J–Y in *year;* Ł–Polish Ł;SS–*sister;* Š–SH in *shut;* U–*boot;* Ų–nasal U as in French *Un;* Ū–long U; Ů–UO; Z– nearly S in *set;* Ž, Ż–ZH or Z in *azure;* or nearly SH in *shut.*

CH–about like in *chorus,* in foreign words: CZ–TSCH: DŻ, DŽ–J in *jam;* SZ–nearly SH in *shut;* IAI–about like A in *date;* UO–WAW. The vowels A, E, I, U, are written long–Ą, Ę, Į, Ų.

LETTISH

A Ā B C Č D E Ē F G Ģ H I Ī J K Ķ L Ļ M N Ņ O P R Ŗ S Š T U Ū V Z Ž Ẓ
a ā b c č d e ē f g ģ h i ī j k ķ l ļ m n ņ o p r ŗ s š t u ū v z ž ẓ
DZ, DŽ, IE. Old characters: G̸, K̸, L̸, N̸, R̸, S̸
Note: Č–Ç, Š–Ş, Ž–Ẓ

Baltic. Roman alphabet. Latvian or Lettish is spoken by about 1,000,000 people in Latvia. Stress usually is on the first syllable. The Gothic alphabet was abandoned by official regulation in 1921.

B, D, F, H, K, L, M, N, P, R, T, Z, are pronounced as in English.

A—*father;* C—TS in *sets;* Č—CH in *church;* DZ—*adze;* DŽ—J in *jam;* E—*yet;* G—*get;* Ģ—DI in *soldier;* I—*tin;* IE—IA; J—Y in *yet;*. Ķ—about like TI in *fortune;* Ņ—*onion;* Ļ—LLI in *million;* O—closed with a slight W sound preceding it; R, Ŗ is rolled on tongue; S—*sister;* Š—SH in *shut;* U—*but;* Ū—OO in *tool;* V—V but U as final; Ž—ZH or as Z in *azure.*

HUNGARIAN

Kezdetben teremté isten a mennyet és a földet. A föld pedig vala ékesseg nélkűl való és puszta, és setétség vala a mélységnek színén, és az Úrnak Lelke táplálja vala a vizeket. Akkor monda az Isten: Legyen világosság: és lett világosság.

A Á B C D E É F G H I Í J K L M N O Ó Ö Ő P R S T U Ú Ü Ű V X Y Z
a á b c d e é f g h i í j k l m n o ó ö ő p r s t u ú ü ű v x y z
Cs, Cz, Ds, Gy, Ly, Ny, Sz, Ty, Zs, Dzs

Ugrian. Roman alphabet. Hungarian or Magyar is spoken by about 8,000,000 people in Hungary and adjoining regions. Distinction must be made between the long and short vowels, for often the meaning of a word depends upon pronunciation. When a consonant is doubled it is pronounced twice or doubly with slight stress on the first syllable. Short final vowels, A, E, are prolonged in words that have affixes.

Hungarian vowels are divided into the following groups: Short—A, E, I, O, Ö, U, Ü, *Long*—Á, É, Í, Ó, Ő, Ú, Ű. These are subdivided into, *Flat*—A, Á, O, Ó, U, Ú, *Sharp*—E, Ő, Ö, Ü, Ű. Mediate, É, I, Í, A rule of Hungarian vowel sounds is harmony—A suffix must sound like a vowel in the root. Stress is always on the first syllable.

B, D, F, H, K, L, M, N, P, T, V, Y, Z, are pronounced as in English.

A–*watch*, or O in *got;* Á–*father;* C, CZ–TS in *sets;* CS–CH in *church;* DS, DZS–J in *jam;* E–about like A in *hat* or as E in *lend;* É–A in *date;* G–*get;* I–*tin;* Í–*machine;* J–Y in *year;* GY–D' or DG; LY–LLI in *million* or like Y in *yet;* NY–NI in *onion;* O–*port;* Ó–*bone;* Ö–about like Er in *her;* Ő–about like UR in *fur;* R–*run* but sounded sharply; S–*shut;* SZ–S in *sister;* TY–T in *tune* with slight consonantal Y intonation after T. (The same rule applies to GY). U–*bull;* Ü–French U; Ú–*rude;* Ű–long U about like in *duty;* X–X in *ox* but rarely used; Y–I or soft sign; ZS–ZH or Z in *azure.*

ALBANIAN

Sepse Perëndia kaqë e deshi botënë, sa dha Birin'e ti të-vetëmlindurinë, që të mos humbashë kushdo që t'i besonjë ati, po të ketë jetë te-përjetëshme.

A B C Ç D E Ë F G H I J K L M N O P Q R S T U V X Y Z
a b c ç d e ë f g h i j k l m n o p q r s t u v x y z
DH, GJ, LL, NJ, RR, SH, TH, XH, ZH

Thraco-Illyrian. Roman alphabet, but formerly written in Greek letters and in three native alphabets–Buthakükye, Elbassan and Veso Bei script. Spoken in Albania. In the Tosk dialect the Gheg letter N is usually pronounced R and sometimes written R. The letter Ë is silent in Gheg. The acute accent lengthens a vowel and the circumflex nasalises it. Stress is usually on the penultimate syllable. Dialects are: Gheg, Calabrian, Sicilian, Tosk.

B, D, F, H, K, L, M, N, P, R, RR, S, SH, Z, ZH, are pronounced as in English.

A–*father;* C–*sets;* Ç–CH in *church;* DH–TH in *father;* E–*end;* E–A in *day;* I–*machine* or short in *pin,* G–*get;* GJ–nearly DG in *edge;* I–*machine* or short I in *pin;* LL–L or Polish Ł; NJ–NI in *onion;* O–*no* or as in *only;* Q–KY or TY; RR–strong R; SH–*shut;* TH–*thick;* XH–J in *jam* or like DJ in *adjective;* Y–German Ü; T–T; V–V. The letter E after U, the letter B after M, and the letter D after N, are silent in Gheg but pronounced in Tosk. The letter Ë has about the value of the neutral vowel E in Tosk but is silent in Gheg.

MINOAN, MYCENAEAN AND HELLENIC LANGUAGES

MINOAN OR CRETAN

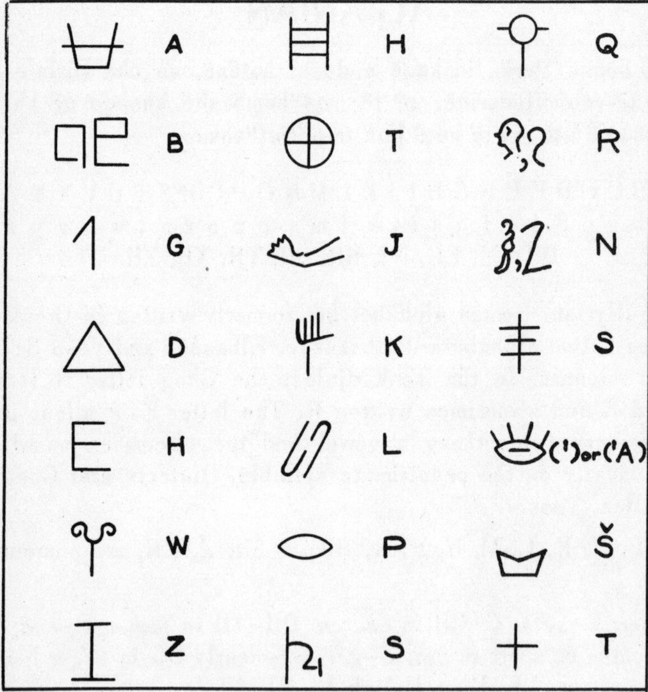

From the island of Crete in the Aegean Sea comes evidence of a native character employed in writing, that was in existence before the Phoenician alphabet had been invented. In ancient Crete a culture apparently indigenous in its primitive stages had been developed many centuries before the coming of the Hellenic race to the mainland. It is believed that there was a period of about 5,000 years of a so-called neolithic period, followed by the bronze age civilization on the island of Crete. Excavations at Knossus have brought to light much evidence of a Cretan culture dating from very early times.

The Minoan period of civilization extended over a period of about 1400 years, beginning about 2500 B. C., and ending with complete destruction, about 1100 B. C. According to Evans, the Minoan bronze age may be divided into three great periods: 1, Early, 2. Middle, 3. Late.

Cretan chronological periods are subdivided into nine cultural phases, designated, EM–I, II, III, MM–I, II, III, LM–I, II, III. Minoan writings of the earliest type were largely pictographic and designated according to apparent chronological groups, class A, class B, etc. In the earliest examples writing was sometimes in boustropheidon but later specimens were usually written from left to right. Linear script seems to have been employed in the late MM period or about the 17th century B.C.

CYPRIOTE

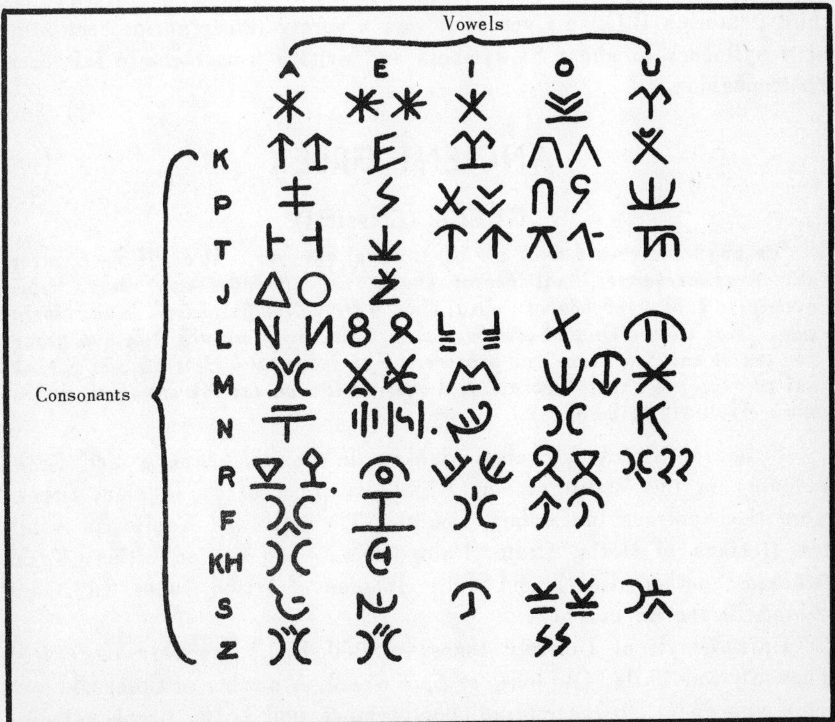

In Cyprus near the coast of Phoenicia another linear script, Cyprian or Cypriote was in use for many centuries. The earliest Cypriote character styled Cypro-Minoan probably borrowed much from the Cretan characters. Professor Petrie writes (The Story of the Alphabet, by Edward Clode), "A great signary (not hieroglyphics, but geometric, in appearance, if not in origin), was in use all over the Mediterranean 5,000 B.C. This signary was employed in Karia with thirty-six signs, and with forty-three signs in Iberia. However, there is little trace of Cretan origins in the Greek alphabet, yet five of the supplementary Greek letters have prototypes in Old Minoan.

In Asia Minor several other alphabets—Lycian and Lydian, were in use prior to the development of the Greek Ionic alphabet. These alphabets retained a number of letters that resembled Phoenician characters and other letters resembling archaic Greek.

Cypro-Minoan, Cypro-Mycenaean. The origin of Cypriote is unknown. The script was once thought to have been derived from various Asiatic sources—Hittite or Assyrian. But now it is generally believed that this character (Cypro-Mycenaean) was derived from the early Cretan via Cypro-Minoan. Cyprian or Cypriote was in use from about the sixth to the third centuries B.C. in Cyprus. It was a purely linear script consisting of a syllabary of about 55 symbols and written from right to left or in bustropheidon.

ANCIENT GREEK

GREEK (Classical)

'Εν ἀρχῇ ἐποίησεν ὁ Θεὸς τὸν οὐρανὸν καὶ τὴν γῆν. Ἡ δὲ γῆ ἦν ἀόρατος καὶ ἀκατασκεύαστος, καὶ σκότος ἐπάνω τῆς ἀβύσσου, καὶ πνεῦμα Θεοῦ ἐπεφέρετο ἐπάνω τοῦ ὕδατος. Καὶ εἶπεν ὁ Θεός Γενεθήτω φῶς. Καὶ ἐγένετο φῶς. Καὶ εἶδεν ὁ Θεὸς τὸ φῶς ὅτι καλόν. Καὶ διεχώρισεν ὁ Θεὸς ἀνὰ μέσον τοῦ φωτὸς καὶ ἀνὰ μέσον τοῦ σκότους. Καὶ ἐκάλεσεν ὁ Θεὸς τὸ φῶς ἡμέραν καὶ τὸ σκότος ἐκάλεσεν νύκτα. Καὶ ἐγένετο ἑσπέρα καὶ ἐγένετο πρωί, ἡμέρα μία.—Genesis 1: 1–5.

Hellenic. Greek alphabet. Spoken in ancient Greece and Greek colonies in the Mediterranean. Chief divisions of the ancient Greeks were the Aeolians of Lesbos, Boeotia, Thessaly and Aeolis (in Asia); the Dorians of Doris, Crete, Peloponnesus and Carian cities; *Magna Graecia* (Southern Italy), and Sicily; Ionians of Attica, Ionia, Sicily and islands in the Aegean Sea.

Epic Greek of Homeric times (c. 850 B.C.) probably came from Thessaly was called Old Ionic or *Epic Greek*. A number of Greek dialects were spoken in Greece and adjacent islands and in the Greek colonies

Α α	a	Ν ν	n
Β β ϐ	b	Ξ ξ	x
Γ γ	g	Ο ο	o
Δ δ	d	Π ϖ π	p
Ε ε	e	Ρ ϱ ρ	r
Ζ ζ ζ	z	Σ σ ς ς	s
Η η	e	Τ τ	t
Θ θ ϑ	th	Υ υ	y.u
Ι ι	i	Φ φ φ	ph
Κ κ κ	k	Χ χ	ch
Λ λ	l	Ψ Ψ ψ	ps
Μ μ	m	Ω ω	o

in Asia minor and Italy. Of these dialects, the most important are: 1. Doric of Peloponnesus, the language of Pindar, c. 500 B.C., spoken in Elis, Sparta, Achaea, Arcadia, Poseidonia. 2. Ionic. a. Epic—the language of Homer and Hesiod. b. New Ionic—spoken in Miletus, Ephesus, Samos, Halicarnassus and in the Euxine and Thracian colonies. 3. *Attic* or classical Greek of Athens, the language of Aeschylus, Sophocles, Euripides, c. 450 B.C.

About 40 local Greek alphabets have been listed by Kirkhoff. These are divided into two divisions: Chalcidian or Old Attic (Western *lambda* ∨), and Ionian, or New Attic (Eastern *lambda* ∧). The chief alphabets are: 1. *Ionian*—Miletus, Ephesus, Samos, Halicarnassus. 2. *Aegean*—Thera, Melos, Paros, Naxos, Thasis, Siphnos. 3. *Corinthian*—Corinth, Megara, Aegina, Anactorium, Syracuse, Leucas, Selinus, Gela, Agrigentum. 4. Attic—Athens. 5. Euboean—Thebes, Plateae, Chalcis, Styra and Magna Graecia. 6. *Peloponnesian*—Elis, Sparta, Achaea, Arcadia, Poseidonia.

Attic Greek (of Athens c. 450 B.C.) or classical Greek was the cultural lingua franca of the Hellenic world but it was supplanted by Alexandrian or the so-called Common Dialect of Egypt about the time of Ptolemy II (c. 285 B.C.). Hellenistic is a form of the Common Dialect of Alexandria used by the translators of the Septuagint version of the Holy Scriptures. Byzantine Greek of the Roman Empire of the East and this side by side with scholastic Greek of the academies gave rise to Romaic, the ancestor of Modern Greek.

The classical Greek alphabet consists of 24 letters of which 7 letters are vowels and 17 letters are consonants. The prehistoric or early Greek letters, *vau* or *digamma* (Ϝ), *koppa* (Ϙ)–90, and *sampi* or *san* (Ϡ) became obsolete. The Greeks borrowed the consonants from the Phoenicians but the vowels seem to have been an invention of their own, or perhaps adaptations of syllables of the Cretan language. In ancient Greece, as in ancient Rome, only capital letters were used–the small letters were invented many centuries later. Classical Greek was written from left to right, but earlier texts were sometimes written from right to left or in *bustropheidon.*

The aspirates or breathings are: Asper (ʽ) which imparts the sound of H to the vowel so marked. Lenis (ʼ) indicates absence of the H sound before the vowel so marked. All words that begin with a vowel have one or the other spiritus over them; but *upsilon* takes only asper when initial. In initial diphthongs the breathing is placed over the second vowel. The letter *rho* takes the asper when an initial,but when two of these letters occur together, the first takes the lenis and the other an asper.

Accents: Acute (´) marks a syllable pronounced in raising tone. Grave (`) marks a syllable pronounced in a lowered tone. Circumflex (~) lengthens the sounds, effects either the ultimate or penultimate syllable of the word on which it occurs. The mark of acope (ʼ) is used for cutting off vowels and diphthongs when they stand at the end of a word and a following word beginning with a vowel. The apostrophe is also used to contract two words into one or to supply the place of a first vowel beginning a word. The diaeresis (¨) over the last of two consecutive vowels show that each vowel is pronounced separately. The diastole (,) is placed between two particles that would bear a different sense without it. Iota subscript (•) written below vowels make them long. In capital letters iota is written in its complete form; it has the same power and is called Iota adscript.

Punctuation; Colon (·), Interrogative point (;). Otherwise Greek punctuation is about as in English and other west European languages.

θῆναι δεῖ τὸν υἱὸν τοῦ ἀνθρώπου, ἵνα πᾶς ὁ πιστεύων εἰς αὐτὸν μὴ ἀπόληται, ἀλλ᾽ ἔχῃ ζωὴν αἰώνιον. οὕτως γὰρ ἠγάπησαν ὁ θεὸς τὸν κόσμον

16 ὁ πιστεύων ἐν αὐτῷ ἔχῃ ζωὴν αἰώνιον. Οὕτως
γὰρ ἠγάπησεν ὁ Θεὸς τὸν κόσμον, ὥστε τὸν Υἱὸν
τὸν μονογενῆ ἔδωκεν, ἵνα πᾶς ὁ πιστεύων εἰς
17 αὐτὸν μὴ ἀπόληται ἀλλ' ἔχῃ ζωὴν αἰώνιον. οὐ
γὰρ ἀπέστειλεν ὁ Θεὸς τὸν Υἱὸν εἰς τὸν κόσμον

ARCHAIC GREEK

GREEK SCRIPTS OF THE MIDDLE AGES

CAPITALS	UNCIALS	CURSIVE	CURSIVE MINUSCULES
Α			
Β			
Γ			
Δ			
Ε			
Ζ			
Η			
Θ			
Ι			
Κ			
Λ			
Μ			
Ν			
Ξ			
Ο			
Π			
Ρ			
Σ			
Τ			
Υ			
Φ			
Χ			
Ψ			
Ω			

Greek writing has undergone many changes through the centuries. The Greek cursive hand of the third century B.C. is notable for its strength and facility. The letters were precise and well formed and the words were well spaced. In later texts words had a tendency to continuity of stroke. In course of time Greek cursive writing became more and more flattened in appearance. About the second century B.C. *alpha* was reduced to mere angles or wedge shapes. The trained clerical hand of the second century B.C. differed from that of the third century. The letters began to be made more perfect and less cursive and the linking of words in texts were marked by less continuity. The characters became more rounded and curves supplanted straight lines in individual letters in the early Roman period. The stage of decadence began about the end of the Ptolomaic period 80–20 B.C. Thereafter, the words became slacker and less exact in structure.

GREEK NUMERALS

		10	20	30	40	50	60	70	80	90
		ιʹ	κʹ	λʹ	μʹ	νʹ	ξʹ	οʹ	πʹ	ϟʹ
1	αʹ	ιαʹ	καʹ	λαʹ	μαʹ	ναʹ	ξαʹ	οαʹ	παʹ	ϟαʹ
2	βʹ	ιβʹ	κβʹ	λβʹ	μβʹ	νβʹ	ξβʹ	οβʹ	πβʹ	ϟβʹ
3	γʹ	ιγʹ	κγʹ	λγʹ	μγʹ	νγʹ	ξγʹ	ογʹ	πγʹ	ϟγʹ
4	δʹ	ιδʹ	κδʹ	λδʹ	μδʹ	νδʹ	ξδʹ	οδʹ	πδʹ	ϟδʹ
5	εʹ	ιεʹ	κεʹ	λεʹ	μεʹ	νεʹ	ξεʹ	οεʹ	πεʹ	ϟεʹ
6	ϛʹ	ιϛʹ	κϛʹ	λϛʹ	μϛʹ	νϛʹ	ξϛʹ	οϛʹ	πϛʹ	ϟϛʹ
7	ζʹ	ιζʹ	κζʹ	λζʹ	μζʹ	νζʹ	ξζʹ	οζʹ	πζʹ	ϟζʹ
8	ηʹ	ιηʹ	κηʹ	ληʹ	μηʹ	νηʹ	ξηʹ	οηʹ	πηʹ	ϟηʹ
9	θʹ	ιθʹ	κθʹ	λθʹ	μθʹ	νθʹ	ξθʹ	οθʹ	πθʹ	ϟθʹ
	100	200	300	400	500	600	700	800	900	1000
	ρʹ	σʹ	τʹ	υʹ	φʹ	χʹ	ψʹ	ωʹ	ϡ	ϙ

Two styles of writing predominated during the second half of the first century A.D: The clear, flowing hand and the small cursive hand. The writings of the Byzantine period are characterized by exaggeration and carelessness in execution of detail. About the fourth century the letters defined as uncials began to be written. In the MSS of the sixth century the uncial letters began to decline, and about the year 600 the Greek uncials had become considerably altered. The circular letters tended to oval forms. In the seventh century the writings began to slope to the right, continuing through the next two centuries. By the tenth century the letters became more upright, had cast off their compressed formation and become again more rounded. Finally, the Greek minuscule book hand had become a well defined cursive style by the end of the fifteenth century.

Some early Greek dialects: *Koine* or common dialect, dating from about 320 B.C. Hellenistic or New Testament Greek, and Byzantine, about 325–1453 A.D.

MODERN GREEK

'Εν ἀρχῇ ἐποίησεν ὁ Θεὸς τὸν οὐρανὸν καὶ τὴν γῆν. Ἡ δὲ γῆ ἦτο ἄμορφος καὶ ἔρημος· καὶ σκότος ἐπὶ τοῦ προσώπου τῆς ἀβύσσου. Καὶ Πνεῦμα Θεοῦ ἐφέρετο ἐπὶ τῆς ἐπιφανείας τῶν ὑδάτων. Καὶ εἶπεν ὁ Θεὸς, Γενηθήτω φῶς· καὶ ἔγεινε φῶς· καὶ εἶδεν ὁ Θεὸς τὸ φῶς ὅτι ἦτο καλόν· καὶ διεχώρισεν ὁ Θεὸς τὸ φῶς ἀπὸ τοῦ σκότους· καὶ ἐκάλεσεν ὁ Θεὸς τὸ φῶς, Ἡμέραν· τὸ δέ σκὸτος ἐκάλεσε, Νύκτα. Καὶ ἔγεινεν ἑσπέρα, καὶ ἔγεινε πρωΐ, ἡμέρα πρώτη.—

Α α	*Α α*	a	Ν ν	*Ν ν*	n, ny, m
Β β	*Β β*	v	Ξ ξ	*Ξ ξ*	ks
Γ γ	*Γ γ*	gh, y, ng	Ο ο	*Ο ο*	o
Δ δ	*Δ δ*	dh	Π π	*Π π*	p, b
Ε ε	*Ε ε*	e	Ρ ρ	*Ρ ρ*	r
Ζ ζ	*Ζ ζ*	z	Σ σ, ς*	*Σ σ ς*	s, z
Η η	*Η η*	i	Τ τ	*Τ τ*	t, d
Θ θ	*Θ θ*	th	Υ υ	*Υ υ*	i, f, v
Ι ι	*Ι ι*	i	Φ φ	*Φ φ*	f
Κ κ	*Κ κ*	k, ky, g, gy	Χ χ	*Χ χ*	kh, ch
Λ λ	*Λ λ*	l, ly	Ψ ψ	*Ψ ψ*	ps, bz
Μ μ	*Μ μ*	m, n	Ω ω	*Ω ω*	o

Hellenic Greek alphabet. Modern Greek is spoken by about 6,000,000 people in Greece. The alphabet of Modern Greek remains unchanged but values ascribed to some of the lettres differ from ancient Greek pronunciation. In Modern Greek the breathings *lenis* or smooth (') and *asper* (') or rough, are written over initial vowels but these have no value as in the ancient tongue. The marks of accent (´ , ` , ~) indicate the stressed syllable, but all have the same value. Accents are not employed when a word is written in capitals. As in ancient Greek *iota subscript* is written below the vowels but *iota adscript* beside and following capital letters, and this is the mark of lengthening the vowel immediately preceding the *iota adscript*. The mark of diaerisis over the second of two vowels indicates that the pair does not form a diphthong but that each vowel is pronounced separately. Punctuation is the same as in ancient Greek.

ADDITIONAL NOTES ON ANCIENT GREEK

Quantity. Vowels *always long*, **η, ω.** Thus *την* = teen, *των* = tone.

Vowels *always short*, **ε, ο.** Thus *μεν* = men, *ον* = on.

Vowels *long or short*, according to the word, *α, ι, υ.*

Aΐ- AI–*aisle*
Eἰ- EI–Ī
Oἰ- OI–*toil*
Yἰ- UI–*quit*
Aΰ- OU–*our*
Eΰ- EU–*feud*
Hΰ- EU–*eureka*
Oὐ- OU–U in *rule*
῞Αι Ā
῞Ηι Ā
᾿Ωι Ō

Lengthening and **Contraction.** When a short vowel has to be made long in the inflection of a word, **ᾰ** becomes **ᾱ** or **η, ε** becomes **η**, sometimes **ει**, and **ο** becomes **ω.** Two vowels, or a vowel and a diphthong occurring together in different syllables, are often contracted into one.

Elision, Crasis, and **Diæresis.** Some words lose a final vowel before an initial vowel in the following. Thus *δια ὡν* becomes *δι᾿ὡν.* In a few instances the vowels are blended, and the two words become one (*crasis* = mixing). Thus *τα αὐτα* becomes *ταὐτα*, the soft breathing (*coronis*) of the initial being retained. *Diæresis* ('division') is the opposite of crasis ; and, by the sign (¨) over the second of two vowels which would otherwise form a diphthong, shows that they are to be pronounced separately. Thus 'Ησαΐας, ὄϊς, Esa-ias, o-is.

SLAVONIC LANGUAGES

OLD SLAVONIC ALPHABETS

GLAGOLITIC

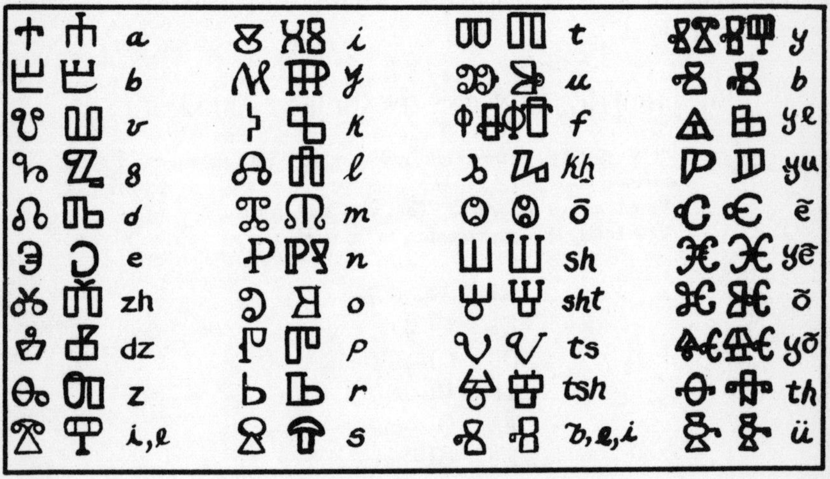

a	i	t	y
b	y	u	b
v	k	f	ye
g	l	kh	yu
d	m	ō	ẽ
e	n	sh	yẽ
zh	o	sht	õ
dz	p	ts	yõ
z	r	tsh	th
i, e	s	ъ, e, i	ü

CYRILLIC

А	a	К	k	Х	kh	Ю	yu
Б	b	Л	l	Ѡ	ō	Ѥ	ye
В	v	М	m	Ч	ch	Ѧ	ẽ
Г	g	Н	n	Ү	tsh	Ѫ	õ
Д	d	О	o	Ш	sh	Ѩ	yẽ
Є	e	П	p	Щ	sht	Ѭ	yõ
Ж	zh	Р	r	Ъ	ъ	Ѯ	(ks)
Ѕ	dz	С	s	Ꙑ	y, v	Ѱ	(ps)
З	z	Т	t	Ь	e	Ѳ	(th)
Н	i	ОУ	u	Ѣ	ě	Ѵ	(ü)
І	ī	Ф	f	Ꙗ	ya	Ц	ts

Glagolitic

Old Slavonic. Liturgical Slovenian of the western Slavic peoples—Croatians, Illyrians, Slovenians of the Roman church. Glagolitic letters are the oldest characters in which the liturgical works of the Slovenian church were written. Glagolitic letters were probably derived from the Greek alphabet with the addition of special characters to render Slavonic sounds; however, Slavonic tradition ascribes the invention of the Glagolitic alphabet to St. Jerome, a Dalmatian, in the fourth century, A. D.

The name Glagolitic is derived from glagoli 'letter.' The alphabet is commonly called *Azbukvitza* because of the names of the first three letters in the alphabet. This character was written in two styles: Round (Bulgarian), and square (Illyrian).

Cyrillic

Old Slavonic. Liturgical Slavonic of the northern Slavic peoples—Bulgarians, Russians, Servians, Ruthenians, of the Eastern or Greek Orthodox church. The Cyrillic alphabet, the ancestor of modern Slavonic alphabets, was invented by the apostles Cyril and Methodius (circa 855-863 A. D.). The earliest Cyrillic alphabet consisted of 30 letters—later increased to 48—of which 24 letters were borrowed from and are almost identical with Greek uncials of the eighth-ninth centuries. Additional letters were added to render Slavonic sounds.

RUSSIAN

Отче нашъ, сущій на небесахъ! Да святится имя Твое; да пріидетъ царствіе Твое; да будетъ воля Твоя и на землѣ какъ на небѣ. Хлѣбъ нашъ насущный дай намъ на сей день; и прости намъ долги наши, какъ и мы прощаемъ должникамъ нашимъ; и не введи насъ въ искушеніе, но избавь насъ отъ лукаваго. Ибо Твое есть царство и сила и слава во вѣки. Аминь.

Slavonic: Eastern. Cyrillic alphabet. Spoken by about 100,000,000 people in the Soviet Union. The modern slavic alphabet in which Russian is written is derived from the Cyrillic letters of Cyril and Methodius,

Slavic Alphabets

Modified Cyrillic		Transliteration U.S.G.B.[1]	Transliteration U.S.L.C.[2]	Russian		Ukrainian		White Russian		Bulgarian		Serbian	
А	а	*a*	*a*	А	а	А	а	А	а	А	а	А	а
Б	б	*b*	*b*	Б	б	Б	б	Б	б	Б	б	Б	б
В	в	*v*	*v*	В	в	В	в	В	в	В	в	В	в
Г	г	*g*[3]	*g*[3]	Г	г	Г	г	Г	г	Г	г	Г	г
Ґ (Ґ)	ґ	*g*	*g*			Ґ	ґ	Ґ	ґ				
Д	д	*d*	*d*	Д	д	Д	д	Д	д	Д	д	Д	д
Ђ (Ђ)	ђ[4]	*dy, d', j*	*đ*									Ђ	ђ
Е	е	*e*[5]	*e*	Е	е	Е	е	Е	е	Е	е	Е	е
Є	є	*ye*	*i͡e*			Є	є						
Ё	ё[6]	*e*	*ë*[7]	Ё	ё			Ё	ё				
Ж	ж	*zh*	*zh*[8]	Ж	ж	Ж	ж	Ж	ж	Ж	ж	Ж	ж
З	з	*z*	*z*	З	з	З	з	З	з	З	з	З	з
И	и	*i*	*i*[9]	И	и	И	и			И	и	И	и
І	і	*i*	*ī*	І[10]	і[10]	І	і	І	і				
Ї	ї	*yi*	*ï*			Ї	ї						
Й	й	*i*[11]	*ĭ*	Й	й	Й	й	Й	й	Й	й		
Ј	ј	*y*	*j*									Ј	ј
К	к	*k*	*k*	К	к	К	к	К	к	К	к	К	к
Л	л	*l*	*l*	Л	л	Л	л	Л	л	Л	л	Л	л
Љ	љ	*ly, l'*	*lj*									Љ	љ
М	м	*m*	*m*	М	м	М	м	М	м	М	м	М	м
Н	н	*n*	*n*	Н	н	Н	н	Н	н	Н	н	Н	н
Њ	њ	*ny, n'*	*nj*									Њ	њ
О	о	*o*	*o*	О	о	О	о	О	о	О	о	О	о
П	п	*p*	*p*	П	п	П	п	П	п	П	п	П	п
Р	р	*r*	*r*	Р	р	Р	р	Р	р	Р	р	Р	р
С	с	*s*	*s*	С	с	С	с	С	с	С	с	С	с
Т	т	*t*	*t*	Т	т	Т	т	Т	т	Т	т	Т	т
Ћ (Ћ)	ћ	*ty, t', ch*	*ć*									Ћ	ћ
У	у	*u*	*u*	У	у	У	у	У	у	У	у	У	у
Ў	ў	*ŭ*	*ŭ*					Ў	ў				
Ф	ф	*f*	*f*	Ф	ф	Ф	ф	Ф	ф	Ф	ф	Ф	ф
Х	х	*kh*	*kh*	Х	х	Х	х	Х	х	Х	х	Х	х
Ц	ц	*ts*	*t͡s*[12]	Ц	ц	Ц	ц	Ц	ц	Ц	ц	Ц	ц
Ч	ч	*ch*	*ch*[13]	Ч	ч	Ч	ч	Ч	ч	Ч	ч	Ч	ч
Џ	џ	*j*	*dž*									Џ	џ
Ш	ш	*sh*	*sh*[14]	Ш	ш	Ш	ш	Ш	ш	Ш	ш	Ш	ш
Щ	щ	*shch*	*shch*	Щ	щ	Щ	щ			Щ	щ		
Ъ[15]	ъ[15]	Omit	″	Ъ	ъ					Ъ	ъ	Ъ	ъ
Ы	ы	*y*[16]	*y*	Ы	ы			Ы	ы				
Ь[17]	ь[17]	Omit	ʼ	Ь	ь	Ь	ь	Ь	ь	Ь	ь		
Ѣ[18]	ѣ[18]	*e*	*i͡e*	Ѣ	ѣ					Ѣ	ѣ		
Э	э	*e*	*ė*	Э	э			Э	э				
Ю	ю	*yu*	*i͡u*	Ю	ю	Ю	ю	Ю	ю	Ю	ю		
Я	я	*ya*	*i͡a*	Я	я	Я	я	Я	я	Я	я		
Ѳ	ѳ	*f*	*ḟ*	Ѳ[19]	ѳ[19]								
Ѵ	ѵ	*i*	*ẏ*	Ѵ[20]	ѵ[20]								
	ѫ	*e*	*ŭ̥*								ѫ		
	і-ѫ	*ya*[21]									і-ѫ		

U.S. Printing Office—*Style Manual.*

adapted forms of Greek uncials of the 8th-9th centuries, with several special characters to render slavonic sounds, taken from Greek ligatures.

The ancient Russian alphabet of the time of Ostromir, Prince of

(Old Orthography)

А а	*А а*	А а	a	Т т	*Т т*	Т т	t
Б б	*Б б*	Б б	b	У у	*У у*	У у	u
В в	*В в*	В в	v	Ф ф	*Ф ф*	Ф ф	f, ph
Г г	*Г г*	Г г	g	Х х	*Х х*	Х х	kh
Д д	*Д д*	Д д	p	Ц ц	*Ц ц*	Ц ц	ts
Е е	*Е е*	Е е	ye, e	Ч ч	*Ч ч*	Ч ч	ch
Ж ж	*Ж ж*	Ж ж	zh	Ш ш	*Ш ш*	Ш ш	sh
З з	*З з*	З з	z	Щ щ	*Щ щ*	Щ щ	shch
И и й	*И и й*	И и	y, i, iy	Ъ ъ	*Ъ ъ*	Ъ ъ	*Hard sign*
І і	*І і*	І і	i	Ы ы	*Ы ы*	Ы ы	i
К к	*К к*	К к	k	Ь ь	*Ь ь*	Ь ь	*Soft sign*
Л л	*Л л*	Л л	l	Ѣ ѣ	*Ѣ ѣ*	Ѣ ѣ	e, ye
М м	*М м*	М м	m	Э э	*Э э*	Э э	e
Н н	*Н н*	Н н	n	Ю ю	*Ю ю*	Ю ю	yu
О о	*О о*	О о	o	Я я	*Я я*	Я я	ya
П п	*П п*	П п	p	Ѳ ѳ	*Ѳ ѳ*	Ѳ ѳ	ph, f
Р р	*Р р*	Р р	r	Ѵ ѵ	*Ѵ ѵ*	Ѵ ѵ	u (v)
С с	*С с*	С с	s				

Novgorod, (c. 1056), was similar to that of liturgical Slavonic or old Cyrillic of the Greek Orthodox Church MSS. The old alphabet was reformed by Elias Kopievich in the reign of Peter the Great. Of the 48 original letters, 14 were discarded, several characters were modified, and one new letter was added.

Russian or "Great Russian" as distinguished from "Little Russian" of the Ukraine, and "White Russian," is the principal language of the Slavonic family of tongues. It is the official language of European Russia and Siberia and is generally understood in all parts of the Soviet Union.

Russian Ё is always accented. Usually a doubled vowel is pronounced as two syllables, except when the second vowel is Й in such combinations. A doubled consonant is prolonged, as in Italian. Italic letters differ greatly from the ordinary characters. See tables of Russian and Slavic alphabets. Stress is irregular but of the greatest importance. It is sometimes indicated by marks of accent in dictionaries and text books of the language, but usually marks of accent are not printed and stressed syllables are determined by knowledge of grammatical rules of inflexion, etc. Strong emphasis is placed upon the stressed syllable when marked by accent.

By decree of the Council of the People's Commissars, Oct. 10, 1918, and the Decrees of the Workers' and Peasants' Government, Oct. 17, 1918, certain reforms were made in Russian orthography, and the new spelling has been introduced in all schools.

1. Replace the letter Ѣ by Е .
2. Replace the letter Ѳ everywhere by Ф .
3. Drop the letter Ъ at the end of words and parts of compound words, but retain it in the middle of words as a sign of division.
4. Replace the letter І everywhere by И .
5. Write certain prefixes before vowels and hard consonants with З , but replace З by С before mute consonants.

Other rules relate to changes of spelling of adjectives and pronouns, for which see, U.S. Printing Office—*Style Manual.*

The Russian alphabet consists of 35 letters, of which 11 letters are vowels, 3 letters are semi-vowels and 21 letters are consonants, but several letters are rarely used.

А-A in *father;* A unstressed about as in *cigarette;* Б —B in *boy,* often nearly like P when final; В —V in *vest,* often nearly like F when final or next to a sharp consonant; Г —G in *get,* but often nearly like K as final, Г —nearly V—sometimes before О ; Д —D in *day;* often like T as final; E in *red,* but like YE in *yet* as initial or after a soft sign; Ё —YAW in *yawn,* but about like AW following one of the hissing sounds–SH (Ш), ZH (Ж), CH (Ч), SHCH (Щ); Ж –ZH or Z in *azure;* З –Z in *zest,* but often nearly SS as final; І , И –I in *machine;* Й –Y in *boy;* К –*kite,* but like Г or Х before some consonants; Л –L in *law;* М –M in *man;* Н –N in *not;* О –about like AW in *law* when stressed, following the stress O is about like O in *ration,* before the stress is shorter; П –P in *pet;* Р –R in *run* but strongly sounded; С –S in *sister;* Т –T in *tent;* У –U in *rule;* Ф –PH in *phonetic;* Х –aspirated H or about like CH in Scotch *loch;* Ц –TS in *sets;* Ч –CH in *church;* Ш –SH in *shut;* Щ SHCH as in *cash-check;* Ы –about like Y in *pity;* It is a difficult letter to pronounce. It resembles I in *hit* pronounced deep in the throat with closed teeth; Ъ –the hard sign, is not pronounced. This hard sign at the end of words is now omitted; Ь –the soft sign. It is difficult to imitate, about like very short E in *here;* Э –nearly E in *there;* Ю –YU in *yule;* Я –YA in *yard;* Θ –F in *far,* now omitted or replaced by Ф ; Ѣ –YE, generally replaced by Е .

The Russian hard Л is pronounced about like W, soft Л is liquid and pronounced about like Spanish LL, more nearly LLI in *million.*

CHIEF LANGUAGES OF THE SOVIET UNION

The Soviet Socialist Republic and European Russia. Chief languages of the Soviet Union–(Russian or Great Russian).

White Russian–Western Russia
Ukrainian–Ukraine
Finnish–Karelian
Lithuanian
Latvian
Esthonian
Lettish
Russian Lapp
Georgian–Caucasus
Votiak
Ziryen
Abkhasian–Caucasus
Cheremiss–Volga region
Perm–East Russia
Mordoff–Sura river region
Bashkir Turkish
Karaite Turkish
Kazan Turkish
Kumuck Turkish
Chuvash Turkish
Slavonic

Chief languages spoken in Russia in Asia or Siberia and territories of Asiatic Russia: (Russian or Great Russian.)

Ararat Armenian
Ossete
Ostiak
Udin
Vogul
Buriat Mongolian
Azerbaijani Turkish
Jagatai Turkish
West Khirghiz Turkish
Altai Turkish
Uzbek
Yakut

LANGUAGES WRITTEN IN THE CYRILLIC ALPHABET

Russian
White Russian
Ukrainian
Bulgarian
Serbian
Karelian Finnish
Bulgarian Romany
Russian Lapp
Gagauzi Turkish
Bashkir Turkish
Chuvash Turkish
Kazan Turkish
Khirghiz Turkish
Yakut Turkish
Vogul
Votiak
Rumanian
Russian Lapp
Perm
Ossetian
Abkhasian
Cheremiss
Buriat Mongolian
Mordoff
Atka Aleut
Kadiak Aleut
Unalaska Aleut

UKRAINIAN

Slavonic: Eastern. Cyrillic alphabet. Ukrainian, Ruthenian or Littl Russian, is spoken by about 20,000,000 people in the Ukraine in th Soviet Union, in parts of Poland, Czecho-Slovakia and parts of Rumani Ukrainian is similar to Great Russian but with several differences i alphabet and orthography (See table of Slavic alphabets).

SERBO-CROATIAN

Jer Bogu tako omilje svijet da je i sina svojega jedinorodnoga dao, da ni jedan koji ga vjeruje ne pogine, nego da ima život vječni.

Croatian Alphabet (Roman)

A B́ V G Ǵ D Đ E Z Ž I·J K L M N O P R S T Ć U F H C Č Š
a b́ v g ǵ d đ e z ž i j k l m n o p r s t ć u f h c č š

DJ, GJ, LJ, NJ, DŽ

Slavonic. Southern. Cyrillic alphabet (Serb) or Roman alphabet (Cro atian). Except for the different alphabets in which they are written Ser and Croatian are practically identical. Serbo-Croatian is spoken by mor than 10,000,000 people in southern and western Yugoslavia. The literar language is understood in all parts of Yugoslavia, but there are thre sub-dialects of this tongue.

1. The "E" dialect (Serbia and north of the Danube)
2. The "YE" dialect (Bosnia, Croatia, Herzegovina)
3. The "I" dialect (Dalmatia)

These dialects are so named because of the variant renderings of the ld Slavonic YE sound and I sound. The letter R may often represent a yllable, about as ER in *herd*, in which the letter R is rolled following ıe semi-vowel. R is sometimes used as a vowel when standing next to nother vowel and forming a dissyllable with it. There are four accents: . Long rising (´). 2. Long falling (⁀). 3. Short rising (`). 4 Short alling (``). Marks of accent are not used except to distinguish two ords of different meaning when spelled alike.

B, V, D, Z, K, L, M, N, P, T, F, are pronounced as in English. A–*father;* A–about as in *idea* when final; G–*get;* Đ , DJ–between and J; E–*end;* Ž–ZH or as Z in *azure;* Z–*zest;* I–*machine;* J–Y in *ear;* LJ–LLI in *million;* NJ–NI in *onion;* O–*note;* R–*run but strongly* ounded; H–CH in Scotch *loch;* S–SS in *glass;* Ć–between T in *tune* nd CH in *church;* C–TS–TS in *sits;* Č–CH in *church;* Š–SH in *shut;* DŽ–J in *jam;* GJ–between D and J. U–*yule;* G–DJ.

The above letters are in *latinitza* or *latinica* spelling of Croatian. Serbian is usually written in Cyrillic characters.

SLOVENE

Kajti tako je Bog ljubil svet, da je dal Sina svojega edinorojenega, da se ne pogubi, kdorkoli veruje vanj, temuč da ima večno življenje.

A B C Č D E Ê F G H I J K L M N O Ô P R S Š T U V Z Ž
a b c č d e ê f g h i j k l m n o ô p r s š t u v z ž

DJ, LJ, NJ, RJ, TJ, KS

Slavonic: Southern. Roman alphabet. The Slovene alphabet is about ıe same as used in Croatian (*latinitza*) except that the letters Đ , Ć , , are not used in Slovene. Slovene or Slovenian is spoken by about ,000,000 people in Yugoslavia in Styria, Carinthia and Carniola, and arts of Hungary.

B, D, F, K, L, M, N, P, R, S, T, V, Z, are pronounced as in English. A–*father;* C–TS in *sets;* Č–*church;* DJ–J in *jam;* E–*yet;* Ê–longer ; G–*get;* H–guttural H sound; I–*machine;* J–Y in *year;* LJ–GLI *(Italian);* J–NI in *onion;* O–*note;* Ô–O; RJ–RJ; Š–SH in *shut;* GJ–DJ; U–*rule;* S–KS; Ž–ZH or Z in *azure;* U–U.

CZECH OR BOHEMIAN

Nebo tak Bůh miloval svět, že Syna svého jednorozeného dal, aby každy, kdož věři v něho, nezahynui, ale měl život věčný.

Á B C Č D Ď E É Ě F G H I Y Í Ý J K L M Ň O Ó P Q R Ř S Š T Ť U Ú Ů V X Z Ž
á b c č d ď e é ě f g h i y í ý j k l m ň o ó p q r ř s š t ť u ú ů v x z ž

Slavonic. Western: Roman alphabet. Czech or Bohemian is spoken by several million people in Czechoslovakia. In Czech the stress is always on the first syllable. The diacritical mark (ʹ) placed over a letter indicates a long vowel and is not used to denote stress. Czech is spoken in Bohemia, Moravia and Silesia. In the eastern part of Czechoslovakia, Slovak is spoken which is very similar to Czech.

Hard and soft letters

1. Soft letters: B, D, D', DZ, DŽ, G, H, V, Z, Ž.
2. Hard letters: P, T, T', C, Č, K, CH, F, S, Š,

Rule 1. The soft letters are sounded at the end of a word or before the hard letters as corresponding hard letters, thus B is pronounced P, D is pronounced T, etc.

Rule 2. Hard letters preceding soft letters (except V) are sounded soft, thus K is pronounced G, but this occurs rarely.

B, D, F, H, K, L, M, N, P, R, S, T, V, X, Z, are pronounced about as in English. C, Č, J, S, Š, Ž, are pronounced as in Croatian. G, Q, X, are used only in foreign words.

A–U in *rug;* Á–*arm;* E–*red;* É–EI in *heir* or about like AI in *air;* Ě–YE in *yet;* I, Y–*tic;* Í, Ý–*pique;* O–*top;* Ó–about like AW in *law;* U–*bull;* Ú, Ů–*rule;* Ď–DG in *edge* but more nearly T' when final; C–TS in *sits;* Č–CH in *church;* G–*get;* Ň–NI in *onion;* Ř-R + Ž or ZH. R sometimes has a syllabic value about like UR in *fur* between two consonants, L sometimes has a syllabic value UL in *cult* between two consonants; Š–SH in *shut;* Ť–TI in *question;* CH–Scotch *loch;* AJ–AI in *aisle;* EJ–EI in *vein;* K is about like G before D and Z. The letters D, N, T, followed by I–D', N', T.' The letter R is strongly sounded.

POLISH

Na początku stworzył Bóg niebo i ziemię. A ziemia była niekształtowna i prózna, i ciemność była nad przepaścią, a Duch Boży unaszał się nad wodami. I rzekł Bóg:

Niech będzie światłość; i stała się światłość. I widział Bóg światłość, że była dobra; i uczynił Bóg rozdział między światłością i między ciemnością. I nazwał Bóg światłość dniem a ciemność nazwał nocą; i stał się wieczór, i stał się zaranek, dzień pierwszy. —Genesis 1: 1–5.

A Ą B C Ć D E Ę F G H I J K L Ł M N Ń O Ó P R S Ś T U W Y Z Ź Ż
a ą b c ć d e ę f g h i j k l ł m n ń o ó p r s ś t u w y z ź ż

Double letters: CH, CZ, DZ, DŻ, DŹ, IE, RZ, RŻ, ŚĆ, SZ (SZCZ)

Slavonic: Western. Roman alphabet. Spoken by about 22,000,000 people in Poland. The letters Ć, Ń, Ś, Ź, have the value of C, N, S, Z, respectively and followed by Y. Soft consonants when final, are pronounced hard (except the softened consonants Ć, Ń, Ś, Ź): thus, final B, D, G, Z, W, become P, T, K, SH, F, respectively. There are no diphthongs. The letters Q, V, X, are not used. In words of more than one syllable the stress is always on the penultimate syllable but accent falls on the antepenult of most words of foreign origin. Polish consonants have many fine distinctions of pronunciation best learned by hearing the language spoken.

B, D, F, H, K, L, M, N, P, R, T, Z, are pronounced as in English.

A—*father;* Ą—nasal sound like French ON in *bon;* C—TS in *sits*, but nearly CH before I; Ć—CH in *church* but softer; CH—Scotch *loch;* CZ—CH in *church* or soft TS; DZ—*adze* but more nearly J before I; DŹ—*adze* or nearly DSH; DŻ—J in *jam;* E—*bed;* Ę—nasal French sound of *En* in *bien;* G—*get;* I—*machine but* pronounced Y before A vowel; J—Y in *yet;* Ł—sound similar to W in *west* (Ł is LL in Galicia); Ń—NI in *onion;* O—*obey* but shorter like open O in *from;* Ó—OO in *book;* RZ—ZH as Z in *azure;* S—*sister;* SZ—SH in *shut;* Ś—SH in *shut* but softer; S—*sister* but pronounced weak SH before I; RŻ—R'ZH; ŚĆ—SH'CH; SZCZ—SH'TSH; U—*rule;* W—V in *vest;* Y—*hardy;* Z—weak Z before I; Ż—ZY or Z' or hard Z in *zig zag;* Z—ZH or Z in *azure;* W—F when final; Ź—Ś when final; IE—YE in *yet.*

SLOVAK

Lebo tak miloval Bóh svet, že svojho jednorodeného Syna dal, aby každý, kto verí v neho, nezahynul, ale mal večný život.

Slavonic. Western: Roman alphabet. Spoken by about 3,000,000 people in Slovakia. Slovak is similar to Czech or Bohemian, but the Czech letters Ě, Ř, Ů are omitted and the letters Ä, Ľ, Ô, are added. Otherwise the

Slovak alphabet is the same as Czech. Slovak orthography was reformed in the middle of the nineteenth century. Stress is always on the first syllable and the accent (ʹ) indicates a long vowel.

The same rules as in Czech apply to hard and soft letters. The letters Ď, N, T before E, I, Í, are pronounced DY, NY, TY. The vowels L' and Ŕ are obsolete. (Semi-vowels).

B, D, F, H, K, L, M, N, P, Q, R, T, X, are pronounced as in English.

A–*father;* Á–German *Haar;* C–TS in *sets;* Č–*church;* Ď–DJ; IE–A; E–German EE; Ě–YE in *yet;* G–*get;* CH–Scotch *loch;* I–E; J–Y in *yet;* Í–*machine;* L' is trilled; Ň–NI in *onion;* O–*long;* Ó–*bow;* R–RSH; S–*sister;* Š–SH in *shut;* Ť–T; U–short U; Ú–OO is *tool;* Ô–OU or OO-O; V–W is *west;* Y–I in *silk;* Ý–EE in *see;* Z–S in *sit;* Ź–SH in *shut;* Ž–ZH.

BULGARIAN

Slavonic: Eastern. Cyrillic alphabet (See Russian). Spoken by about 5,000,000 people in Bulgaria. Bulgarian is closely akin to Russian though somewhat simplified. Bulgarian is sometimes mistaken by speakers of Russian for old Russian.

бесните? [13] И никой не е възлязъл
на небето, освен тоя, който е слязъл
от небето, *сиреч*, Човешкия Син, който
е на небето. [14] И както Моисей из-
дигна змията в пустинята, така трябва
да бъде издигнат Човешкия Син, [15] та
всеки, който вярва в него [да не по-
гине, но] да има вечен живот. [16] За-
щото Бог толкоз възлюби света, щото
даде своя единороден Син, за да не
погине ни един, който вярва в него,
но да има вечен живот. [17] Понеже
Бог не е пратил Сина в света да съди

WHITE RUSSIAN

Slavonic. Cyrillic alphabet (See table of Slavic alphabets.) White Russian is a dialect of Russian and is spoken by about 12,000,000 people in parts of Poland, Lithuania and western Russia.

KASZUB

Slavonic. Cyrillic alphabet. Kaszub or Kashube is spoken by a few people dwelling along the Baltic coast near Pomerania. Kaszub is related to Polish but with additional nasal sounds not used in the latter language. Stress is mobile.

WEND

Slavonic, Western German Gothic characters or Roman alphabet. Wend or Serbian or Lusatian, as it is sometimes called, is spoken by about 100,000 people in the Spreewald and Bauzten in Germany. Wend is related to Czech. Dialects are: High Wend or High Lusatian, Low Wend.

OLD SLAVONIC

Гла҃, г҃. за҃, и҃.

ѣже чл҃къ ѿ фарїсеи, нико
димъ имѧ емꙋ, кнзь жи
довскыи, сеи прїиде къ іс҃ꙋ
нощїю, и рече емꙋ. равви,
вѣмъ, ꙗко ѿ бг҃а пришелъ
еси оучитель. никтоже бо можетъ
ѕнаменїи сихъ творити, иже ты

SLAVONIC NUMERALS

1 — а҃.
2 — в҃.
3 — г҃.
4 — д҃.
5 — є҃.
6 — ѕ҃.
7 — з҃.
8 — и҃.
9 — ѳ҃
10 — і҃.
11 — а҃і.
12 — в҃і
13 — г҃і
14 — д҃і
15 — є҃і.

16 — ѕ҃і.
17 — з҃і
и т. д.
20 — к҃.
21 — к҃а.
22 — к҃в.
23 — к҃г
и т. д.
30 — л҃.
31 — л҃а
и т. д.

40 — м҃.
50 — н҃.
60 — ѯ҃.
70 — ѻ҃.
80 — п҃.
90 — ч҃.
100 — р҃.
101 — р҃а
и т. д.
111 — ра҃і
и т. д.
120 — р҃к.
121 — рк҃а
и т. д.

200 — с҃.
300 — т҃.
400 — ѵ҃.
500 — ф҃.
600 — х҃.
700 — ѱ҃.
800 — ѡ҃.
900 — ц҃.
1000 — ҂а.
1800 — ҂аѡ.
1874 — ҂аѡ҃ѻд.
2000 — ҂в.
3000 — ҂г.

MISCELLANEOUS LANGUAGES

BASQUE

Zergatic aiñ naite izan du Jaungoicoac mundua, non eman duen bere Seme Bácarra beragan fedea duan guzia galdu ez dedin baizic izan dezan betico bizia. Jn. 3.16.

Basque (Eskuara). Roman alphabet. Basque, a language of unknown origin, is spoken in the region of the Pyrenees mountains between France and Spain. Basque is not related to any other language of western Europe. Some Basque dialects are: Biscayan, Central dialect, Guipuzcoan, Labourdin, Eastern Low Navarese, South High Navarese, and Souletin. The above specimen is written in the Guipuzcoan dialect.

R.G.S. II. phonetics: All vowels and consonants in Basque are pronounced as in R. G. S. II.

Variants: Z–S; J–Y in French Basque; J–H in Spanish Basque; CH is written TCH in French Basque; CH is written X in Spanish Basque; palatal N–N' or Spanish Ñ.

MALTESE

Ghaliex Alla hecca hab id dinia illi tâ l'Iben tighu unigenitu, sabiex collmin jemmen bih ma jintilifx, izda icollu il haja ta dejem. Jn. 3.16.

Maltese is a dialect of Arabic, spoken in the Island of Malta in the Mediterranean. Maltese pronunciation is much influenced by Italian.

ROMANY

Andiar sangue penelo, que sinará osuncho anglal es majares dé Undebél por yeque chor sos querela aberuco. Lk. 15. 10.

Gypsy. Roman alphabet. Romany is spoken by various bands of Gypsies living in Europe. Some Romany dialects are: Bulgarian, Lettish, North German, South German, Moravian, Yugoslav and Spanish Romany or Gitano. The above specimen is written in Spanish Romany. The Romany dialects differ widely and pronunciation is much influenced by the languages of the countries in which the Romany tongues are spoken.

UNIVERSAL LANGUAGES

Because of the great number of tongues spoken in the world philologists and scholars have long dreamed of a universal language or an artificial auxiliary tongue as a medium of communication and speech between all of the nations of the world. Perhaps one of the earliest attempts to provide an artificial auxiliary language was the *Ars Signorum* (Art of Symbol) of George Delgarno, written in 1661. This was followed by Wilkin's *Real Character and a Philosophical Language* (London, 1669), but these proposals like various other linguistic systems published since have not been attended with any great success.

In 1887 Doctor Ludwig Zamenhoff of Warsaw gave to the world the international tongue known as Esperanto. This artificial auxiliary language enjoyed considerable popularity several years among language enthusiasts in Europe and elsewhere. A number of Esperanto societies were formed and the New Testament was translated into that tongue in 1912, by a committee of the International Congress of Esperanto and the British Esperanto association. Thus, the Esperanto movement seemed ushered into being under the happiest auspices, but the tongue is not very extensively used today.

Other artificial languages are: Idiom Neutral of the *Akademi international de lingua universal,* for a time the only formidable contender with Esperanto. Volapük, invented by Johann Schleyer, a German, in 1880, created considerable interest and a number of grammars and dictionaries were published on that tongue. These are, perhaps, the best known universal tongues. Some others are: Interlingua, invented by Giusseppe Paeno, an Italian in 1908, Novial, invented by Jespersen, a Dane, in 1928, Ro and Ido.

ESPERANTO

A B C Ĉ D E F G Ĝ H Ĥ I J Ĵ K L M N O P R S Ŝ T U Ŭ V Z
a b c ĉ d e f g ĝ h ĥ i j ĵ k l m n o p r s ŝ t u ŭ v z

The letters B, D, F, H, K, L, M, N, O, P, R, T, V, Z, are pronounced as in English. A long as in *father;* A short as in *fat;* E–*bed;* I–*machine;* U–*rude;* C–TS as in *nets;* Ĉ–CH in *church;* G–*get,* never as in *gem;* Ĝ–J or G in *gem;* Ĥ–CH in Scotch *loch;* J–Y in *yet;* Ĵ–ZH or as Z in *azure;* R is always clearly pronounced; S–*sing;* Ŝ–SH in *shut;* Ŭ–W in *wine.* Diphthongs: AJ–AI in *aisle;* EJ–EI in *vein;* OJ–OI in *toil;* UJ–UI in ruin; AU–OW in *cow;* EU is pronounced Ā–O͝O. Stress usually falls on the penultimate syllable.

VOLAPÜK

A Ä B C D E F G H I J K L M N O Ö P R S T U Ü V X Y Z
a ä b c d e f g h i j k l m m o ö p r s t u ü v x y z

B, D, F, H, K, L, M, N, P, R, T, V, X, are pronounced as in English. A–*father;* Ä–*care;* C–J in *jam;* E–*obey;* G–get; I–*machine;* O–*go;* Ö–U in *fur;* S–*sun,* but as S in *rose* in BS, DS, GS, LS: U–*rude;* Ü–German Ü; Y–*yet;* Z–TS in *sets.*

DIACRITICAL MARKS OF EUROPEAN LANGUAGES

Albanian
(Baskimi)
ÂÉ âé

Anglo-Saxon
Đǒ (Thorn) Þþ (Sithan)
Ʒʒ (Yid)

Bohemian
ÁČĎÉĚÍŇÓŘŠŤÚŮÝŽ
áčďéěíňóřšťúůýž

Croatian
ĆČŠŽ ćčšž

Danish and Norwegian
ÆØ æø

Dutch
ẅÿ

Esperanto
ĈĜĤĴŜŬ ĉĝĥĵŝŭ

Finnish
ÄÖ äö

French
ÀÂÇÉÈÊËÎÏÔÙÛÜ
àâçéèêëîïôùûü

German
With English Characters
ÄÖÜ äöü

Hungarian
ÁÉÍÓÖŐÚÜŰ
áéíóöőúüű

Italian
ÀÈÌÎÒÙ àèìîòù

Lithuanian
ÁÀÂĆÉÈÊÍÌÎŁÓÒÔ
ÚÙÛÜŻ
áàâćéèêíìîłóòôúùûüż

Polish
ĄĆĘŁŃÓŚŹŻ
ąćęłńóśźż

Portuguese
ÁÃÇÉÊÍÑÓÔÕÚÜ
áãçéêíñóôõúü

Roumanian
ÂĂÉÊĔÎĬÓŞŢ
âăéêĕîĭóşţ

Slovakian and Slovenian
ÁÄČĎÉÍĹĽŇÓÔŔ
ŠŤÚÝŽ
áäčďéíĺľňóôŕšťúýž

Spanish
ÁÉÍÑÓÚÜ áéíñóúü

Swedish
ÅÄÖ åäö

Welsh
ÂÄÊÔÛŴỲŶ
âäêôûŵỳŷ

PART II

NON-EUROPEAN LANGUAGES

CUNEIFORM WRITING, ETC.

CUNEIFORM WRITING

The earliest clues to the decipherment of ancient cuneiform inscriptions came from the work of early investigators of old Persian inscriptions. Grotefend first succeeded in deciphering the names Xerxes, Darius and Hystaspes in 1802. But the phonetic values of a number of the cuneiform characters were shown by Sir Henry Rawlinson who discovered the Persian cuneiform alphabet in 1837. Since this time very creditable advance has been made in transliterating and translating these ancient writings by scholars of Europe and America.

PERSIAN ALPHABET

Foreign characters of doubtful meaning:

a̧	ka,i	ḱu	χa,(i),u	ga,i ?	ǵu	-	ha,i,u		yu,i,u			
a	ča,i,(u)	-	ša,i,u	ǰa,(u)	-	ži	śa,i,(u)		ra,i	ŕa		
i, ē	ta,i	ťu	θa,i,u	da,i	ďu	δi	sa,i,(u).	za,i,(u)	w i	ẃu,a	na,i	ńu
u, ō	pa,i,u	-	-	ba,i,u	-	-	fr,a					
ai				ma	ḿu	vi						
au												

Lepsius

Cuneiform (the words means "wedge") writing was a system of inscribing lines or wedges on stone or other materials; and on tablets of wet clay which were later baked. Many thousands of these tablets, some dating from the dawn of recorded history, are in the museums of the world. Most of the tablets known consist of receipts for taxes, bills of sale and various other commercial recordings and many of these have impressions upon them made by cylinder seals—ancient prototypes of the modern rubber stamp.

Cuneiform writing became a conventionalized script. In the earliest examples of cuneiform, these lines or wedges were discernible vestiges of pictorial objects. But in time the pictographs tended to simplification and superfluous lines were omitted. Because of the practise of writing with a stylus upon moist clay, the lines soon became adapted to the function of the writing instrument; the lines became modified into wedge like shapes; and the characters finally lost all resemblance to their original forms.

THE EVOLUTION OF CUNEIFORM WRITING

Reed

Dagger

Ox

Man

This evolution may be seen in the Sumerian word *lugul*—King (Akkadian) *Sharru* ( ) of about 3,000 B.C.; ( ) Babylonian, about 2,000 B.C.; ( ) Assyrian, about 1,200 B.C.; and ( ) New Babylonian, about 600 B.C.

The ancient name of Nineveh, the capital of the Assyrians, meant the house of fish, which might be written ( ). In the earliest inscriptions Nineveh was written ( ) in line characters, but the name became ( ) in later cuneiform writings.

The early inscriptions were largely pictorial and were probably invented by the Akkado-Sumerian peoples. In the most ancient tongues the sounds of words seemed to have been derived from names of objects indicated by specific signs. But in later writings signs were generally employed as phonetic syllables or speech phonograms, and with other characters to convey abstract ideas, called ideographs. Some of the phonetic syllabics were homophones; others were polyphones (with more than one sound). Determinatives were added to avoid ambiguity. The earliest writings are sometimes referred to as old line character and are usually read, as in Chinese, from top to bottom of text; whereas later cuneiform characters became a conventionalized linear script.

The cuneiform inscriptions may be conveniently classified in six chronological groups, or periods: 1. Early Accadia and Ur III, c. 25th-22nd centuries B.C. 2. Early Babylonian, c. 19th-20th centuries B.C. 3. Kassite period, 17th-11th centuries B.C. 4. Assyrian, 12th-7th centuries B.C. 5. Neo-Babylonian, 6th century B.C. 6. Final period, 3rd-1st century B.C.

The ancient Assyrian language did not possess an alphabet but a number of phonetic signs and other characters were used: 1. Vocals or simple vowels. 2. Simple syllables or consonants with inherent vowels. 3. Compound consonants and syllables with inherent vowels. 4. Ideograms, indicating meaning or word class. 5. Determinatives.

Cuneiform was the official script of the Achaemenid dynasty in Persia (6th-3rd centuries B.C.). Early Persian which was probably based upon Neo-Babylonian, consisted of a simplified "alphabet" of 41 symbols, of which 4 were ideograms, 1 a sign of division between words, etc. and the remainder phonetic.

NUMERALS

1	𒁹	11	𒌋𒁹	100	𒁹 𒈨
2	𒈫	12	𒌋𒈫	200	𒈫 𒈨
3	𒐈	20	𒎙	300	𒐈 𒈨
4	𒐉	30	𒌍	400	𒐉 𒈨
5	𒐊	40	𒐏	500	𒐊 𒈨
6	𒐋	50	𒁹	600	𒐋 𒈨
7	𒐌	60	𒁹𒌋	700	𒐌 𒈨
8	𒐍	70	𒁹𒎙	800	𒐍 𒈨
9	𒐎	80	𒁹𒌍	900	𒐎 𒈨
10	𒌋	90	𒁹𒐏	1000	𒁹 𒌋𒈨

Cuneiform writings were used from about 3,000 B.C. (the dates are uncertain) to the beginning of the Christian era, in many nations in Mesopotamia and adjacent regions—the Sumerians, Elamites, Babylonians, Neo-Babylonians, Assyrians, Hittites, Syrians.

ASSYRIAN AND MEDE CUNEIFORM CHARACTERS

First Columns—Assyrian. Second Columns—Mede.

Assyrian	Mede		Assyrian	Mede		Assyrian	Mede	
		a			*ya*			*ta*
		i			*ka*			*ti*
		u			*ki*			*tu*
		ā			*ku*			*da*
		ī			*ġa*			*du*
		ū			*gi*			*at*
		ha			*ak*			*ut*
		hi			*ik*			*ṯu*
		hu			*uk*			*pa*
		pi			*ni*			*ul*
		ba			*nu*			*ša*
		bī			*an*			*ši*
		bu			*in*			*šu*
		ap			*un*			*šī*
		ip			*ra*			*aš*
		up			*ri*			*iš*
		ma, va			*ru*			*sa*
		mi, vi			*ir*			*s̱a*
		mu, vu			*ur*			*s̱i*
		im			*la*			*s̱u*
		um			*li*			*aṣ*
		na			*lu*			*is*

HITTITE

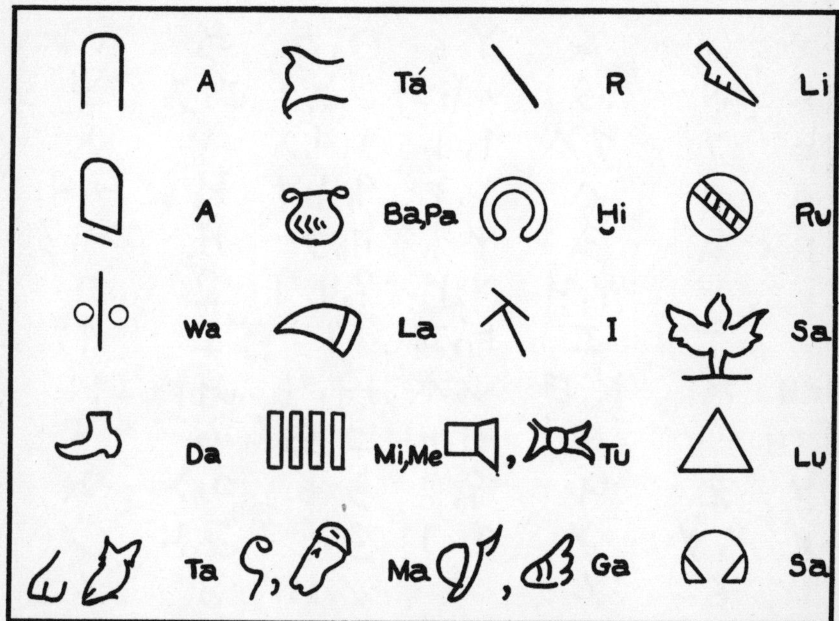

Hamitic. Written in Hittite hieroglyphics. In 1812 a stone bearing unknown inscriptions was discovered at Hamah in Syria near Kadesh, the ancient Hittite capital. Later, other fragments with undeciphered characters written upon them were found at Hamah and in places between the Black Sea and Southern Palestine, and from the Levant to the Euphrates. These writings were identified as Hittite, and the character in which the language was written seemed to be a syllabary consisting of pictographs or ideographs, of which over 400 symbols are known, but the language remains undeciphered.

The ancient Hitites were called by the Egyptians the Khatte and several records in Egyptian hieroglyphics are preserved that attest to the magnitude of this power that was at its zenith of culture perhaps about 1400-1200 B.C. The Royal archives at Boghaz-Koey (ancient Hattushash) has been the main source of the study of this writing.

OTHER EARLY ALPHABETS OF ASIA

The early alphabets of Asia, however dissimilar in form they appear, are but the result of different developments of the same primitive letters. Among the earliest alphabets are Moabite and the Tyrian type of the

	MOABITE	PHOENICIAN	HAURANTIC	NABATHEAN	PALMYRENE	ARAMAIC
A						
B						
G						
D						
H						
V						
Z						
KH						
TH						
Y						
K						
L						
M						
N						
S						
'A						
P						
S̱						
Q						
R						
SH						
T						

Phoenician alphabet. The Sidonian type of Phoenician inscriptions belongs to the same chronological group. Other alphabets of about this date or later, are the Siloam letters which resemble Samaritan.

After the downfall of the Phoenician power the heritage of its letters succeeded to the Aramean which in turn became the parent of the Semitic alphabets—Hebrew, Arabic, Syriac, and to the Western Hellenic and Roman.

THE SEMITIC ALPHABET

I. Phoenician: a. *Cadmean* (Hellenic, Italic, Lycian, Carian). b. *Tyrian* (Moabite, Samaritan). c. *Sidonian* (Punic, Aramean: 1. Palmyrene-Hebrew, 2. Estrangelo-Syrian, 3. Haurantic. 4. Nabathean-Arabic. 5. Iranian-Pehlevi).

II. South Semitic: a. *Sabean* (Himyaritic-Ethiopic). b. Thamudene. c. Indic (Nagari, Pali, Dravidian).

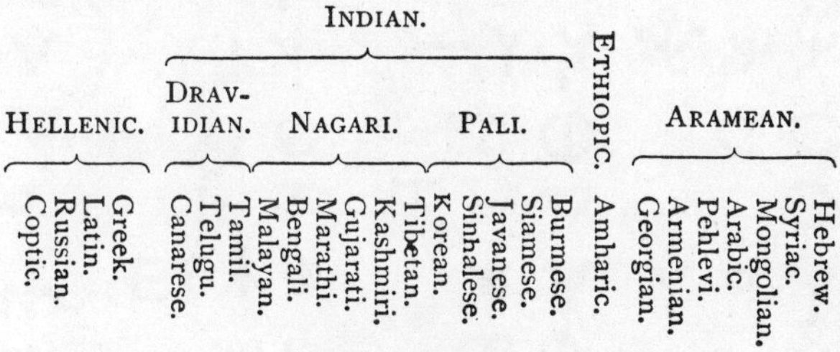

INDIAN.

HELLENIC. Greek. Latin. Russian. Coptic.

DRAVIDIAN. Canarese. Telugu. Tamil. Malayan.

NAGARI. Bengali. Marathi. Gujarati. Kashmiri.

PALI. Tibetan. Korean. Sinhalese. Javanese. Siamese. Burmese.

ETHIOPIC. Amharic.

ARAMEAN. Georgian. Armenian. Pehlevi. Arabic. Mongolian. Syriac. Hebrew.

HIMYARITIC

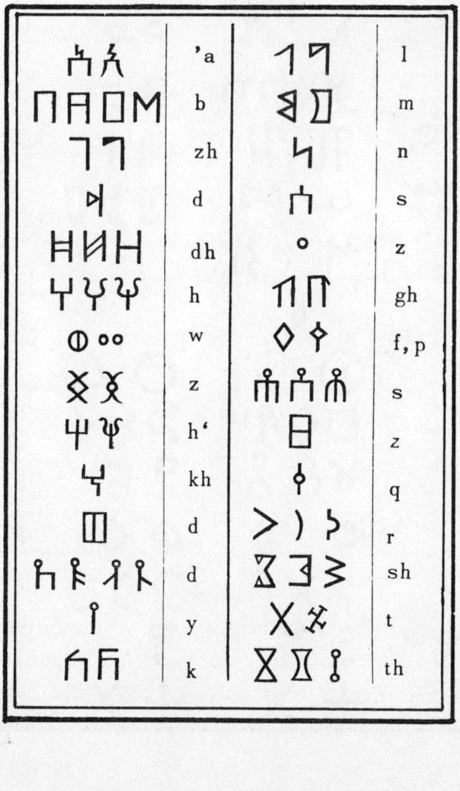

	'a		l
	b		m
	zh		n
	d		s
	dh		z
	h		gh
	w		f, p
	z		s
	h'		z
	kh		q
	d		r
	d		sh
	y		t
	k		th

SINAITIC LETTERS AND COMPARATIVE ALPHABETS

	SINAITIC SCRIPT	THAMUDENE	SAFTAIC	ABYSSINIAN
ʾ				
b				
g				
d				
h				
w				
z				
h				
t				
j				
k				
l				
m				
n				
s				
o				
p,f				
s				
q				
r				
sh				
t				

THE LANGUAGES OF AFRICA

NOTES ON THE LANGUAGES OF AFRICA

The great language families of Africa are: Sudan languages (about 450 languages and dialects) spoken by 50,000,000 people in central Africa and Sudan—Ful and Wolof in Senegal, Nubian and Hausa in the east. Bantu family of languages (about 100 languages and dialects) spoken by 50,000,000 people in equitorial Africa—Herero, Kaffir, and Zulu; Bushman and Hottentot languages, spoken by about 300,000 people in Southwest Africa.

Swahili, Coast Swahili or Union Swahili, a trade language developed by Arabic slave traders and containing a mixture of Arabic and native African words, is spoken in Congo, Mombasa, Kenya, Zanzibar, in many parts of central Africa and along the east coast of the continent. Zulu is spoken in Zululand and Natal in South Africa.

Yoruba is spoken by about 2,500,000 people in western Nigeria, West Africa, Tswa or Sheetswa is used by about 3,000,000 people in northern Transvaal and southern Mozambique, southeast Africa. In Tanganyika various dialects of Nyanja are used.

Ganda or Luganda, an important member of the Bantu language family, is the chief tongue of Uganda. In Bechuanaland Chuana or Sechuana is spoken. Some native languages spoken in the Congo are: Kongo, Luba, Lualube—Ngwana, and a trade language—Ngala. Mbundu is spoken in Angola, Ashanti is used on the Gold Coast.

Algerian, Tunisian Colloquial and Arabic are the chief languages of northern Africa and the Mediterranean coast. Amharic, or Ge'z, Tigre and Galla are spoken in Abyssinia or Ethiopia, Malagasy is the language of about 3,000,000 people in Madagascar.

The chief language of central Sudan and parts of Nigeria is Hausa, spoken by about 12,000,000 people. Hausa is sometimes written in Roman letters, Arabic characters or Aljemi Arabic letters.

English is spoken in the Union of South Africa and other British colonies and in the Republic of Liberia. In South Africa many descendants of the Dutch colonists speak a dialect of Dutch called Cape Dutch or Afrikaans. English, Spanish, French and Portugese is spoken by settlers and traders in most of the coast towns.

Few of the languages of Africa have written characters of their own; most of the tongues of the continent are written in the Roman alphabet with a few modified letters, diacritics to represent peculiar African sounds—clicks, etc. The Sudan languages of the north are usually written in Arabic characters. Amharic is written in the old Ethiopic alphabet, derived from South Semitic Himyaritic. Several little known scripts have recently been discovered in West Africa: Nsibidi script of the Ibo and Efik peoples of South Nigeria (Maxwell, 1905); Bamum script of Cameroons, a syllabic character, of which little is known definitely, Mende, and the Vai script discovered by Commodore Forbes (1848). The Vai script is an ideographic and pictographic character consisting of about 226 symbols. It was finally reduced to syllabic writing by a native—Momolu Duwalu Bukele. This script was first discovered at Bohmar on, the Western coast of Africa, near Liberia, and an outline grammar of this tongue was published in 1849.

SOME LANGUAGES OF AFRICA

Accra or Ga	Gold Coast	Galla	Ethiopia
Agni	Ivory Coast	Ganda or Luganda	Uganda
Akunakuna	Nigeria	Giryama	Kenya
Ashanti	Gold Coast	Gu	Dahomey
Bali	Cameroon		
Bambara	Senegal	Hausa	Sudan
Banu	Equitorial Africa	Herero	Damaraland
Bari	Sudan		
Bemba	N. Rhodesia	Ibo, Ijo	Nigeria
Bobangi	Congo	Ila	S. Rhodesia
Bondei	Tanganyika		
Bulu	Cameroon	Karenga	Mashonaland
Burum	Nigeria	Kikuyu	Kenya
		Konde	Nyasaland
Chuana	Bechuanaland	Kongo	Congo
Chokwe	Angola		
		Luba	Congo
Dagbane	Gold Coast	Luba-Lulua	Congo
Darkkarkari	Nigeria		
Duala	Cameroon	Malagasy	Madagascar
		Mambwe	Tanganyika
Ewe	Togoland	Mandingo	Sierra Leone
		Mbundu	Angola
Fernando Po	Nigeria	Meninka	Senegal
Fula	Cameroon, Nigeria	Mongo	Congo

Nandi	Kenya
Ngala	Congo
Ngombe	Congo
Nyanja	Nyasaland
Nyore	Kenya
Omyene	Equitorial Africa
Ragoli	Kenya
Ronga	E. Africa
Sango	Congo
Shamba (Kitchen Swahili)	Uganda, Kenya
Shambala	Mozambique
Shilha	Morocco
Shona	S. Rhodesia
Somali	Somaliland
Songoi	French W. Africa
Susu	Sierra Leone
Suto	Basutoland
Swahili	East and Central Africa
Tigre	Eritrea
Tonga	Nyasaland
Tswa or Sheetswa	Transvaal
Xosa or Kaffir	S. Africa
Yoruba	Nigeria
Zulu	Zululand, Natal

EGYPTIAN

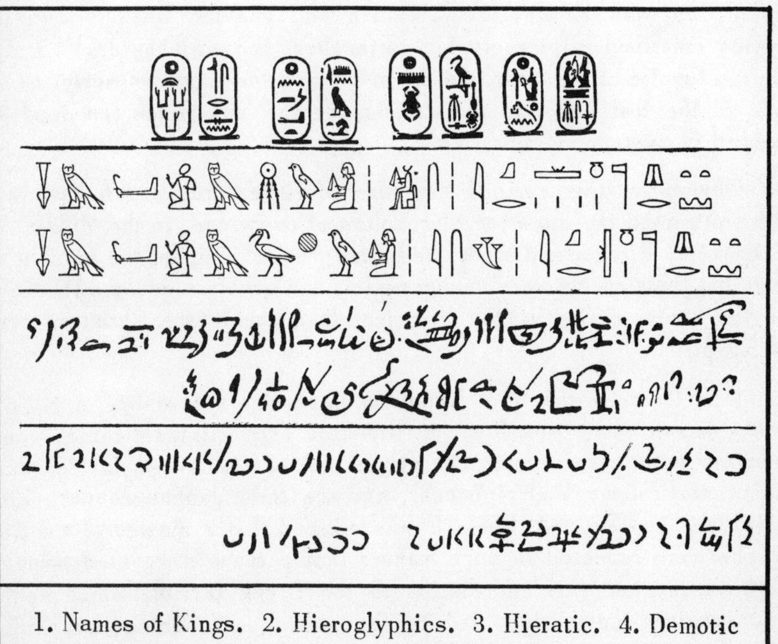

1. Names of Kings. 2. Hieroglyphics. 3. Hieratic. 4. Demotic

Hieroglyphics—the name means "sacred writings"—were written in Egypt from perhaps the earliest dynasties. The use of this character is sometimes believed to date from the reign of Menes or Mena—the first dynastic ruler (ca. 3000 B.C.?), or earlier. Certainly, there is evidence that this script was in use in the fourth dynasty and the time of Cheops. Inscriptions upon the Nar-mer palette (c. 3000 B.C.) attest to the great antiquity of this writing. Herodotus in the 6th century B.C., wrote on the Egyptian picture language and even at that date the land of Egypt was rich in the lore of the monuments and had been so 1000 years before. The cartouches of *Men-kheper-Ra* (Thothmes III), and *User-maat Ra-sotep-en Ra, Ramesu-meri-Amen* (Ramses II) inscribed on the columns of the temples were evidence of the great antiquity of this writing, and because of the peculiar nature of Egyptian ritual much of this evidence has been preserved.

The hieroglyphic character was employed during all of the Egyptian dynasties. It was in use long before the Hyksos invasion and continued until the Christian era. It was still in use at the time of the Tanite and Bubastic kings and even into the Ptolemaic era at which time its use was contemporary with other scripts, hieratic, demotic and Greek of the Alexandrines. As late as the time of Vespasian some knowledge of the characters was known; the Claudian and Flavian Caesars had their names inscribed in hieroglyphic cartouches. But with the decline of the Roman Empire of the West, the art of reading the Egyptian script became one of the lost arts and the writings on the monuments remained submerged in mystery for centuries.

Obviously, this curious language of little birds and fishes should have attracted the attention of scholars of every age. In the Middle Ages Athanasius Kircher and others had attempted to decipher the ancient writings but their efforts were unsuccessful, and scholars devoted themselves to the study of Coptic, the liturgical language of the Christian church of Egypt.

In 1799 as a result of Napoleon Bonaparte's invasion of Egypt, a black basalt stone was found at Rosetta. This trilingual tablet was inscribed with a decree of the priesthood of the synod in Memphis in honor of Ptolemy V (Epiphanes), and the three languages were hieroglyphics, demotic and Greek. It was noticed that a number of the hieroglyphs were repeated in such manner that perhaps suggested some phonetic uses, and this in relation to the Greek text of which scholars had retained knowledge, led to the subsequent decipherment of the Egyptian letters.

Thomas Young, an English mathematician, and Francois Champollion, a French scholar, independently of each other, began the study of the inscriptions and eventually succeeded in deciphering the Royal names. These discoveries were later augmented by Champollion and others; particularly, by Richard Karl Lepsius, a German Egyptologist, who succeeded in translating the inscription on the decree of Canopus, found at Tanis in 1867.

THE EGYPTIAN ALPHABET

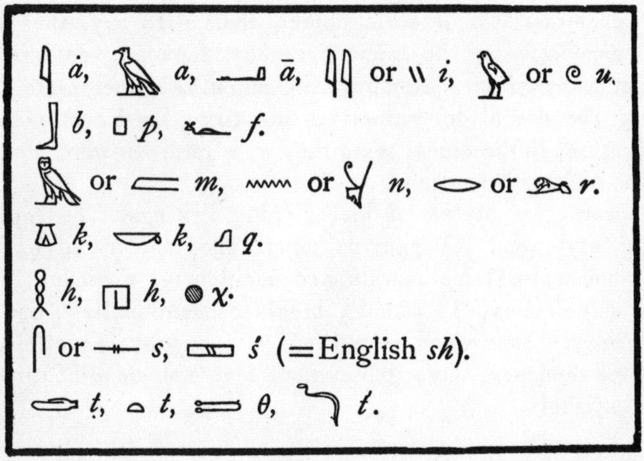

ȧ, a, ā, or i, or u.
b, p, f.
or m, or n, or r.
ḳ, k, q.
ḥ, h, χ.
or s, ś (=English sh).
ṭ, t, θ, ṯ.

It became clear that some of the signs in the hieroglyphic texts were used in the sense of an alphabet; some signs were employed as syllabics; others were ideographic and many were supplementary pictographs or ideographs employed as determinatives. The alphabet consisted of 24 consonants and vowels with several variant letters. The alphabet contained the vowels—*a*, *i*, *u*, but it was evident that another vowel, conveniently called *e* by archaeologists and grammarians, was inherent in the consonants when no other vowel was written after them.

The earliest Egyptian inscriptions were largely phonetic. Writings of the fourth dynasty and perhaps earlier, were characterized by simplicity compared with the practice of the scribes of later dynasties. The old lapidary hieroglyphics were usually carefully executed and clearly cut in every detail. But the quality of Egyptian epigraphy seemed to decline gradually; the writings of the later periods lack much of the simple precision of the characters on the older monuments and the bold simple hand of the earlier papyrii.

Syllabic signs used for phonetic values were derived from the spoken language or colloquial—sounds similar to those which the scribe wished to render. However, some symbols were employed for simplification of text, and eventually many symbols superseded other forms hitherto used for phonetic values alone.

Some words could not be drawn; therefore, other words with the same sounds were substituted. Many words soon lost their original meanings, thus becoming syllabic signs which might be employed in any word with a similar sound. To simplify the texts pictographs or ideographs were added to words. These are called determinatives, and they are of two orders; a general determinative was a picture of some object or characteristic of some object, that is to say, the character might be suggestive or abstract. Specific determinatives were pictographs. But many of the determinatives might be either pictographs or ideographs. The use of determinatives in writing the Egyptian text was a late invention. In the oldest texts they were rare, but were abundant in inscriptions of later dynasties.

There were two styles of hieroglyphic writings: The lapidary or monumental style and the papyrus hand. The lapidary style, usually seen on monuments, large murals and sepulchers, engraved in incuse intaglio or cavo relievo is usually highly conventionalized and clearly cut. The papyrus hand seen in writings on papyrus was characterized by a cursive tendency, more abbreviated text and simplification of the letters and symbols.

THE EVOLUTION OF HIERATIC FROM HIEROGLYPHICS

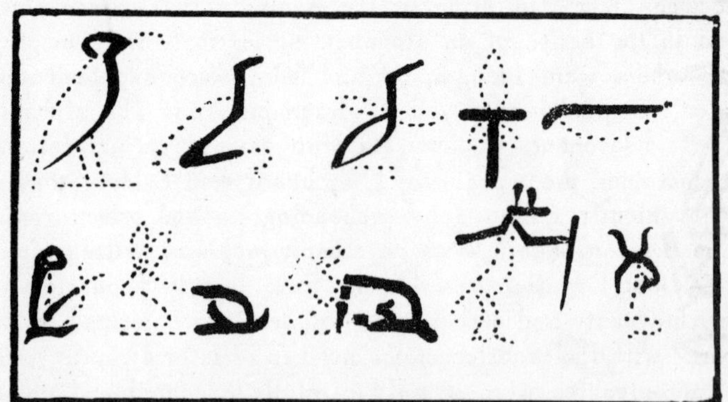

The cursive papyrus hand or linear hieroglyphics led to hieratic, a more abbreviated style of writing which began to be employed in writing profane texts, about 1700 B.C. The use of hieratic was very common in the later dynasties. Demotic was a simplified style derived from hieratic which was widely used in late dynasties until the Christian era, when it was supplanted by Coptic, a native Egyptian tongue with an alphabet modeled after Greek.

Hieroglyphics were written from left to right, right to left or in perpendicular columns. The texts are read in the order facing the images (birds, animals, etc.). Words were not divided.

EGYPTIAN ALPHABET

HIEROGLYPHICS HIERATIC DEMOTIC HIEROGLYPHICS HIERATIC DEMOTIC

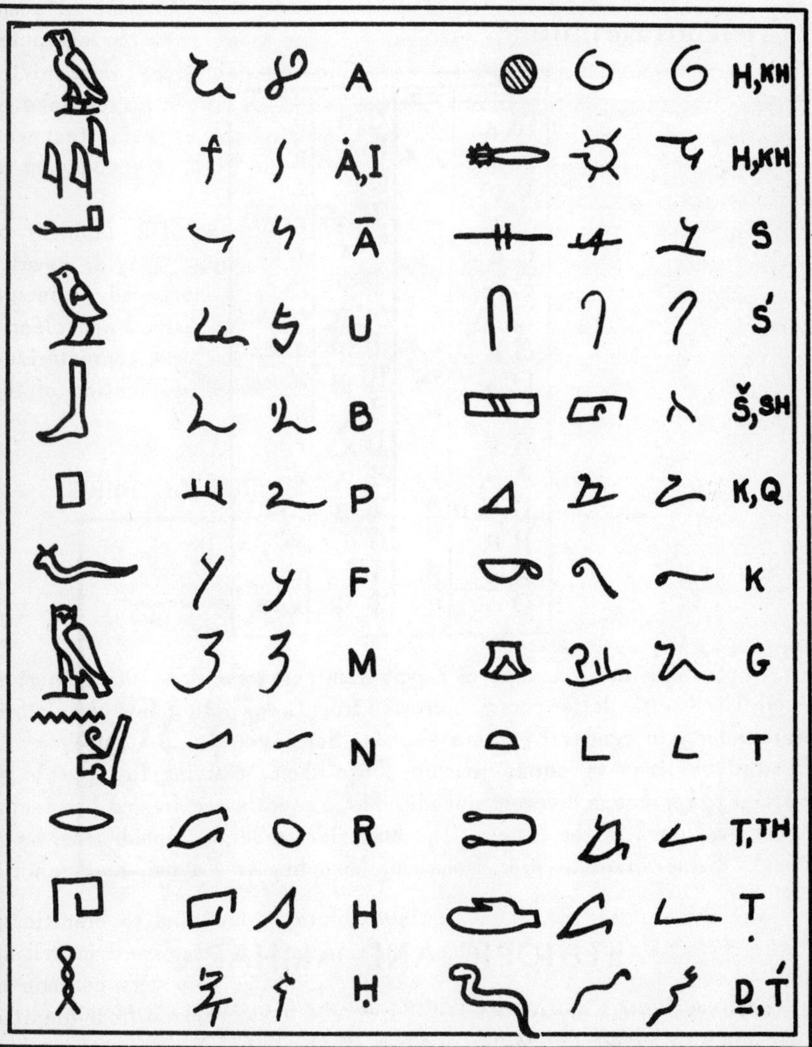

COPTIC

Ⲓⲏ̅ⲥ̅ ⲇⲉ ⲉ̀ⲧ ⲁⲩⲙⲁⲥϥ ϧⲉⲛ Ⲃⲏⲑⲗⲉⲉⲙ ⲛ̀ⲧⲉ ϯ ⲓⲟⲩⲇⲉⲁ̀ ϧⲉⲛ ⲛⲓ ⲉ̀ϩⲟⲟⲩ ⲛ̀ⲧⲉ ⲏ̀ⲣⲱⲇⲏⲥ ⲡⲟⲩⲣⲟ ϩⲏⲡⲡⲉ ⲓⲥ ϩⲁⲛ ⲙⲁⲅⲟⲥ ⲁⲩⲓ̀ ⲉ̀ⲃⲟⲗ ⲥⲁ ⲡⲉⲓⲉⲃⲧ ⲉ̀ ⲓ̀ⲗ̅ⲏ̅ⲙ̅ ⲉⲩϫⲱ ⲙ̀ⲙⲟⲥ.
2. ϫⲉ ⲁϥ ⲑⲱⲛ ⲫⲏ ⲉ̀ⲧ ⲁⲩⲙⲁⲥϥ ⲡⲟⲩⲣⲟ ⲛ̀ⲧⲉ ⲛⲓ ⲓⲟⲩⲇⲁⲓ ⲁⲛⲛⲁⲩ ⲅⲁⲣ ⲉ̀ ⲡⲉϥⲥⲓⲟⲩ ⲥⲁ ⲡⲉⲓⲉⲃⲧ ⲟⲩⲟϩ ⲁⲛⲓ̀ ϫⲉ ⲛ̀ⲧⲉⲛⲟⲩⲱϣⲧ ⲙ̀ⲙⲟϥ.

Figure.	Power.	Figure.	Power.
Ⲁ ⲁ	A.	Ⲡ ⲡ	P.
Ⲃ ⲃ	B. V.	Ⲣ ⲣ	R.
Ⲅ ⲅ	G.	Ⲥ ⲥ	S.
Ⲇ ⲇ	D.	Ⲧ ⲧ	T.
Ⲉ ⲉ	E.	Ⲩ ⲩ	Y. U.
Ⲋ ⲋ	S.	Ⲫ ⲫ	Ph.
Ⲍ ⲍ	Z.	Ⲭ ⲭ	Ch. Gr.
Ⲏ ⲏ	I. Æ.	Ⲱ ⲱ	O long.
Ⲑ ⲑ	Th.	Ϣ ϣ	Sh.
Ⲓ ⲓ	J.	Ϥ ϥ	F.
Ⲕ ⲕ	K.	Ϧ ϧ	Kch.
Ⲗ ⲗ	L.	Ϩ ϩ	H.
Ⲙ ⲙ ⲙ	M.	Ϫ ϫ	g, soft j
Ⲛ ⲛ	N.	Ϭ ϭ	Sh.
Ⲝ ⲝ	X.	Ϯ ϯ	D.
Ⲟ ⲟ	O	Ⲯ ⲯ	Bs.

Coptic was the language of Egypt from about the 3rd–10th centuries, A.D. The Coptic letters were borrowed from Greek, but a few new letters were added to render Egyptian sounds. Some vowels in Coptic are indicated by lines or points written above them, causing the vowels so marked to represent different sounds. The numerals are formed by placing a bar over each of the letters. The numerical order is alphabetical as in Greek. Some dialects are: Bohairic, Memphis or Fayum, and Sahidic.

ETHIOPIC AND AMHARIC

በቀዳሚ ፡ ገብረ ፡ እግዚአብሔና ፡ ሰማየ ፡ ወምድረ ። ወምድርሰ ፡ ኢታስተርኢ ፡
ወኢኮነት ፡ ድሉተ ፡ ወጽልመት ፡ መልዕልተ ፡ ቀላይ ፡ ወመንፈሰ ፡ እግዚአብሔር ፡

ይጼልል : መልዕልተ : ማይ :: ወይቤ : እግዚአብሔር : ለይኩን : ብርሃን : ወኮነ : ብርሃን :: ወርእዮ : እግዚአብሔር : ለብርሃን : ከመ : ሠናይ : ወፈለጠ : እግዚአብ
ሔር : ማእከለ : ብርሃን : ወማእከለ : ጽልመት :: ወሰመዮ : እግዚአብሔር : ለብር
ሃን : ዕለተ : ወለጽልመት : ሌሊተ : ወኮነ : ሌሊተ : ወጸብሐ : ወኮነ : መዓልተ : ፩ ::

Gen. 1, 1—5.

ETHIOPIC ALPHABET

	with ă	with û	with î	with â	with ê	with ĕ	with ô
h	ሀ	ሁ	ሂ	ሃ	ሄ	ህ	ሆ
l	ለ	ሉ	ሊ	ላ	ሌ	ል	ሎ
ḥ	ሐ	ሑ	ሒ	ሓ	ሔ	ሕ	ሖ
m	መ	ሙ	ሚ	ማ	ሜ	ም	ሞ
s	ሠ	ሡ	ሢ	ሣ	ሤ	ሥ	ሦ
r	ረ	ሩ	ሪ	ራ	ሬ	ር	ሮ
s	ሰ	ሱ	ሲ	ሳ	ሴ	ስ	ሶ
q	ቀ	ቁ	ቂ	ቃ	ቄ	ቅ	ቆ
b	በ	ቡ	ቢ	ባ	ቤ	ብ	ቦ
t	ተ	ቱ	ቲ	ታ	ቴ	ት	ቶ
kh	ኀ	ኁ	ኂ	ኃ	ኄ	ኅ	ኆ
n	ነ	ኑ	ኒ	ና	ኔ	ን	ኖ
'a	አ	ኡ	ኢ	ኣ	ኤ	እ	ኦ
k	ከ	ኩ	ኪ	ካ	ኬ	ክ	ኮ
w	ወ	ዉ	ዊ	ዋ	ዌ	ው	ዎ
a	ዐ	ዑ	ዒ	ዓ	ዔ	ዕ	ዖ
z	ዘ	ዙ	ዚ	ዛ	ዜ	ዝ	ዞ
y	የ	ዩ	ዪ	ያ	ዬ	ይ	ዮ
d	ደ	ዱ	ዲ	ዳ	ዴ	ድ	ዶ
g	ገ	ጉ	ጊ	ጋ	ጌ	ግ	ጎ
ṭ	ጠ	ጡ	ጢ	ጣ	ጤ	ጥ	ጦ
p	ጰ	ጱ	ጲ	ጳ	ጴ	ጵ	ጶ
ts	ጸ	ጹ	ጺ	ጻ	ጼ	ጽ	ጾ
dz	ፀ	ፁ	ፂ	ፃ	ፄ	ፅ	ፆ
f	ፈ	ፉ	ፊ	ፋ	ፌ	ፍ	ፎ
p	ፐ	ፑ	ፒ	ፓ	ፔ	ፕ	ፖ

Amharic is the vernacular speech of about 3,000,000 people in Ethiopia. The alphabet consists of 33 radicals—each radical character has 7 vowels. Amharic is written from left to right. Ethiopic is the ancient liturgical language of the Ethiopian church. These letters were invented in the 5th century A.D. Ancient Ethiopic, like Amharic, is written from left to right.

NUBIAN AND LIBYAN

b	⊙	t	≻—	m	]	r	○
g	⟨	y	≷	n	|	sh	≻
d	⊓	K	⇋ ⇌ ≦	s	(⧖ ⋈	t	+ ∃
w ⊓⊓ = ÷		l	||	p	ⴳ	?	>HM

African. Nubian characters. Nubian or Libyan, is the mother script of the North African nomads. It is spoken by about 300,000 people in the Nile valley between Aswan and Seyala, and in Dongela, Heiban and in Kordofan province, Anglo-Egyptian Sudan. Some dialects are: Kunuzi, Fiadidja, Heiban and Nirore.

TAMACHEK

i,u,a	•	z	ⵣ ⵣ	l	||	sh	ⵛ
b	⊞ ⦶	r	□ ○	m	]	h	⁞
t	+	s	⊡ ⊙	n	|	d	∃
d	⊔ Λ ⊓	s	Ï !	K	∴	x	∷
zh	I	ś	⋈	q	⋯	ū,w	:
z	#	f	ⵊ ⵊ	y	⋮	ī	{

African. Tiffinag alphabet. Spoken by the Taureg tribes in the Tamanrasset region of central Sahara, North Africa.

MOGREBI

African: Arabic dialect. Mogrebi or Arabic of the West, is spoken in Algeria, Morocco, Tunis, and other parts of northwest Africa. The North African Arabic dialects are written in several styles of the Arabic character: Neskhi, Tunisian, Carshuni and Aljemi Arabic letters. Arabic of the West is similar to the tongues spoken in the East, but the chief differences of pronunciation is the accent, although the North African dialects have a number of dialectical peculiarities not shared by the spoken tongues of Egypt, Iraq and Syria.

In Mogrebi accent is free and is not controlled by long vowels or double closure, and there is a tendency to drop or slur over the short vowels preceding the accent; whereas, in Egypt, Syria and to some extent, in Iraq, accent or stress generally recedes from the end of the word until it falls upon a long vowel or a short vowel followed by two consonants. Otherwise Mogrebi colloquial is very similar to Eastern colloquial. However, certain sections of north Africa have local peculiarities of pronunciation influenced by speakers of Berber tongues–the Kabyle and Riffi of the mountains.

AFRIKAANS

Afrikaans or Cape Dutch or the Taal, is a dialect of Holland Dutch, spoken by the Afrikaners or Boers in the Union of South Africa. It is one of the three official languages of the Union and is in very general use throughout the country. Afrikaans is based upon Netherlands Dutch but the language contains a considerable admixture of English and Bantu words.

Consonants generally are pronounced as in Dutch. The letters C and X are rarely used. The letter G has a guttural sound of CH in Scotch *loch.* The letter H has the power of H in *hat* and is never aspirated. The letter Q is not used, KW is employed instead.

A–closed–about like A in *hat* but A open like A in *father;* DJ–TJ: E closed–*get;* E open–about E in *mere;* F is nearly W in various inflectional forms; GH–*get;* GHW–GUA; I–*wit* in an accented syllable, otherwise I–*machine;* IE–English EE but shorter; O in closed syllables–*top;* O in open syllables– OO in *moor;* Ô–AW in *law;* OO–OO in *foot;* SCH–SK but more nearly S as *final;* SJ–SH in *shut;* U–*luck* when closed; U open–German *über;* V–F; Z–S in *sit;* AI–I in *high;* AAI–I in *try;* Ë denotes a separation of syllables. In Afrikaans A sometimes has the sound of U as in *cup.* Often the letter N has a slight nasal sound as in French.

HAUSA

Gama Allah ya yi ḳamnar duniya har ya bada Ḍansa, haifaffe shi kaḍai, domin dukan wanda yana bada gaskiya gareshi kada ya lalache, amma ya sami rai na har abada. —Jn. 3.16

African. Sudan. Hausa is spoken by about 12,000,000 people in northern Nigeria and central Sudan. Chief dialects are; Katsena, Kano, Sokoto. The Kano dialect is most widely spoken in Hausaland but the Katsena dialect of the north is the purest. Hausa is perhaps the most widely spoken language of continental Africa. Like Arabic and Swahili it is a lingua franca of much of eastern and western tropical Africa. Although Hausa contains many words imported into the language from Arabic, it is not a Semitic tongue.

Hausa is usually written in the Roman alphabet or the Arabic alphabet. Several diacritical marks are provided for sounds of the language when written in the Roman letters. These are Ḅ, Ḍ, Ḳ.

B, CH, D, F, G, H, J, K, L, M, N, P, R, SH, T, W, Z, are pronounced as in English. Note: CH always has the sound of CH as in *church.*

A—*father* but short A as in *fat* in a closed syllable; Ḅ—hard B with point of tongue touching upper teeth; Ḍ—hard D with point of tongue touching upper teeth; E—A in date; F sometimes has power of FH; G—G in *get,* never as G in *gem;* I—*machine* but short I as in *fit* in a closed syllable; Ḳ—sub-palatal guttural K or "watery" K so-called because the mouth is placed in a position for shooting out water from the throat; L sometimes has a sound intermediate between R and L; O—*note;* P is often interchangeable with F or B; U—*flute* or as OO in *fool,* but short U as in *but* in a closed syllable; Y—*yet,* never used as a consonant; AI—*aisle;* AU—OW in *cow.*

BOBANGI

Nowele Nyambe aliki nde o tinda o Mwana w'o molongo na ntin'ete atendele molongo ka, nde na ntin'ete molongo mokoswibwa bokoswibwaka na Yeye.

A B C D E Ê G I K L M N O Ô P S T U W Y Z
a b c d e ê g i k l m n o ô p s t u w y z

African: Bantu. Bobangi is spoken in the Bolobo region, or near the south bank of the Congo river.

B, D, K, L, M, N, P, T, W, Y, are pronounced as in English.

A—*father;* C—TSE in *itself;* E—A in *date;* Ê—between E and I; G—*get;* I—*machine;* O—OU in *ought;* Ô—*note;* S—*set;* U—OO in *pool;* Z—DZ in *adze.*

LUBA-LULUA

Buala bua Nzambi wakatamba kusua be ha buloba, yeye wakabaha Muan'andi umuehele mulela ne, wamuit abuxa, kena ufua, neikale ne muoyo wa cendelele.

A Ă Ä B C D E Ĕ F G H I Ĭ Ī J K L M N O P S T U Ŭ V W X Y Z
a ă ä b c d e ĕ f g h i ĭ ī j k l m n o p s t u ŭ v w x y z

African: Bantu. Spoken by about 3,000,000 people between the Kasai and Lulua Rivers, Belgian Congo.

B, D, F, K, L, M, N, P, T, V, W, Y, Z, are pronounced as in English. A—*father;* Ă—*hat;* Ä—*ball;* C—CH in *church;* E—*they;* Ĕ—*met;* G—*get;* H—breathing sound between F and P, but must be heard to be understood; I—*machine;* Ĭ—*hit;* Ī—*line;* J—ZH or as Z in *azure;* O—*note;* S—*sister;* U—*rule;* Ŭ—*but;* X— sh in *shut.*

KONGO

Kadi bonso bwabu Nzambi wazola nza, vo wavana Mwan' andi mosi kaka, mpasi wonso ukunlekilanga minu kabungwa ko, kansi kala moyo wamvu ya mvu.

Buende or Fioti dialect.

A B D E F G I J K L M N O P S T U V W X Y Z
a b d e f g i j k l m n o p s t u v w x y z

African: Bantu. Spoken in the regions of Brazzaville, Manyanga, Mbanza, Lukungu, and the south bank of the Congo river, Belgian Congo.

B, D, F, K, L, M, N, P, T, V, W, Y, Z, are pronounced as in English. A—*father;* E—A in *date;* G—*get;* I—*machine;* J—ZH or Z in *azure;* O—*toy* or as OU in *ought;* S—*sister;* U—OO in *tool;* X—SH in *shut.*

Dipthongs: AU—OU in *cow;* AI—*aisle;* TI—CH—*cheese.* Every syllable ends with a vowel and no two consonants come together except nasals prefixed to other consonants, or W and Y which may follow a consonant. A as final in a word is elided before A in another word. A before I combines with it to form E.

Nasal combinations: MB, MF, MP, ND, NG, NJ, NK, NL, NS, NT, NX, NZ.

LUGANDA

Kubanga Katonda bweyayagala ensi bwati, nokuwayo nāwayo Omwānanawe eyazālibwa omu ye'ka, buli muntu yena amu'kirza aleme okubula, naye abēre nobulamu obuta'gwāwo.

A AI B C D E F G I J K L M N NG' NY O P R S T U V W Y Z
a ai b c d e f g i j k l m n ng' ny o p r s t u v w y z

African: Bantu. Spoken in Uganda, East Africa. Ganda or Luganda is the most northerly of the Bantu family of languages.

B, D, J, K, L, M, N, P, T, W, Y, Z, are pronounced as in English.

A–*father;* AI–*aisle;* C–CH in *church;* E–*were;* F–FW or VW; G–*get;* I–*machine;* NG'–*singer*; NY–NI in *onion;* O–*hold;* S–*sister;* U–*rule;* V–FWA or VWA. L after A, O, U, and R after E, I, are nearly identical in sound.

Emphatic consonants, pronounced with explosive force: K', G', T', D', P', B', S', Z', F', V', J', M', N'.

YORUBA

Nitori Ọlọrun fẹ araiye tobẹ̃ gẹ, ti o fi Ọmọ bíbi rẹ̀ kanṣoṣo funni, ki ẹnikẹni ti o ba gbà a gbọ́ ma ba ṣegbé, ṣugbọn ki o le ni ìye ainipẹkun.

A AI AU B C D E Ẹ F G H I J K L M N O Ọ OI P Q R S Ṣ T U
a ai au b c d e ẹ f g h i j k l m n o ọ oi p q r s ṣ t u

V W X Y Z
v w x y z

African. Spoken by about 2,500,000 people in Western Nigeria.

D, F, J, K, L, M, N, P, Q, R, S, T, V, W, X, Y, Z, are pronounced as in English.

A–*at;* AI–*aisle;* AU–OU in *round;* B, GB–nearly B but this sound must be heard; C–*cut;* E–A in *date;* Ẹ Ẹ–*let;* G–*get;* H is aspirated; I–*machine;* O–*bone;* Ọ–A in *war;* OI–O in *long;* Ṣ–SH in *shut;* U–OO in *boot.* The tilde (˜) over a letter usually indicates contraction of a word.

ZULU

Ngoba uNkulunkulu wa wu tanda unhlaba kangaka, ngangoba wa pa ngeNdodana yake ayizalayo e yodwa, ukuba bonke abakolwa iyo ba nga bubi, ba be nokupila okumiyo njalo.

A B C D E F G H I J K L M N O P Q R S T U V W X Y Z
a b c d e f g h i j k l m n o p q r s t u v w x y z

African: Bantu, Spoken in Zululand, Natal, Cape Colony, and southeast coast of Africa.

B, D, F, H, J, K, L, M, N, P, S, T, V, W, Y, Z, are pronounced as in English.

A—*father;* C—click sound; E—*there;* G—*get;* I—*machine;* O—*pole;* Q—click sound; U—*rule;* X—*click sound;* AU—OU. Accent is usually on the penult.

NAMA

ǁNatigoseb gu̥m Eloba ǃhūb-eiba gye ǀnamo, ob gye ǁẽib di ǀguise ǃnai hã ǀgõaba gye ma, ǁẽib ǃna ra ǂgomn hoan gā-ǁō tite se, χawen nĩ lamö ũiba ū-ha se.

A B C D E (F) G GH H I K KH (L) M N O P Q R S T U V W X (Y) Z
a b c d e (f) g gh h i k kh (l) m n o p q r s t u v w x (y). z

African: Hottentot-Bushman. Spoken by about 50,000 natives in Southwest Africa. Characters of the Nama tongue are the clicks sounded in speaking the language. These must be heard to be properly understood.

B, D, F, H, K, L, M, N, P, R, S, T, W, Y, Z, are pronounced as in English.

A—*father;* E—A in *date;* G—*get;* GH—guttural; KH—*deep guttural;* I—*pin;* O—*bone*. AE—A in *day;* AI—*aisle;* AU—OW in *how;* EI—*eight;* OI—*toil;* OU in OW in *sow;* UI— Dutch *tuin*.

The clicks are: C, Q, V, X. These are made by drawing the breath inward until the sound is combined with another sound. The clicks are sometimes written with special characters. Dental click C—press tip of tongue against front upper teeth, then withdraw suddenly. Palatal click C—press tip of the tongue flat against end of palate at gums and remove suddenly. Cerebral click Q—curl tip of tongue against roof of palate, then withdraw suddenly. Click X—same as Q. The letters, F, L, Y, are not used. W is a semi-vowel at beginning of syllables.

SWAHILI

Kwani Mwenyiezi Mngu jinsi alivyoupenda ulimwengu amewapa watu Mwanawe mzaliwa pekee killa mwenyi kuamini kwakwe asipotee, awe na uzima we milele.

Mombasa dialect.

A B CH D E F G H I J K L M N O P R S T U V W Y Z
a b ch d e f g h i j k l m n o p r s t u v w y z

African: Bantu. Swahili, a trade language, developed by Arabic slave traders, is spoken along the eastern coast of Africa and in many parts of Central Africa. Swahili is written in the Roman alphabet or in Arabic letters. Chief dialects are: Zanzibar, Kingwana or Ituri of Congo, Mombasa of Kenya.

B, CH, D, F, H, J, K, L, M, N, P, R, S, T, V, W, Y, Z, are pronounced as in English.

A—*father;* E—first E in *there;* CH—*church;* G—*get,* never as in *gem;* I—*machine;* O—*boy;* U—OO in *tool;* GH—Arabic ghain; KH—as CH in Scotch *loch;* TH—TH or Z; KW—QU in *quick;* M often has a syllabic sound (*mu*) before consonants, except before B or W, but M before A or E has the sound of MW; M before O frequently omits the syllabic sound; N followed by CH, F, H, M, N, S, has nasal semivocal sound like NI in *onion;* NG or GN—NG in *singing;* SH—*shut;* P, T, K, often have an explosive or aspirated sound of a suppressed N.

MALAGASY OF MADAGASCAR

16 Fa toy izao no nitiavan' Andriamanitra izao tontolo izao: nomeny ny Zanani-
lahy Tokana, mba tsy ho very izay rehetra
mino Azy, fa hanana fiainana mandrakizay.
17 Fa Andriamanitra tsy naniraka ny
Zanaka ho amin' izao tontolo izao haname-
loka [1] izao tontolo izao, fa mba hamonjeny
izao tontolo izao. 18 Izay mino Azy dia
tsy helohina [2]; fa izay tsy mino kosa dia efa

SEMITIC LANGUAGES

ARABIC

1. *Cufic.* 2. *Karmathian.* 3. *Neskhi.* 4. *Sulus.*

Semitic. Arabic alphabet. The Arabic letters are written in four styles or forms: The letter as initial, as medial, as final; and the letter when isolated or standing alone. With few exceptions consonants only are written; the vowels are supplied by points written above or below the consonants and sounded after the consonant so marked. Unpointed Arabic, written without vowel points is unintelligible except to natives and scholars who have profound knowledge of the language.

There are many Arabic colloquials but the literary language or written Arabic, as it is called, is generally understood in all of the countries that have adopted the Moslem faith—about 30,000,000 people in Syria, Iraq, Palestine, Trans-Jordan, Mesopotamia, Egypt, Algeria, Tunisia, Morocco; Saudi-Arabia, and Sudan.

4	3	2	1		4	3	2	1	
ـا			ا	’a	ـط	ـطـ	طـ	ط	t
ـب	ـبـ	بـ	ب	b	ـظ	ـظـ	ظـ	ظ	dh
ـت	ـتـ	تـ	ت	t	ـع	ـعـ	عـ	ع	‘
ـث	ـثـ	ثـ	ث	th	ـغ	ـغـ	غـ	غ	gh
ـج	ـجـ	جـ	ج	j	ـف	ـفـ	فـ	ف	f
ـح	ـحـ	حـ	ح	h‘	ـق	ـقـ	قـ	ق	k
ـخ	ـخـ	خـ	خ	kh	ـك	ـكـ	كـ	ك	k
ـد			د	d	ـل	ـلـ	لـ	ل	l
ـذ			ذ	th	ـم	ـمـ	مـ	م	m
ـر			ر	r	ـن	ـنـ	نـ	ن	n
ـز			ز	z	ـه	ـهـ	هـ	ه	h
ـس	ـسـ	سـ	س	s	ـة			ة	t
ـش	ـشـ	شـ	ش	sh	ـو			و	w
ـص	ـصـ	صـ	ص	s	ـى	ـيـ	يـ	ى	y
ـض	ـضـ	ضـ	ض	dh	ـلا			لا	la

4. Final 3. Medial 2. Initial 1. Isolated

The alphabet contains 27 consonants: ’ , ‘ , B, T, TH, G, H, KH, D, DH, R, Z, S, SH, *S*, *D*, *T*, *Z*, GH, F, Q, K, L, M, N, H, W, Y. There are no sounds of P or V. Letters shown (not in italics) are pronounced about as in English. The italic letters sometimes present difficulties to foreigners. Arabic speakers attach quite different sound values to these letters which are best learned by hearing the language spoken. The letter H is an aspirated consonant with a guttural sound. TH is pronounced about as in *thick;* DH is similar to TH in *these,* except in Egypt where TH–T, and DH–D, and in Syria where these letters also may have the sounds of S and Z respectively, as well as Egyptian sounds. The letter KH is similar to Scotch *loch.* Three guttural consonants are represented by ', ', GH. The letter GH is sometimes described as an attempt at gargling; we may describe ' as an effort to utter the word A in *and* but with contraction of the throat; the letter ' is more emphatic, pronounced as if one had a catch in the throat.

In Iraq the letter K with I sometimes has the value of CH as in *church.* In Upper Egypt, among the desert Arabs, and to some extent in Iraq, Q has the value of G in *get.* In Egypt, the Sudan and Sinai, the letter J has the power of J in *jam* but is pronounced about like ZH or Z in *azure* in North Africa. The letter R is pronounced with a rolling sound. Egyptian G is about as in *get* but elsewhere sometimes nearly as in *gem.* In Upper Egypt G is sometimes pronounced like DY, and along the Euphrates G may have the value of Y as in *yet.*

The vowels (Mesopotamian sounds) are: Â–*father:* A–*along;* À–*hat;* Ê–A in *day;* E–*let;* Î–*machine;* I–*pin;* Ô–*bone;* O–*forest;* Û–*blue;* U–OO in *good;* AI–*aisle;* AW–OU in *how.* The short vowels are pronounced as if somewhat thrust back in the throat but there are many different soundings of the letters among the Arabic speaking peoples. And to the Arabic ear the sounds of the short vowels often indicate the speaker's province, nation or town, and whether he be Moslem, Christian or Jew. Usually a consonant is sounded with the aid of an auxiliary vowel, and when three consonants come together, it is necessary to insert a vowel. This is the general practice in the colloquials except in West Arabic where the unaccented vowel is usually shortened, almost as if omitted, before the accent. Every syllable is pronounced distinctly otherwise.

Accent: In the colloquial of Lower Egypt and Syria accent is on the last syllable when that syllable has a long vowel or a short vowel followed by two consonants; but accent is on the penultimate syllable if that syllable is short and closed by one consonant. Generally (in Mesopotamia) the accent usually falls on the first long syllable counting from the end of a word, or the first closed syllable; otherwise, accent falls on the first syllable of a word except when beginning with *wasl*–then accent is on the second syllable.

Vowel points and diacritics

1. *Fetha* (ـَـ) A is written above the consonant and sounded after the consonant so marked. When *alif* is added to the consonant A becomes long A; then *fetha* is indicated by a vertical stroke (ـٰ) written above the consonant.

2. *Kesra* (ـِـ) –I is written below the consonant after which it is sounded. When YA is added to the consonant with *kesra,* I becomes long I.

3. *Dhumma* (ـُ) U is written above the consonant and sounded after the consonant so marked. When WAW is added to the consonant with *dhumma*, U becomes long U.

4. *Hemza*—usually written above initial *alif* (ـٔ) indicates a sound in the throat resembling guttural H. When *hemza* is written above initial *alif*, the letter has no value of its own. When the following vowel is *fetha*, the mark *hemza* is written above *alif*, but when the following word is *kesrah*, *hemza* is written below *alif*. *Hemza* is also written over WAW and YA.

5. *Wasl* (ٱ) is written above one of two consecutive consonants t form a bridge between them. *Wasl* also serves to link the final vowel of a preceding word to the first consonant of a second word. When *wasl* is written above *alif*, that letter has no value of its own.

6. *Shedda* or *tashdid* (ـّ) written above a consonant indicates that the letter is doubled except in final IYA.

7. *Medda* (ـٓ) written above the letter indicates the combined power of *alif* with *hemza* followed by a second *alif* with *hemza*. *Medda* also is used sometimes when *alif* is followed by *hemza*.

8. *Jasm* (ـْ) written above a letter indicates contraction or that no vowel sound follows the consonant so marked. Similarly *shukun* (ـْ) indicates that the consonant has no vowel sound following it. *Shukun* is written above WAW or YA when either are part of diphthongs.

9. *Tanwin* (ـٍ) written below the letter adds the sound of N to final vowels.

10. *Dhummaten* (ـٌ) written above the letter indicates the final sound of UN.

11. *Kesraten* (ـٍ) written below the letter indicates the final sound of IN.

12. *Fethaten* (ـً) written above the letter indicates the final sound of AN.

The vowels and *jasm* are not always written but sometimes implied. In unpointed Arabic the reader is expected to know these sounds. *Ali* *maqsura* (ى)—A. The article EL (Western Arabic) or AL (Eastern Arabic is assimilated in pronunciation before D, DH, N, R, S, SH, T, TH, Z; thus *esh shem*—not, *el shem*. *Lam-alif* is obsolete, now written *lam, alif*.

When WAW and YA are preceded by heterogeneous vowels, diphthongs result: A—WAW—AW or colloquial Ô; A—YA—AI or colloquial Ê.

The Arabic alphabet is also used with modifications and specia diacritics in Persia (Iran), in old Turkish, in India (Sindhi, Urdu, etc.), in Pushto or Pashto (Afghanistan), Balochi, Brahui, Kabyle, Kurdish Mandingo, Shilha, More, Malay, Hausa and Swahili.

ARABIC TYPES

سُورَةُ ٱلْبَقَرَةِ بِسْمِ ٱللَّهِ ٱلرَّحْمَٰنِ ٱلرَّحِيمِ .1 ذَٰلِكَ ٱلْكِتَابُ لَا
رَيْبَ فِيهِ هُدًى لِلْمُتَّقِينَ .2 ٱلَّذِينَ يُؤْمِنُونَ بِٱلْغَيْبِ وَيُقِيمُونَ
ٱلصَّلَوٰةَ وَمِمَّا رَزَقْنَاهُمْ يُنْفِقُونَ .3 وَٱلَّذِينَ يُؤْمِنُونَ بِمَا أُنْزِلَ إِلَيْكَ
وَمَا أُنْزِلَ مِنْ قَبْلِكَ وَبِٱلْآخِرَةِ هُمْ يُوقِنُونَ

The various styles of script sometimes employed in writing Arabic letters are: 1. *Cufic* or the ancient square character. 2. *Karmathian.* 3. *Neskhi* or common character. 4. *Ta'alik.* 5. *Rika'a.* 6. *Diwanny.* 7. *Sulus,* a character often employed in chapter headings, etc. 8. *Jeritsi.* 9. *Qalm rash'd.* 10. *S'yakat.* 11. *Mogreb* or *Mauretanian.* 12. *Shekesteh.* 13. *Aljemi.*

HEBREW

וַיְכֻלּוּ הַשָּׁמַיִם וְהָאָרֶץ וְכָל־צְבָאָם׃
וַיְכַל אֱלֹהִים בַּיּוֹם הַשְּׁבִיעִי מְלַאכְתּוֹ אֲשֶׁר עָשָׂה וַיִּשְׁבֹּת
בַּיּוֹם הַשְּׁבִיעִי מִכָּל־מְלַאכְתּוֹ אֲשֶׁר עָשָׂה׃
וַיְבָרֶךְ אֱלֹהִים אֶת־יוֹם הַשְּׁבִיעִי וַיְקַדֵּשׁ אֹתוֹ כִּי בוֹ שָׁבַת
מִכָּל־מְלַאכְתּוֹ אֲשֶׁר־בָּרָא אֱלֹהִים לַעֲשׂוֹת׃

Semitic. Hebrew alphabet. Hebrew was spoken by the ancient Israelites of the Hebrew nation. Except for some passages of Daniel, Ezra and Jeremiah, written in Aramaic (Chaldee) Hebrew was the original language of the Old Testament. Ancient Hebrew was written without vowels, only the consonants were written—the vowels were supplied by the reader whose knowledge of the language was usually profound. At some time between the 6th and 11th centuries a group of Jewish scholars known as the Massoretes supplied the traditional vowels called Masoretic points now ordinarily used in writing Hebrew.

Masoretic points are written after or below the consonant but sounded after the letter so marked—with the exception of furtive patakh, a vowel sound which precedes the consonant so marked. Five of the Hebrew letters have final forms differing from the letters used as initial or medial. Eight letters have more than one sound which is indicated by dots written over them or within the letter.

א	H in hour	1
ב or בּ	B, V	2
ג or גּ[1]	Gh, G	3
ד or דּ	Dh, d, as	4
ה	in he or that	5
ו	V	6
ז	Z	7
ח	Kh or Hh	8
ט	T	9
י	Y	10
כ or כּ final ך or ךְ	Kh, K	20
ל	L	30
מ final ם	M	40
נ final ן	N	50
ס	S	60
ע	Almost silent Sound unknown.	70
פ or פּ final ף	Ph, P	80
צ final ץ	Ts	90
ק	K or Q	100
ר	R	200
שׁ or שׂ	Sh, S	300
ת or תּ	Th, T	400

MASORETIC POINTS

ָ	Kamets	בָּ	ba	*a* in *all.*
ָ	Khatuph	בָּד	bod	*o* in *holiday, not,* and *son.*
ֵ	Tsere	בֵּ	be	*e* in *they.*
ִי	Khirik Gadol (long)	בִּי	bi	*i* in *machine.*
ִ	Khirik Katon (short)	בִּד	bid	*i* in *pin, estimate.*
וֹ	Kholem	בּוֹ	bo	*o* in *go, no, so.*
וּ	Shurek	בּוּ	bu	*u* in *rule.*
ַ	Pathakh (long)	בַּד	bad	*a* in *father.*
	Pathakh (short)	בַּד		*a* in *fair.*
ֶ	Segol (long)	בֶּד	bed	*e* in *prey.*
	Segol (short)	בֶּד		*e* in *met, men.*
ֻ	Kibbuts (long)	בֻּד	bud	*u* in *rue.*
	Kibbuts (short)	בֻּד		*u* in *full.*

Sheva (simple) מְ *e* in *begin.*

Kateph Pattahh חֲ *a* in *litany.*

Kateph Segol אֱ *e* in *begin.*

Kateph Kamets חֳ *o* in *ivory.*

The *sheva* (indicates that the letter above the point is coalescent or silent. Infrequently *sheva* takes the sound of short E. The vowel in *furtive patakh* precedes the marked consonant as described before. There are about 21 marks of accent in Scriptural Hebrew.

According to the Babylonian Talmud, the ancient Jews attributed their alphabet to Ezra—that is, the adoption of the present letters derived from the ancient Aramean alphabet for the older letters as written upon Maccabean coins. Modern square Hebrew letters called *Kitab Merubba* probably were first used during the 1st century B.C. In the early codex Odessa the Hebrew letters have practically the same forms as of modern writings, but the punctuation marks, etc., are those of the Babylonian Masoretic school.

Besides *Kitab Merubba* or square Hebrew letters of the rolls of the synagogues and printed books, there are several more cursive and simplified styles: 1. Rabbinical of Germany and Italy (Raschi), and Spanish-Levantine; and the cursive hand script.

The Hebrew language and alphabet (somewhat modified) is spoken in the new Jewish state of Israeli in Palestine.

HEBREW ALPHABETS

1	2	3		1	2	3	
א	א	א	A	ל	ל	ל	L
ב	ב	ב	B	מ ם	מ ם	מ ם	M
ג	ג	ג	G	נ ן	נ ן	נ ן	N
ד	ד	ד	D	ס	ס	ס	S
ה	ה	ה	H	ע	ע	ע	'
ו	ו	ו	V	פ ף	פ ף	פ ף	F
ז	ז	ז	Z	צ ץ	צ ץ	צ ץ	TS
ח	ח	ח	KH	ק	ק	ק	K
ט	ט	ט	T	ר	ר	ר	R
י	י	י	Y	ש	ש	ש	S,SH
כ ך	כ ך	כ ך	KH	ת	ת	ת	TH

1. Square characters 2. Rabbinical 3. Cursive

CHALDEE

מֵאַרְעָא דְמִצְרַיִם מִבֵּית עַבְדוּתָא׃ וְיַת יְיָ אֱלָהָךְ יייייייייייייי ייייייייייייי
תִדְחַל וּקְדָמוֹהִי תִפְלַח וּבִשְׁמֵיהּ תְּקַיֵּים׃ לָא תְהָכוּן בָּתַר טָעֲוַת עַמְמַיָּא

Chaldee is an Aramaic vernacular which superseded Hebrew among the Jewish population of Palestine and Babylon.

YIDDISH

6 דָאס וָואס אִיז גֶעבּוירֶען פוּן דֶעם פְלֵייש אִיז פְלֵייש, אוּן
דָאס וָואס אִיז גֶעבּוירֶען פוּן דֶעם גֵייסְט אִיז גֵייסְט. 7 פֶערְוְואוּנְדֶער דִיךְ נִיט
אַז אִיךְ הָאבּ דִיר גֶעזָאגְט, אִיהְר מוּזְט פוּן אוֹיבֶּען גֶעבּוירֶען וֶוערֶען. 8 דֶער
וִוינְד בְּלָאזְט וְואוּ עֶר וִויל, אוּן דוּא הֶערְסְט זֵיין קוֹל, אָבֶּער דוּא וֵוייסְט נִיט
פוּן וַואנֶען עֶר קוּמְט, אוּן וְואוּ אַהִין עֶר גֶעהְט; אַזוֹי אִיז אִיטְלִיכֶער וָואס אִיז
גֶעבּוירֶען פוּן דֶעם גֵייסְט. 9 נִיקוֹדִימוֹס הָאט גֶעעֶנְטְפֶערְט אוּן הָאט צוּ אִיהְם
גֶעזָאגְט, וִויא אַזוֹי קֶען דָאס זֵיין? 10 יֵשׁוּעַ הָאט גֶעעֶנְטְפֶערְט אוּן הָאט צוּ

Hebrew characters or Rabbinical characters. Spoken by many Jews in Europe and America. Yiddish, Jewish or Judaeo-German is based upon German with a small admixture of Hebrew words and additions from other languages. Some vowels are indicated by certain consonants and the language, like Hebrew, is written from right to left. Capital letters are not used, letters of lower case but of larger body are used as in Hebrew at beginnings of chapters, sentences, etc.

LADINO

פורקי אנסי אמו איל דייו אֵי מונדו, קי דיאו אה סו
איזו אוניג׳יניטו, פארה קי טודו איל קי קריאי אין איל
נו סי דיספיירדה, סינו קי טינגה בֿידה די סיימפרי. פורקי
נו איגבֿייו איל דייו אה סו איזו אל מונדו פארה קונדי-
נאר אל מונדו, סינו פארה קי איל מונדו סיאה סאלבֿא-
דו פור איל. איל קי קריאי אין איל נו איס קונדינאדו;
מאה איל קי נו קריאי ייה איס קונדינאדו, פורקי נו קרייו
אין איל נומברי דיל אוניג׳יניטו איזו דיל דייו.

Ladino is a Spanish Jewish tongue spoken by the Sephardim or Spanish Jews as distinguished from the Ashkenazim or the Jews of central and eastern Europe. Pronunciation of some letters in Ladino differ from

Yiddish or Hebrew. Hebrew veth (B) has the power of V in Spanish and Portugese Jewish. Silent *ayin* in Hebrew has the power of NG in Spanish Jewish. *Thav* (T) has the power of T in Spanish Jewish but is variously pronounced S or TH in Hebrew.

SYRIAN

1. ܒܪܫܝܬ ܒܪܐ ܐܠܗܐ ܝܬ ܫܡܝܐ. ܘܝܬ ܐܪܥܐ. 2. ܘܐܪܥܐ
ܗܘܬ ܬܘܗ ܘܒܘܗ. ܘܚܫܘܟܐ ܥܠ ܐܦܝ ܬܗܘܡܐ. ܘܪܘܚܗ ܕܐܠܗܐ
ܡܪܚܦܐ ܥܠ ܐܦܝ ܡܝܐ. 3. ܘܐܡܪ ܐܠܗܐ. ܢܗܘܐ ܢܘܗܪܐ. ܘܗܘܐ
ܢܘܗܪܐ. 4. ܘܚܙܐ ܐܠܗܐ ܠܢܘܗܪܐ ܕܫܦܝܪ. ܘܦܪܫ ܐܠܗܐ ܒܝܢ
ܢܘܗܪܐ ܠܚܫܘܟܐ. 5. ܘܩܪܐ ܐܠܗܐ ܠܢܘܗܪܐ ܐܝܡܡܐ. ܘܠܚܫܘܟܐ
ܩܪܐ ܠܠܝܐ. ܘܗܘܐ ܪܡܫܐ ܘܗܘܐ ܨܦܪܐ ܝܘܡܐ ܚܕ.

Gen. 1, 1 – 5.

ܐ			ܐ	'a	ܠ	ܠ	ܠ	ܠ	l
ܒ	ܒ	ܒ	ܒ	b, v	ܡ	ܡ	ܡ	ܡ	m
ܓ	ܓ	ܓ	ܓ	g, γ	ܢ	ܢ	ܢ	ܢ	n'
ܕ			ܕ	d, ð	ܣ	ܣ	ܣ	ܣ	s
ܗ			ܗ	h	ܥ	ܥ	ܥ	ܥ	ʒ
ܘ			ܘ	w, u	ܦ	ܦ	ܦ	ܦ	p, f
ܙ			ܙ	z	ܨ			ܨ	ṣ
ܚ	ܚ	ܚ	ܚ	χ	ܩ	ܩ	ܩ	ܩ	q
ܛ	ܛ	ܛ	ܛ	ṭ	ܪ			ܪ	r
ܝ	ܝ	ܝ	ܝ	y	ܫ	ܫ	ܫ	ܫ	š
ܟ	ܟ	ܟ	ܟ	k, χ	ܬ			ܬ	t, θ

Aramean script: Syriac alphabet. Syrian is the speech of the Christian peoples of the East. The Syrian alphabet is descended from ancient Aramean via Estrangelo. Modern Syriac is spoken by about 100,000 people in Iraq and adjacent parts of Turkey and Iran. Vowels are not written but are provided by points which are added to the consonants as in Arabic.

The Vowels are expressed by Points,
placed either over or under the Letters:

Petock..(*a*) ܒܰ or ܒܱ	Zekoph.(*o*) ܒܳ .. ܒܴ
Rebotz.(*e*) ܒܶ .. ܒܷ	Eztotz..(*u*) ܒܽ .. ܒܾ
Chebotz (*i*) ܒܺ .. ܒܻ	

ESTRANGELO

The name Estrangelo is derived from satar (writing) and evangelo (evangelist). It was a form of the old Syriac character employed in the writings of Christian missionaries of the East in the early Middle Ages. Estrangelo was the only Syriac script in use until the 5th century. Some secondary scripts based upon Estrangelo are: Nestorian, Jacobite and Peshito.

VARIANT FORMS OF SYRIAN, CHALDEE AND OLD ESTRANGELO

	Estrangelo		Jerusalemic	Modern Majuscules			Minuscules	
a	[illegible]	[illegible]	[illegible]	[illegible]	[illegible]	[illegible]	[illegible]	[illegible]
b	[illegible]	[illegible]	[illegible]	[illegible]	[illegible]	[illegible]	[illegible]	[illegible]
g	[illegible]	[illegible]	[illegible]	[illegible]	[illegible]	[illegible]	[illegible]	[illegible]
d.dh	[illegible]	[illegible]	[illegible]	[illegible]	[illegible]	[illegible]	[illegible]	[illegible]
h	[illegible]	[illegible]	[illegible]	[illegible]	[illegible]	[illegible]	[illegible]	[illegible]
v.u	[illegible]	[illegible]	[illegible]	[illegible]	[illegible]	[illegible]	[illegible]	[illegible]
z	[illegible]	[illegible]	[illegible]	[illegible]	[illegible]	[illegible]	[illegible]	[illegible]
hh	[illegible]	[illegible]	[illegible]	[illegible]	[illegible]	[illegible]	[illegible]	[illegible]
t	[illegible]	[illegible]	[illegible]	[illegible]	[illegible]	[illegible]	[illegible]	[illegible]
i.y	[illegible]	[illegible]	[illegible]	[illegible]	[illegible]	[illegible]	[illegible]	[illegible]
k	[illegible]	[illegible]	[illegible]	[illegible]	[illegible]	[illegible]	[illegible]	[illegible]
l	[illegible]	[illegible]	[illegible]	[illegible]	[illegible]	[illegible]	[illegible]	[illegible]
m	[illegible]	[illegible]	[illegible]	[illegible]	[illegible]	[illegible]	[illegible]	[illegible]
n	[illegible]	[illegible]	[illegible]	[illegible]	[illegible]	[illegible]	[illegible]	[illegible]
s	[illegible]	[illegible]	[illegible]	[illegible]	[illegible]	[illegible]	[illegible]	[illegible]
ʿ	[illegible]	[illegible]	[illegible]	[illegible]	[illegible]	[illegible]	[illegible]	[illegible]
p.f.	[illegible]	[illegible]	[illegible]	[illegible]	[illegible]	[illegible]	[illegible]	[illegible]
ts	[illegible]	[illegible]	[illegible]	[illegible]	[illegible]	[illegible]	[illegible]	[illegible]
q	[illegible]	[illegible]	[illegible]	[illegible]	[illegible]	[illegible]	[illegible]	[illegible]
r	[illegible]	[illegible]	[illegible]	[illegible]	[illegible]	[illegible]	[illegible]	[illegible]
sh	[illegible]	[illegible]	[illegible]	[illegible]	[illegible]	[illegible]	[illegible]	[illegible]
t.th.	[illegible]	[illegible]	[illegible]	[illegible]	[illegible]	[illegible]	[illegible]	[illegible]

The first was named for Nestorius, Bishop of Constantinople. Nestorian missionaries spread the Gospel among the peoples of Egypt, Arabia, India, Tartary and China during the 6th and succeeding centuries. The second script is called Jacobite for the followers of Jacob Baradaeus, Bishop of Edessa (died 578 A.D.). Peshito is a Syriac word meaning common or simple—applied to this script to distinguish it from the archaic and elaborate writings intended for liturgical use. Modern Syriac is called *Serta,* or linear script.

The Nestorian or Syro-Chaldaic alphabet as used during the Sassanian dynasty, was carried to India where it is sometimes written in a composite character with additions from other alphabets, in a style called Carshuni. The Nestorians also penetrated eastern Asia, and the modern Mongolian, Kalmuck and Manchu alphabets are evolutionary forms of Nestorian letters. However, modern Syriac *serta* is a direct descendant of Jacobite but the writings of the 12th century differ considerably from modern Syriac.

ܐ			ܐ	a	ܠ	ܠ	ܠ	ܠ	l
ܒ	ܒ	ܒ	ܒ	b, v	ܡ	ܡ	ܡ	ܡ	m
ܓ	ܓ	ܓ	ܓ	g, γ	ܢ ܢ	ܢ	ܢ	ܢ	n
ܕ			ܕ	d, ð	ܣ	ܣ	ܣ	ܣ	s
ܗ			ܗ	h	ܥ	ܥ	ܥ	ܥ	ʒ
ܘ			ܘ	w	ܦ	ܦ	ܦ	ܦ	p, f
ܙ			ܙ	z	ܨ			ܨ	ṣ
ܚ	ܚ	ܚ	ܚ	χ	ܩ	ܩ	ܩ	ܩ	q
ܛ	ܛ	ܛ	ܛ	t̲	ܪ			ܪ	r
ܝ	ܝ	ܝ	ܝ	y	ܫ	ܫ	ܫ	ܫ	š
ܟ	ܟ	ܟ	ܟ	k, χ́	ܬ			ܬ	t, θ

TURKISH

ای اوغل شویله بلمش اول که حقّ سبحانه و تعالی آشکار و نهانده
و یرده و کوکده و بو جهانده و اول جهانده عقل ایله ادراک اولنور ٭
امّا کندونک ذات شریفی تصوّر عقلدن منزّهدر ٭ امّا اکر دیلرسن که
اللّه تعالی‌نی بله‌سن اوّل کندو کندوکی بیل و کندو حالکدن

4	3	2	1		4	3	2	1	
ـا			ا	’a	ـض	ـضـ	ضـ	ض	z
ـب	ـبـ	بـ	ب	b, p	ـط	ـطـ	طـ	ط	t, th
ـپ	ـپـ	پـ	پ	p	ـظ	ـظـ	ظـ	ظ	z
ـت	ـتـ	تـ	ت	t	ـع	ـعـ	عـ	ع ع	‘
ـث	ـثـ	ثـ	ث	th, s	ـغ	ـغـ	غـ	غ غ	g
ـج	ـجـ	جـ	ج	j	ـف	ـفـ	فـ	ف	f
ـچ	ـچـ	چـ	چ	ch	ـق	ـقـ	قـ	ق	q, kh
ـح	ـحـ	حـ	ح ح	h‘	ـك	ـكـ	كـ	ك	k’
ـخ	ـخـ	خـ	خ	kh	ـگ	ـگـ	گـ	ک	g’
ـد			د	d, t	ـڭ	ـڭـ	ڭـ	ڭ	n
ـذ			ذ	z	ـل	ـلـ	لـ	ل	l
ـر			ر ر	r	ـم	ـمـ	مـ	م	m
ـز			ز	z	ـن	ـنـ	نـ	ن	n
ـس	ـسـ	سـ	س	s	ـه	ـهـ	هـ	ه	h
ـش	ـشـ	شـ	ش	sh	ـو			و	v
ـص	ـصـ	صـ	ص	s	ـى	ـیـ	یـ	ى	y, i

1. Isolated. 2. Initial. 3. Medial. 4. Final

VOWEL POINTS

ـَ ـُو و ى *a o u i̤*

ـَ و ـُ ـِى,ـِ *e o̤ ṳ ı*

Turanian or Ural Altaic. Arabic characters or Roman characters. When written in Arabic characters, Turkish is written from right to left and vowels are indicated by points and diacritical marks as in Arabic; in Roman characters, Turkish is written from left to right. Turkish is spoken by about 13,000,000 people in Turkey. The language is sometimes written in Armenian, Greek, Hebrew and Cyrillic characters. The new Turkish alphabet consists of twenty nine Roman letters. There are no silent letters, every letter is distinctly pronounced. When two vowels occur together, each must be pronounced separately.

NEW TURKISH ALPHABET

Zira Allah dünyayı öyle sevdi ki biricik Oğlunu verdi; ta ki ona her iman eden helâk olmayıp ancak ebedî hayata malik olsun.

A long as in *far*, short as in *fat;* B as in *bat;* C as J in *justice;* Ç—CH as in *church;* D as in *day;* E long as in *fete*, short as in *met;* F as in *fat;* G as in *good;* Ğ—GH as in *through* pronounced softly; H as in *hat;* Î as in *machine;* I as in *dirt;* J has sound of ZH as in *azure;* K as in *kite;* L as in *law;* M as in *man;* N as in *not* but with slight nasal tone; O as in *not* or long; O as in *no;* Ö equal to German Ö or nearly French EU; P as in *put;* R as in *run;* S as in *son;* Ş as SH in *shut;* T as in *ton;* U as in *bull* or long Û as in *rule;* Ü resembles German Ü or French U; Y as in *yet;* Z as in *zest;* V—V; K—KY before a vowel with circumflex.

Some of the various styles employed in writing old Turkish are: *Neskhi, Diwanny, Talik, Kirma, Sulus, Iakouti* and *Rejhani.* Some dialects of Turkish are: *Osmanli, Azerbaijani, Bashkir, Chuvash, Jagatai, Gaguazi, Karaite, Kashgar, Kumuck, Qazaq, Turki* or *Altai, Negai, Uzbek* and *Yakut.*

"Arabesque"

IRANIAN LANGUAGES, ETC.

PEHLEVI AND ZEND

ZEND

a ā gh ą ą̄	p f bh
ä ä̅ ĕ ē å	b
i ī y y g	m nh
u ū v v	n ṅ ṅh ń
h kh χw	ž
k γ	o ō r rh
tš dž th	ś
t θ dh δ d	s š z ž

The non-Semitic Iranian scripts are derived from Phoenician via Aramean. Among these are Armenian, Georgian, Zend, Pehlevi. The Zend or Avesta language is an ancient Iranian tongue in which the *Zend Avesta*—the holy book of the cult of Zoroaster, was written. The Zend alphabet was later adopted from the prevailing Pehlevi script. Pehlevi and Avesta are descended from Palmyrene letters. The earliest Pehlevi scripts are: Achaemanian, Arsacidan or proto-Pehlevi, and Sassanian.

The key to the decipherment of the old Zend character was first discovered by Anquetil Duperron, a young French student, who in the 18th century learned the language from the Parsi priests of Surat—a tongue hitherto unknown to the savants of Europe.

PEHLEVI (Arsacidan, Sassanian, etc.)	AVESTA
a	*a*
b	*b*
g	*g*
d	*d*
h	*h*
v	*u*
z	*z*
ḥ	
j	*i*
k	*k*
l,r	*r*
m	*m*
n	*n*
s	*s*
f,p	*p*
č,ch	*č*
q	
r	
š,sh	*š*
t	*t*

PERSIAN

زیرا که خدا جهانرا اینقدر محبّت نمود که پسر یگانهٔ خودرا داد تا
هر که بر او ایمان آورد هلاك نگردد بلکه حیات جاودانی یابد ◆

4	3	2	1			4	3	2	1		
ـا ـأ			ا أ	*a, æ*	a	ـض	ـضـ	ضـ	ض	*z*	z, z
ـب	ـبـ	بـ	ب	*b*	b	ـط	ـطـ	طـ	ط	*t*	t
ـپ	ـپـ	پـ	پ	*p*	p	ـظ	ـظـ	ظـ	ظ	*z*	z
ـت	ـتـ	تـ	ت	*t*	t	ـع	ـعـ	عـ	ع	*'*	ʻ
ـث	ـثـ	ثـ	ث	*s*	th, s	ـغ	ـغـ	غـ	غ	*g*	gh
ـج	ـجـ	جـ	ج	*j*	j	ـف	ـفـ	فـ	ف	*f*	f
ـچ	ـچـ	چـ	چ	*c*	ch	ـق	ـقـ	قـ	ق	*q*	q, g
ـح	ـحـ	حـ	ح	*h*	h', h	ـك	ـکـ	کـ	ك	*k*	k
ـخ	ـخـ	خـ	خ	*x*	kh	ـگ	ـگـ	گـ	گ	*g*	g
ـد			د	*d*	d	ـل	ـلـ	لـ	ل	*l*	l
ـذ			ذ	*z*	z	ـم	ـمـ	مـ	م	*m*	m
ـر			ر	*r*	r	ـن	ـنـ	نـ	ن	*n*	n
ـز			ز	*z*	z	ـه ـهٔ	ـهـ	هـ	ه هٔ	*h*	h
ـژ			ژ	*z*	zh	ـو			و	*v, w*	w
ـس	ـسـ	سـ	س	*s*	s	ـی	ـیـ	یـ	ی	*y, í*	i
ـش	ـشـ	شـ	ش	*s*	sh	ـلا			لا	*la*	la
ـص	ـصـ	صـ	ص	*s*	s, s						

1. Isolated. 2. Initial. 3. Medial 4. Final.

Aryan, Iranic. Arabic alphabet with additional letters, written from right to left. Persian is spoken by about 10,000,000 people in Iran or Persia. Vowel points written above or below the consonants are:

Zaharr (◌َ)–Ă; *Zeerr* (◌ِ)–Ĕ; *Pish* (◌ُ)–Ŭ; *Madd* (◌ٓ)–over *alif* at the beginning of a word–A. The vowel E is not written but is indicated by *zaharr*. *Djazm* (◌ْ) placed over a letter is used to indicate that no vowel is sounded after the letter. *Tashdid* (◌ّ) placed over a letter indicates that the letter is doubled. The vowel shown by zaharr or zabar is sometimes pronounced Ŭ before M and N. The vowel O is rarely used. *Zer-i-izafat*, the sign of a possessive or an attribute is written I followed by a capital.

Several Persian scripts are: *Talik* or *Ta'alik* or hanging script, used in poetry. *Shekesteh* or broken script used in rapid writing, and *Neskhi* or common book hand script.

ARMENIAN

ՄԻՆՉ չեւ բնաւ էր ինչ, ասեն, ոչ երկինք և ոչ երկիր և ոչ այլ ինչ արարածք՝ որ յերկինս կամ յերկրի, Զրուան ոմն անուն էր, որ թարգմանի բախտ կամ փառք։ Զհազար ամ յաշտ արար՝ զի թերեւս որդի մի լինիցի նմա, որում անուն Որմիզդ, որ զերկինս և զերկիր և զամենայն որ 'ի նոսա՝ առնիցէ. և յետ հազար ամի յաշտ առնելոյ՝ սկսաւ ածել զմտաւ, ասէ. օգո՞ւտ ինչ իցէ յաշտս զոր առնեմ, և լինիցի՞ ինձ որդի Որմիզդ, եթէ 'ի զուր ինչ ջանայցեմ։ Եւ մինչ դեռ նա զայս խորհէր, Որմիզդ, և Արհմն յղեցան յարգանդի մօր իւրեանց.

Iranian. Armenian alphabet, written from left to right. Spoken by Armenians in Asia Minor. The ancient Armenian tongue was reduced to written form by Mesrop who invented 36 of the 38 characters of the alphabet. Dialects are: Western or Constantinople dialect and Eastern or Araret dialect. Armenian scripts; Zaghachir or flowery capitals. *Chelhhachir* or animal letters, also called *Chassanochir*. *Erghhachir*–iron writing or stony script. *Poloverchir* or small round script, and *Notrchir*, or cursive script.

Ա	Բ	Գ	Դ	Ե	Զ	Է	Ը	Թ	Ժ	Ի	Լ	Խ	Ծ	Կ	Հ	Ձ	Ղ	Ճ	Մ	Յ	Ն
a	*b*	*g*	*d*	*e*	*z*	*ē*	*e̥*	*tt*	*ž*	*i*	*l*	*χ*	*ts*	*k*	*h*	*dz*	*γ*	*tš*	*m*	*y*	*n*
1	2	3	4	5	6	7	8	9	10	20	30	40	50	60	70	80	90	100	200	300	400

ARMENIAN

Capitals.	Minuscules.	Cursives	Values.
Ա	ա	ա	*a*
Բ	բ	բ	*b, p*
Գ	գ	գ	*g, k*
Դ	դ	դ	*d, t*
Ե	ե	ե	*e, y*
Զ	զ	զ	*z*
Է	է	է	*ē*
Ը	ը	ը	*ĕ*
Թ	թ	թ	*tt, th*
Ժ	ժ	ժ	*zh*
Ի	ի	ի	*i*
Լ	լ	լ	*l*
Խ	խ	խ	*kh*
Ծ	ծ	ծ	*ts, dz*
Կ	կ	կ	*g, k*
Հ	հ	հ	*h*
Ձ	ձ	ձ	*dz, ts*
Ղ	ղ	ղ	*gh*
Ճ	ճ	ճ	*j, jh*

Capitals.	Minuscules	Cursives.	Values.
Մ	մ	մ	*m*
Յ	յ	յ	*h', y*
Ն	ն	ն	*n*
Շ	շ	շ	*sh*
Ո	ո	ո	*oo, wo*
Չ	չ	չ	*jh, j*
Պ	պ	պ	*p, b*
Ջ	ջ	ջ	*ch*
Ռ	ռ	ռ	*rr*
Ս	ս	ս	*s*
Վ	վ	վ	*v*
Տ	տ	տ	*t, d*
Ր	ր	ր	*r*
Ց	ց	ց	*ṭs, ḍz*
Ւ	ւ	ւ	*u*
Փ	փ	փ	*pp, ph*
Ք	ք	ք	*kk, kh*
Օ	օ	օ	*o*
Ֆ	ֆ	ֆ	*f*

GEORGIAN

Khutsuri. Capitals.	Minuscules.	Mkhedruli. Cursives.	Values.
Ⴀ	ⴀ	ა	*a*
Ⴁ	ⴁ	ბ	*b*
Ⴂ	ⴂ	გ	*g*
Ⴃ	ⴃ	დ	*d*
Ⴄ	ⴄ	ე	*e*
Ⴅ	ⴅ	ვ	*w, v*
Ⴆ	ⴆ	ზ	*z*
Ⴡ	ⴡ	ჱ	*h'*
Ⴇ	ⴇ	თ	*th*
Ⴈ	ⴈ	ი	*i*
Ⴉ	ⴉ	კ	*kk*
Ⴊ	ⴊ	ლ	*l*
Ⴋ	ⴋ	მ	*m*
Ⴌ	ⴌ	ნ	*n*
Ⴢ	ⴢ	ჲ	*y*
Ⴍ	ⴍ	ო	*o*
Ⴎ	ⴎ	პ	*pp*
Ⴏ	ⴏ	ჟ	*zh*
Ⴐ	ⴐ	რ	*r*
Ⴑ	ⴑ	ს	*s*

Khutsuri. Capitals.	Minuscules.	Mkhedruli. Cursives.	Values.
Ⴒ	ⴒ	ტ	*tt*
Ⴓ	ⴓ	უ	*u*
Ⴣ	ⴣ	ჳ	*vi*
Ⴔ	ⴔ	ფ	*p*
Ⴕ	ⴕ	ქ	*k*
Ⴖ	ⴖ	ღ	*gh*
Ⴗ	ⴗ	ყ	*q*
Ⴘ	ⴘ	შ	*sh*
Ⴙ	ⴙ	ჩ	*ch*
Ⴚ	ⴚ	ც	*ts*
Ⴛ	ⴛ	ძ	*dz*
Ⴜ	ⴜ	წ	*tts*
Ⴝ	ⴝ	ჭ	*ttsh*
Ⴞ	ⴞ	ხ	*kh*
Ⴤ	ⴤ	ჴ	*kkh*
Ⴟ	ⴟ	ჯ	*j*
Ⴠ	ⴠ	ჰ	*h*
Ⴥ	ⴥ	ჵ	*hoi*
Φ	φ	ჶ	*f*
		ჷ	*ĕ*

GEORGIAN

Khutsuri.

[illegible]

Mkhedruli.

მამაო : ჩუენო : რომელი : ხარ : ცათა : შინა :
წმიდა : იყავნ : სახელი : შენი : მოვედინ : სუფევა :
შენი : იყავნ : ნება : შენი : ვითარცა : ცათა : შინა :

Iranian. Khutsuri or ecclesiastical characters, and Mkhedruli or civil characters. The alphabet is called *anban* which is derived from the names of the first two letters. Mkhedruli letters have no capitals but are written in minuscule only. The Khutsuri alphabet was invented by Mesrop in the 5th century. Georgian is written from left to right.

Ⴀ	Ⴁ	Ⴂ	Ⴃ	Ⴄ	Ⴅ	Ⴆ	Ⴡ	Ⴇ	Ⴈ	Ⴉ	Ⴊ	Ⴋ	Ⴌ	Ⴢ	Ⴍ	Ⴎ	Ⴏ	Ⴐ	Ⴑ	Ⴒ	Ⴓ
a	*b*	*g*	*d*	*e*	*w*	*z*	*h*	*th*	*i*	*k*	*l*	*m*	*n*	*y*	*o*	*p*	*ž*	*r*	*s*	*t*	*u*
1	2	3	4	5	6	7	8	9	10	20	30	40	50	60	70	80	90	100	200	300	400

PASHTO

ځکه چه الله له جهان سره داسي مينه

وکړه چه ابن وحيد خپل يې ورکړ تا چه هر څوک چه

په ده ايمان راوړي هلاک نه شي بلکه ابدي ژوندون

Aryan: Iranian. Arabic or Persi-Arabic alphabet. Pashto or Pushto is spoken by about 10,000,000 people in Afghanistan, Punjab Province, Quettah District and northern Baluchistan. Pashto is written from right to left. Dialects are: Dir, Tirhai, Laghmani, Pashai, Kandahari, and Peshawuri.

ه å, ا a, آ ā, اې ē, اِ i, اِى ī, او o, اُ u, اُو ū, اَى ai, اَو au.

THE LANGUAGES OF INDIA

त्वं यदुक्तस्तत्राश्चर्य्यं मा मन्यस्व। आत्मरूपो वायु र्यत्रेच्छति तत्र ८
वाति, तत्स्वनस्त्वया श्रूयते, न ज्ञायते तु स कुत आयाति कुत्र
याति वा। आत्मतो जातः सर्व्वमनुष्यस्तादृग्भूतः। नीकदीमः प्रति- ९
भाषमाणस्तमवादीत्, सर्व्वमेतत् कथं भवितुं शक्नोति ? यीशुः प्रति- १०

—Sanskrit

The earliest scripts of India of record are the Proto-Indian semi-pictographic writings and seal inscriptions of the Indus Valley, which are believed to date from perhaps as early as 2000 B.C. Among these early characters are the scripts of Harappa and Mohenjo-daro. Some effort has been made to show a collateral relationship between these ancient Indian scripts and the alphabets of the West. According to the *Lalita Vistara* 64 alphabets were in use in India at the time of the Buddha. However, it is generally conceded that the Brahmi (attributed to Brahma) alphabet is the traditional ancestor of all the Indian scripts.

Early Indian alphabets are the letters of Maghada and the Mauryan characters of Asoka. Early Indian characters inscribed upon a rock near Kapur-di-giri, are believed to date from this period of Indian writing, c. 260 B.C. These are conveniently placed in chronological Group I, together with Kalinga, the Dravi letters of about 150 B.C., Andra or West Deccan, Late Maurya, Sunga, North Indian and South Indian prototypes.

Chronological Group II includes North Indian Gupta (4th-6th century A.D.), cursive Gupta, Khotanese, Agnean, Kuchan, Tibetan, Lepcha. The Siddhamatrka character, a derivative of Eastern Gupta, of about this date, is the immediate ancestor of the Devanagari letters—the parent script of most of the alphabets of Modern India. South India produced another script called Nandi-nagari.

The Sarada alphabet of Kashmiri was derived from West Gupta (8th century). Proto-Bengali is an evolutionary style of Nagari of East India (11th century). Nevari or "hooked letters", the ancestor of modern Bengali probably came into use about the 12th century. The Oriya letters are related to Bengali, but because of the nature of the materials upon which the languages of the south were written, the horizontal lines or *matru* were omitted; this elimination of line in writing the alphabets of the Pali group of the south is the chief feature that distinguishes the forms of these letters from the Nagari alphabets of the north.

Other Indian scripts are: Manipuri, from Bengali (700 A.D.), Kaithi a north Indian corrupted form of Nagari, Gujarati or refined Kaithi. Other Kaithi scripts were: Bhojpuri, Magahi and Tirhuti of which the last is called the elegant script. Modi or "twisted" script is adapted from southern Nagari. Dogri, Chameali and Manddali are Indian alphabets akin to Takri. Landa or "clipped" alphabet is the character of Punjab and Sindh. Banya is a "trade" script, used by merchants. Lepcha of the Rong of the Sikkim in the Himalayas, is an Indian script, akin to Tibetan.

The South Indian or Dravidian group includes: Kanarese, Late Kalinga, Grantha (14th century), Tulu-Malayalam, Tamil, Vatteluttu, Maldivian, Syro-Malabaric and Sinhalese of Ceylon. The further India group consists of the alphabets of the Chams or Kmers (Cambodian), the Mons (Burmese, Peguan), and the Shans (Siamese, Laos, Ahom, Miao), and basic script of South India—Pali (Pali-Burmese, Pali-Siamese, Pali-Cambodian).

ALPHABETS AND LANGUAGES OF INDIA

DEVANAGARI

Bhatneri
Bhili
Bihari
Bikaneri
Garhwali
Gondi
Gujarati
Harauti
Hindi
Ho
Jaipuri
Jaunsari
Kanauri
Kulu
Kumaoni
Kurku
Kurukh
Malvi
Manipuri
Marathi
Marwari
Mewari
Mundari
Nepali
Palpa
Prakrit
Sanskrit
Sindhi
Urdu (Hindustani)

BENGALI

Assamese
Bengali
Bodo
Garo
Khasi
Manipuri
Rabha
Santali

BALBODH

Marathi

BANYA

Sindhi

BURMESE

Burmese
Karen
Maghi
Pali
Talaing
Taungthu

CAMBODIAN

Cambodian

GRANTHA

Marathi
Panjabi
Sindhi
Gujarati

GUJARATI

Gujarati
Urdu (Hindustani)

GURMUKHI

Panjabi
Sindhi

KAITHI

Bihari
Gujarati
Hindi

ORIYA
Orissa
Khondi
Mundari
Santali

QUÔC NGŪ
Assamese

SARADA
Kashmiri

SIAMESE
Siamese
Miao
Yao

SINHALESE
Sinhalese
Pali

TAMIL
Kanarese
Tamil
Toda

KANARESE
Kanarese
Tulu

LEPCHA
Lepcha or Rong

MALAYALAM
Malayalam

MODI
Marathi

PALI
Pali

TANKRI
Chambiali
Kanauri
Jaunsari

TELUGU
Gondi
Telugu

LANDA
Khudawadi

BIHARI

ALPHABETS OF INDIA AND FURTHER INDIA

	1	2	3	4	5	6
a						
i						
u						
e						
o						
ā						
ka						
kha						
ga						
gha						
ṅa						
ča						
čha						
ja(ǧa)						
jha(ǧh)						
ña						
ṭa						
ṭha						
ḍa						
ḍha						
ṇa						
ta						
tha						
da						
dha						
na						
pa						
pha						
ba						
bha						
ma						
ya						
ra						
la						
va						
śa						
sa(ša)						
sa						
ha						

	7	8	9	10	11	12	13	14
a								
i								
u								
e								
ā								
ka								
kha								
ga								
gha								
ṅa								
ča								
čha								
ǧa								
ǧha								
ña								
ta								
tha								
ḍa								
ḍha								
ṇa								
ta								
tha								
da								
dha								
na								
pa								
pha								
ba								
bha								
ma								
ya								
ra								
la								
va								
śa								
ṣa								
sa								
ha								

1. Brahmi (Asoka)
2. Gupta (Allahabad)
3. Gupta (Cursive)
4. Tocharian
5. Siddhamatrka
6. Modi
7. Barmani
8. Patimokkha
9. Siamese
10. Boromat
11. Laos
12. Cambodian
13. Peguan or Mon
14. Ahom

ALPHABETS OF INDIA AND FURTHER INDIA

	15	16	17	18	19	20	21	22
a								
i								
u								
e								
o								
ā								
ka								
kha								
ga								
gha								
ṅa								
ča								
čha								
ǧa								
ǧha								
ña								
ṭa								
ṭha								
ḍa								
ḍha								
ṇa								
ta								
tha								
da								
dha								
na								
pa								
pha								
ba								
bha								
ma								
ya								
ra								
la								
va								
śa								
ṣa								
sa								
ha								

	23	24	25	26	27	28
a						
i						
u						
e						
ā						
ka						
kha						
ga						
gha						
ṅa						
ča						
čha						
ǧa						
ǧha						
ña						
ṭa						
ṭha						
ḍa						
ḍha						
ṇa						
ta						
tha						
da						
dha						
na						
pa						
pha						
ba						
bha						
ma						
ya						
ra						
ḷa						
va						
śa						
ṣa						
sa						
ha						
ṛa						
ḻa						

15. Sarada
16. Kashmiri
17. Tankri-Jaunsari
18. Tankri-Chambiali
19. Landa-Khudawadi
20. Landa-Sindhi
21. Multani
22. Gurmukhi
23. Telugu
24. Kanarese
25. Cera
26. Grantha
27. Malayalam
28. Tamil

MODERN ALPHABETS OF INDIA

The phonetic system of transcribing native characters of the languages of India, into the Roman alphabet. Proposed by the Hon. C. W. Bradley in the Journal of the American Oriental Society, Vol. IV, No. 2, and published in: A Glossary of Judicial and Revenue Terms of Useful Words Occuring in Official Documents, etc.—of British India. (Pp. x-xi.) By H. H. Wilson. London: Wm. H. Allen, 1855.

ENGLISH	ARABIC PERSIAN PASHTO URDU	SANSKRIT HINDI MARATHI	GUJARATI	BENGALI	ORISSA	TELUGU	KANARESE	TAMIL	MALAYALAM
A a	ـَ ا	अ . .	અ . .	অ . . .	ଅ . . .	అ ✓ .	ಅ ✓ .	அ . . .	അ
Á á	ا آ	आ ा .	આ ા .	আ . া .	ଆ ା .	ఆ ా .	ಆ ಾ .	ஆ ா .	ആ ാ
Â â	ع ء	—	—	—	—	—	—	—	—
Ai ai	اي ـَي	ऐ ै .	ઐ ૈ .	ঐ ৈ .	ଐ ୈ .	ఐ ై	ಐ ೈ .	ஐ ை	ഐ ൈ
Au au	او ـَو	औ ौ .	ઔ ૌ .	ঔ ৌ	ଔ ୌ	ఔ ౌ	ಔ ೌ	ஔ ௌ	ഔ ൌ
B b	ب ـِ	ब . . .	બ . . .	ব . . .	ବ . . .	బ . . .	ಬ . . .	ப . . .	ബ
Bh bh	بھ	भ . . .	ભ . . .	ভ . . .	ଭ . . .	భ . . .	ಭ . . .	—	ഭ
Ch ch	چ ـچ	च . . .	ચ . . .	চ . . .	ଚ . . .	చ . . .	ಚ . . .	ச . . .	ച
Chh chh	چھ . . .	छ . . .	છ . . .	ছ . . .	ଛ . . .	ఛ . . .	ಛ . . .	—	ഛ
D d	د . . .	द . . .	દ . . .	দ . . .	ଦ . . .	ద . . .	ದ . . .	த . . .	ദ
Dh dh	دھ . . .	ध . . .	ધ . . .	ধ . . .	ଧ . . .	ధ . . .	ಧ . . .	—	ധ
Ḍ ḍ	ڈ . . .	ड . . .	ડ . . .	ড . . .	ଡ . . .	డ . . .	ಡ . . .	ட . . .	ഡ
Ḍh ḍh	ڈھ . . .	ढ . . .	ઢ . . .	ঢ . . .	ଢ . . .	ఢ . . .	ಢ . . .	—	ഢ
E e	ي ـِ	ए े	એ ે	এ ে .	ଏ େ .	ఎ ె .	ಎ ೆ .	எ ெ .	എ െ
É é	—	—	—	—	—	ఏ ే .	ಏ ೇ	ஏ ே .	—

F	f	ف	—	—	—	—	—	—	—	—
G	g	گ	ग	ગ	গ	ଗ	గ	ಗ	க	ഗ
Gh	gh	گھ	घ	ઘ	ঘ	ଘ	ఘ	ಘ	—	ഘ
G̣h	g̣h	غ	—	—	—	—	—	—	—	—
H	h	ح	ह	હ	হ	ହ	హ	ಹ	—	ഹ
Ḥ	ḥ	ه	—	—	—	—	—	—	—	—
H̤	h̤	—	ः	ઃ	ঃ	ଃ	ః	ಃ	—	ഃ
I	i	اِ ي	इ ि	ઇ િ	ই ি	ଇ ି	ఇ ి	ಇ ಿ	இ ி	ഇ ി
Í	í	اِي	ई ी	—	ঈ ী	ଈ ୀ	ఈ ీ	ಈ ೀ	ஈ ீ	ഈ ീ
J	j	ج	ज	જ	জ	ଜ	జ	ಜ	—	ജ
Jh	jh	—	झ	ઝ	ঝ	ଝ	ఝ	ಝ	—	ഝ
K	k	ک	क	ક	ক	କ	క	ಕ	க	ക
Ḳ	ḳ	ق	—	—	—	—	—	—	—	—
Kh	kh	خ	ख	ખ	খ	ଖ	ఖ	ಖ	—	ഖ
Kḥ		کھ	—	—	—	—	—	—	—	—
L	l	ل	ल	લ	ল	ଲ	ల	ల	ல	ല
Ḷ	ḷ	—	ळ	—	—	—	ళ	ಳ	ள	ള
L̤	l̤	—	—	—	—	—	—	—	ழ	—
M	m	م	म	મ	ম	ମ	మ	ಮ	ம	മ
N	n	ن	न	ન	ন	ନ	న	ನ	ந	ന
N̥	n̥	—	ं	ં	ং	—	—	—	—	—
Ṇ	ṇ	—	ण	ણ	ণ	ଣ	ణ	ಣ	ண	ണ
N̤	n̤	—	—	—	—	—	—	—	ன	—
N̬	n̬	—	ङ	—	ঙ	ଙ	ఙ	ಙ	ங	ങ
N̈	n̈	—	ञ	—	ঞ	ଞ	ఞ	ಞ	ஞ	ഞ

ENGLISH		ARABIC PERSIAN PASHTO URDU	SANSKRIT HINDI MARATHI	GUJARATI	BENGALI	ORISSA	TELUGU	KANARESE	TAMIL	MALAY-ALAM
O	o	او و	ओ ो .	ઓ ો	ও ো	ଓ ୋ	ఒ ొ	ಒ ೊ	ஒ ொ	ഒ ൊ
Ó	ó	—	—	—	—	—	ఓ ో	ಓ ೋ	ஓ ோ	—
P	p	پ ﭙ	प . . .	પ . . .	প . . .	ପ . . .	ప . . .	ಪ . . .	ப . . .	പ
Ph	ph	پھ . .	फ . . .	ફ . . .	ফ . . .	ଫ . . .	ఫ . . .	ಫ . . .	—	ഫ
R	r	ر . .	र . . .	ર . . .	র . . .	ର . . .	ర ◡	ರ ◡	ர . . .	ര
Ṛ	ṛ	ڑ . .	—	—	—	—	ఱ . .	ಱ . . .	ற . . .	റ
R̤	r̤	—	—	—	—	—	—	—	—	ഠ
Ṛi	ṛi	—	ऋ ृ .	—	ঋ ৃ	ଋ . . .	ఋ ృ	ಋ ೃ	—	ഋ ൃ
Ṛí	ṛí	—	ॠ ॄ .	—	ৠ ৄ	ୠ . . .	ౠ ౄ	ೠ ೄ	—	ൠ ൄ
S	s	س سـ	स . . .	સ . . .	স . . .	ସ . . .	స . . .	ಸ . . .	ச . . .	സ
Ṣ	ṣ	—	श . . .	શ . . .	শ . . .	ଶ . . .	శ . . .	ಶ . . .	—	ശ
S̤	s̤	ص صـ	—	—	—	—	—	—	—	—
Ş̣	ş̣	ث ثـ	—	—	—	—	—	—	—	—
Sh	sh	ش شـ	ष . . .	ષ . . .	ষ . . .	ଷ . . .	ష . . .	ಷ . . .	—	ഷ
T	t	ت تـ	त . . .	ત . . .	ত . . .	ତ . . .	త . . .	ತ . . .	த . . .	ത
Th	th	تھ . . .	थ . . .	થ . . .	থ . . .	ଥ . . .	థ . . .	ಥ . . .	—	ഥ
Ṭ	ṭ	ٹ ٹـ	ट . . .	ટ . . .	ট . . .	ଟ . . .	ట . . .	ಟ . . .	ட . . .	ട
Ṭh	ṭh	ٹھ . .	ठ . . .	ઠ . . .	ঠ . . .	ଠ . . .	ఠ . . .	ಠ . . .	—	ഠ
T̤	t̤	ط ط	—	—	—	—	—	—	—	—
U	u	و و	उ ु .	ઉ ુ	উ ু	ଉ . . .	ఉ ు	ಉ ು	உ ு	ഉ ു
Ú	ú	—	ऊ ू .	ઊ . . .	ঊ ূ	ଊ . . .	ఊ ూ	ಊ ೂ	ஊ ூ	ഊ ൂ

V W	v w	و . .	व . . .	વ . . .	—	—	వ . . .	ವ . . .	வ . . .	വ
X	ksh	—	क्ष . . .	—	क्ष . . .	କ୍ଷ . . .	క్ష . .	క్ష . .	—	—
Y	y	ي . .	य . . .	ય . . .	য . . .	ଯ . . .	య [illegible]	ಯ . .	ய . . .	യ
Z	z	ز . .	—	—	—	—	—	—	—	—
Zh	zh	ژ . .	—	—	—	—	—	—	—	—
Ẓ	ẓ	ذ . .	—	—	—	—	—	—	—	—
Z̤	z̤	ض ض	—	—	—	—	—	—	—	—
Z̥	z̥	ظ ظ	—	—	—	—	—	—	—	—

Coalescent Vowels

1	ক ka, কা kā, কি ki, কী kī, কু ku, কূ kū, কৃ kṛ, কৢ kḷ, কে ke, কৈ kai, কো ko, কৌ kau.
2	𑘎𑘰 kā, 𑘎𑘲 ki, 𑘎𑘳 ku, 𑘎𑘹 ke, 𑘎𑘺 kai, 𑘎𑘻 ko, 𑘎𑘼 kau, 𑘨𑘿𑘎 rk, 𑘎𑘽 kā.
3	ਕਾ kā, ਕਿ ki, ਕੀ kī, ਕੁ ku, ਕੂ kū, ਕੇ ke, ਕੈ kai, ਕੋ ko, ਕੌ kau, ਕਂ kā, ਕ੍ਰ kra.
4	ક ka, કા kā, કિ ki, કી kī, કુ ku, કૂ kū, કે ke, કો ko, કૌ kau, કં kā, અર્ક ark.
5	का kā, कि kī, कु ku, के ke, कं kā, कः k.
6	का kā, कि ki, की kī, कु ku, कू kū, कृ kṛ, कॄ kṝ, कॢ kḷ, कॣ kḹ.
7	କା kā, କି ki, କୀ kī, କୁ ku, କୂ kū, କୃ kṛ, କ୍ରୁ kru, କେ ke, କୈ kai, କୋ ko, କୌ kau, କଁ kā, କଃ kaḥ.
8	కా kā, కి ki, కీ kī, కు ku, కూ kū, కృ kṛ, కౄ kṝ, కె ke, కే kē, కై kai, కొ ko, కో kō, కౌ kau.
9	க கா கி கீ கு கூ கெ கே கை கொ கோ கௌ *ka kā ki kī ku kū ke kē kai ko kō kau*
10	ക ka, കാ kā, കി ki, കീ kī, കു ku, കൂ kū, കെ ke, കൈ kai, കൊ ko, കൌ kau.
11	කා kā, කි ki, කී kī, කු, කු, කු ku, කූ, කූ kū, කෙ ke, කේ kē, කෛ kai, කො ko, කෝ kō, කෘ kṛ, කෲ kṝ, කං kā, ක් k.
12	က် k, ကာ kā, ကိ ki, ကီး kī, ကု ku, ကူး kū, ကေး ke, ကဲ့ kai, ကော့ ko, ကော် kau, ကံး kā, ကား kaḥ.
13	ก ka, กา kā, กิ ki, กี kī, กึ kị, กื kị̄, กุ ku, กู kū, เก ke, แก kē, ไก kai, ใก kei, โก ko, เกา kau, กำ kā, กะ kaḥ, กน kŏn, กัน kăn, กอน kōn, กวน kven, เกียน kyen, เกือน kuīen, เกิน keun. Accent : กฺ kạ, ก่ kā, ก้ kà, ก๊ kạ, ก๋ ká.
14	က ka, ကာ kā, ကိ ki, ကီ kī, ကု ku, ကူ kū, ကေ ke, ကဵ kē, ကော ko, ကေဴ kō, ကဳ kị, ကဲ kai, ကဲ kaị, ကဵု kau, ကံဴ keu, ကို koi.
15	ᰀ ᰀᰦ ᰀᰧ ᰀᰧᰦ ᰀᰨ ᰀᰩ ᰀᰪ ᰀᰫ ᰀᰬ k'a, kā, ki, kī, ko, ḳō, ku, kū, ke. ᰀᰭ ᰀᰮ ᰀᰯ ᰀᰰ ᰀᰱ ᰀᰲ ᰀᰳ ᰀᰴ ᰀᰵ kak, kam, kal, kan, kap, kar, kat, kañ, ḳaṅ.

1. Bengali
2. Marathi
3. Panjabi
4. Gujarati
5. Kashmiri
6. Nepali
7. Orissa
8. Telugu
9. Tamil
10. Malayalam
11. Sinhalese
12. Burmese
13. Siamese
14. Peguan or Mon
15. Lepcha

SANSKRIT

THE DEVANAGARI ALPHABET

यत ईश्वरो जगतीत्थं प्रेम चकार, यन्निजमेकजातं पुत्रं ददौ, तस्मिन् विश्वासो सर्व्वमनुष्यो यथा न विनश्यानन्तं जीवनं लप्स्यते।

अ	a	ऌ	l̥	ग	ga	ट	ṭa	ध	dha	र	ra
आ	ā	ॡ	l̥̄	घ	gha	ठ	ṭha	न	na	लल	la
इ	i	ए	e	ङ	ṅa	ड	ḍa	प	pa	ळ	la
ई	ī	ऐ	ai	च	tša	ढ	ḍha	फ	pha	व	va
उ	u	ओ	o	छ	tšha	ण	ṇa	ब	ba	स	sa
ऊ	ū	औ	aů	ज	dža	त	ta	भ	bha	श श्	ša
ऋ	r̥	क	ka	झ	džha	थ	tha	म	ma	ष	ša
ॠ	r̥̄	ख	kha	ञ	ńa	द	da	य	ya	ह	ha

का kā, कि ki, की kī, कु ku, कू kū, कृ kr̥, कॄ kr̥̄, कॢ kl̥, कॣ kl̥̄, के ke, कै kai.

को ko, कौ kau, कं kã, कँ kã, कः kaḥ, क+ kaχ, क‿ kaf, र्क rk, र्के rke, क् k.

Aryan, Indic. Devanagari or nagari alphabet. The term *sanskrit* was intended to imply the literary idiom of India as established by conventional rules. The name is probably derived from *sam* (together) and *kr* (to make). Sanskrit is the literary language of the Brahman cult of India and is one of the oldest tongues (Vedic) of the Aryan language family. The character in which Sanskrit is usually written is called devanagari (sacred writing or town script). Most of the alphabets of central India are modified forms of nagari such as Gurmukhi, Bengali, Tankri, Sarada, Modi, Balbodh, Sindhi, Kaithi, Manipuri, Nevari, Banjin-Mola, Ranja, Urya, etc.

Sanskrit is written from left to right. The alphabet consists of 10 vowels, 4 diphthongs, 33 consonants including 4 semi vowels, Y, R, L, V or W, the soft aspirate H, the consonants Ś, Ş (sh) Ñ, Ṇ, Ṇ̄. The simple vowels are: A, Ā, I, Ī, U, Ū, Ṛ, Ṝ, Ḷ, Ḹ. The letters E, Ō are classed as diphthongs. Vowels, except when initial, are usually indicated by vowel marks or points above or below the consonants and sounded after the consonants so marked. Consonants usually contain an inherent A vowel which is sounded if not otherwise elided or changed by vowel points. The A vowel is of very frequent occurence in Sanskrit.

Coalescent Vowels and Points

ा â	follows the consonant	ॢ ḷ	under the consonant
ि i	precedes the consonant	ॣ ḹ	under the consonant
ी î	follows the consonant	े e	over the consonant
ु u	under the consonant	ै ai	over the consonant
ू û	under the consonant	ो o	follows the consonant
ृ ṛ	under the consonant	ौ au	follows the consonant
ॄ ṝ	under the consonant		

Nasal sounds and diacritics are: *Anusvâra* (ं) and *Anunâsika* (ँ) which are sometimes substituted for M and N respectively. *Anunâṣika* is written above the letter. *Visarga* (ः) or (8) is sometimes used to substitute for S and R. *Jihvâmuliya* (+) and *Upadhmâniya* (ᳵ) are strong final aspirates. *Ardhavisarga* is *visarga* when used for S and R. *Virama* (्) under a final consonant indicates absence of the inherent A vowel sound.

The close of a sentence ending in a vowel, a diphthong or a *visarga,* is shown by (।). The mark is doubled (॥) at the end of a verse. The mark of hïatus (ऽ) is often used to indicate elision of the vowel A after E or O. It is also used to mark coalescence of two consecutive A vowels. The mark of abbreviation is (॰). Marks of accent are: *Anudâtta* or grave (—) under the accented letter, and *Svarita* or circumflex (\ ) over the accented letter. Brevity is sometimes indicated by (\ ); the sign (5) may be used to indicate length.

GRANTHA CHARACTERS

[illegible]

[illegible]

[illegible]

[illegible]

PRAKRIT

Prakrit is a name applied to the vernacular tongues of India as opposed to Sanskrit, the literary idiom, although Sanskrit was derived from *Aryavarta,* a primary prakrit of the Midland about 300 B.C. The chief differences in Sanskrit-Prakrit phonetics are: Sanskrit Ē and Ō may be either long or short vowels in Prakrit. The diphthongs ĀI, ĀU in Sanskrit may become Ē, Ō, AÏ and AÜ respectively. Sanskrit R becomes A, I, or U in Prakrit. Sanskrit long vowels are shortened and I and U are changed to E O respectively before two consonants in Prakrit. Except in Maghadi Prakrit Sanskrit initial Y may become J. In Prakrit the letters K, C, G, J, T, D, are commonly elided. Sanskrit KH, CH, TH, DH, BH are modified to H. TH becomes ḌH; Ṭ becomes Ḍ. L and V are usually elided when first or last in any compounded word, but then the remaining letter is doubled. K, G, T, Ḍ, D, P, S, Ś, S, when standing first in a compounded word are usually doubled.

The chief prakrits are: *Maghadi, Ardhamaghadi, Maharastri, Paisaci.* Pali and Jains prakrit are derived from a secondary vernacular called *Apabhramsa* (corrupt language). *Sauraseni* prakrit of the Midland was another early vernacular of the Gangetic Doab.

PALI

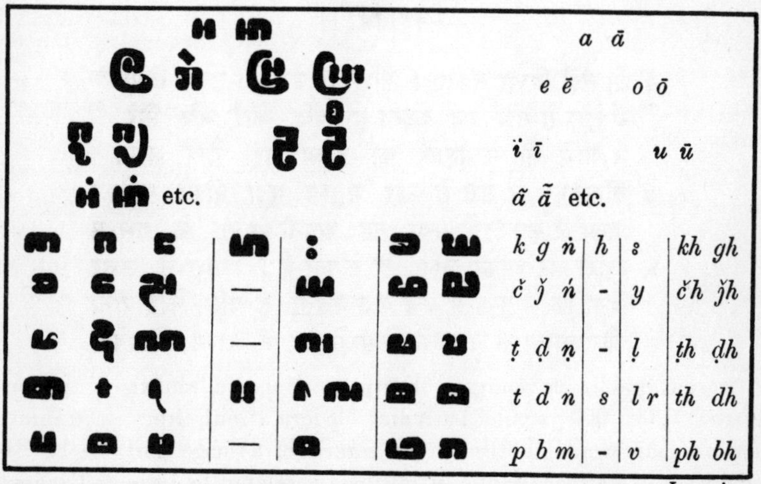

a ā		
e ē		*o ō*
ï ī		*u ū*
ã ã̄ etc.		
k g ṅ	*h*	*ꞩ*	*kh gh*
č ǰ ń	-	*y*	*čh ǰh*
ṭ ḍ ṇ	-	*ḷ*	*ṭh ḍh*
t d n	*s*	*l r*	*th dh*
p b m	-	*v*	*ph bh*

Lepsius

Pali, the language of the Buddhist literature in Burma, Ceylon, Siam, is the script in which the Buddhist *Tripitaka* texts were written, and was used as a language of daily intercourse from about the 7th

1	2	3		1	2	3	
		အ	*a*			ပ	*pa*
		က	*ka*			ဖ	*pha*
		ခ	*kha*			မ	*ma*
		င	*ṅa*			ယ	*ya*
		စ	*tša*			ရ	*ra*
		ဉ	*ńa*			လ	*la*
		တ	*ta*			ဝ	*wa*
		ထ	*tha*			သ	*sa*
		န	*na*			ဟ	*ha*

1.–2. Pali. 3. Burmese

century B.C. and was retained many centuries as a literary language in southern India. Alphabets or scripts, etc., of many of the languages of southern India, etc., are written are derived from Pali. Other styles or scripts are: Pali-Siamese, Pali-Burmese, Pali-Cambodian. Pali is written in several styles: round characters, and square characters.

HINDI

३ तो नहीं दिखा सकता। यीशु ने उस को उत्तर दिया कि
मैं तुझ से सच सच कहता हू यदि कोई नये सिरे से
न जन्मे तो परमेश्वर का राज्य नहीं देख सकता।
४ नीकुदेमुस ने उस से कहा मनुष्य बूढ़ा होकर क्योंकर
जन्म ले सकता है क्या वह अपनी माता के गर्भ में
५ दूसरी बार जाकर जन्म ले सकता है। यीशु ने उत्तर
दिया कि मैं तुझ से सच सच कहता हूं यदि कोई पानी
और आत्मा से न जन्मे तो परमेश्वर के राज्य में प्रवेश

Aryan, Indic. Devanagari, Kaithi or Mohajun alphabet. Spoken by about 100,000,000 people in India. Modern Hindi, free of Arabic and Persian loan words .is the lingua franca of a large part of the Hindu population of northern India. It is closely related to Urdu or Hindustani and follows substantially the same grammatical rules. However, Hindi which is usually written in nagari characters from left to right, is a more nearly sanscritized idiom for the use of non-Moslems in Hindustan.

1. BURMESE. 2. PALI-BURMESE. 3. PALI-SIAMESE.							
	1	2	3		1	2	3
a	အ			*ḍa*	ဍ		
ā	အာ			*ḍha*	ဎ		
i	ဣ			*ṇa*	ဏ		
ī	ဤ			*ta*	တ		
u	ဥ			*tha*	ထ		
ū	ဦ			*da*	ဒ		
e	ဧ			*dha*	ဓ		
o	ဪ			*na*	န		
ka	က			*pa*	ပ		
kha	ခ			*pha*	ဖ		
ga	ဂ			*ba*	ဗ		
gha	ဃ			*bha*	ဘ		
ṅa	င			*ma*	မ		
tša	စ			*ya*	ယ		
tšha	ဆ			*ra*	ရ		
dža	ဇ			*la*	လ		
džha	ဈ			*wa*	ဝ		
ńa	ဉ			*sa*	သ		
ṭa	ဋ			*ha*	ဟ		
tha	ဌ						

Persian Letters with their Nagari Equivalents

ع अ़	غ ग़	ح ह़	خ ख़	ط त़	ظ स
ص स़	ض स़	ث स़	ذ ज़	ز ज़	ف फ़

Some Hindi dialects are: Chhattisgarhi, Braj Basha, Awadhi, Kanauji, Kuswari, Durahi, Gadi, Bhili, Chentsu, Hulba, Nimari, Lambadi.

URDU OR HINDUSTANI

۰کیونکہ خدا نے دُنیا سے ایسی محبت رکھی کہ اُس نے اپنا اکلوتا بیٹا

بخش دیا تاکہ جو کوئی اُس پر ایمان لائے ہلاک نہ ہو۔ بلکہ ہمیشہ کی زندگی پائے۰

4	3	2	1		4	3	2	1	
ا	ـا	ـا	ا	a	س	ـس	ـسـ	سـ	s
ب	ـب	ـبـ	بـ	b	ش	ـش	ـشـ	شـ	sh
پ	ـپ	ـپـ	پـ	p	ص	ـص	ـصـ	صـ	ṣ
ت	ـت	ـتـ	تـ	t	ض	ـض	ـضـ	ضـ	ẓ
ٹ	ـٹ	ـٹـ	ٹـ	ṭ	ط	ـط	ـطـ	طـ	ṭ
ث	ـث	ـثـ	ثـ	ṣ	ظ	ـظ	ـظـ	ظـ	ẓ
ج	ـج	ـجـ	جـ	j	ع	ـع	ـعـ	عـ	ʻ
چ	ـچ	ـچـ	چـ	ch	غ	ـغ	ـغـ	غـ	gh
ح	ـح	ـحـ	حـ	ḥ	ف	ـف	ـفـ	فـ	f
خ	ـخ	ـخـ	خـ	kh	ق	ـق	ـقـ	قـ	ḳ
د	ـد	ـد	د	d	ک	ـک	ـکـ	کـ	k
ڈ	ـڈ	ـڈ	ڈ	ḍ	گ	ـگ	ـگـ	گـ	g
ذ	ـذ	ـذ	ذ	z̤	ل	ـل	ـلـ	لـ	l
ر	ـر	ـر	ر	r	م	ـم	ـمـ	مـ	m
ڑ	ـڑ	ـڑ	ڑ	ṛ	ن	ـن	ـنـ	نـ	n
ز	ـز	ـز	ز	z	و	ـو	ـو	و	w,o,u
ژ	ـژ	ـژ	ژ	zh	ہ	ـہ	ـہـ	ہـ	h
					ی	ـی	ـیـ	یـ	y,e,i

1. Initial. 2. Medial. 3. Final. 4. Isolated.

Aryan, Indic. Persi-Arabic alphabet. Spoken by about 70,000,000 people (chiefly Moslems) in western India or Pakistan. Urdu retains many Persian and Arabic words, introduced into India by Moslem invaders who brought with them their holy book, the Koran. Urdu is closely related to Hindi and Panjabi. It is written from right to left. Early Urdu poetical texts were written in a style called *rekhta.* Dakkhani is the chief dialect.

B, D, F, G, H, J, K, L, M, N, P, R, S, T, V, Z, are pronounced about as in English. BH, CHH, KH, GH, JH, PH, ṚH=B, CH, K, G, J, P, Ṛ respectively but with aspiration.

A—nearly u in *cup;* Ā—*father;* AI—*aisle;* AU—Ou in *how;* CH—*church;* Ḍ—d in *day* but with tip of tongue pressed against palate; E—*where* or as A in *day;* Ḥ—strong H; I—*sin;* Ī—ee in *see;* K̲H̲—about as ch in Scotch *loch;* Ḳ—k in *kite* but with tongue making a slight clicking sound; Ṇ—nasal Ṅ, almost ng; O—*bone;* Ṛ—hard r; Ṣ—*sister;* Ṭ, Ṭ̈,—soft T; ṬH—Ṭ+H; U—*full;* Ū—*rule;* W, V—interchangeably W or V as in English; Y—*yet* (not used as a vowel); Z̲, Ẓ, Z̤—Z in *zest;* ZH—Z in *azure.*

ZABER	U	MADA	Ä
ZAR	I	HAMZA	Ū
PASH	Ū	TASHDED	Double

SINDHI

Aryan; Indic. Arabic, Devanagari, Banya, Kaithi, Multani or Gurmukhi characters. Spoken by about 3,000,000 people in Sindh in western India. Sindhi contains many old Prakrit forms and is descended from Abrahamsa Prakrit. Dialects: Jathki, Sirai, Lari, Vicholi, Jagdali, Tharel and Mendh.

PANJABI

ਹੇ ਸੁਰਗਮੈਂ ਰਹਣੇਵਾਲੇ ਹਮਾਰੇ ਪਿਤਾ ਤੇਰਾ ਨਾਮ ਪਵਿਤ੍ਰ ਹੋਵੇ। ਤੇਰਾ ਰਾਜ ਆਵੇ ਤੇਰਾ ਇਛਾ ਜਿਸਪ੍ਰਕਾਰ ਸਰਗਮੈਂ ਤਿਸਪ੍ਰਕਾਰ ਪ੍ਰਿਥੀਵਿਚ ਕੀਤਾ ਜਾਵੇ। ਅਸਾਡੇ ਜੀਵਣਲਾਇਕ ਖਾਣਾ ਅਸਾਡਤਾਂਈ ਅਜੁ ਦੇਵਹੁ। ਅਤੇ ਜਿਸਪ੍ਰਕਾਰ ਅਸੀ ਆਪਣਿਆਂ ਕਰਜ਼ਾਈਆਂਕੋ ਮਾਫ਼ ਕਰਦੇਹਾਂ ਤੈਸੇ ਅਸਾਡੇਤਾਂਈ ਮਾਫ਼ ਕਰੁ। ਅਤੇ ਅਸਾਨੂ ਪਰੀਖਿਆਵਿਚ ਪ੍ਰਾਪਤ ਮਤ ਕਰਹੁ ਹੋਰਕੀ ਅਸਾਨੂ ਬੁਰੇਤੇ ਛੁਡਾਉ ਕਿਉਂਕੇ ਰਾਜ ਅਤੇ ਪਰਾਕਰਮ ਅਤੇ ਮਹਾਤਮ ਸਭ ਕਾਲਵਿਚ ਤੇਰਾਹੀ। ਆਮਿਨ॥

Neo-Aryan: Indic. Gurmukhi or Devanagari alphabet. Spoken by about 17,000,000 people in the Punjab. Panjabi is the vernacular of the Sikhs. Dialects: Multani, Uch, Jugdwali, Jathki, Pethwari, Chibhali, Dogri and Puhari.

GUJARATI

કેમકે દેવે જગત પર એટલી પ્રીતિ કીધી કે તેણે પોતાનો એકાકીજનિત દીકરો આપ્યો એ સારૂ કે, જે કોઈ તેના પર વિશ્વાસ કરે તેનો નાશ ન થાય, પણ તે અનંત જીવન પામે.

Aryan: Semi-Tibeto-Burman. Gujarati, Devanagari, Balbodh or Kaithi characters. Spoken by about 11,000,000 people in India. Some dialects: Surari, Bhil, and Kattiawari.

MARATHI

[illegible]

Aryan: Semi-Tibeto-Burman. Devanagari, Balbodh, Modi, or Kanarese characters. Spoken by about 16,000,000 people in Bombay Presidency, India. Dialects: Modi, Konkani, Dakhini and Gomantaki.

BENGALI

হে আমারদের স্বর্গস্থ পিতা তোমার নাম পবিত্র
মান্য হউক। তোমার রাজ্য প্রকাশ হউক। যেমন স্বর্গে
তেমন পৃথিবীতে তোমার ইচ্ছা ক্রিয়া করা যাউক। অদ্য
আমারদের নিত্য ভক্ষ্য আমারদিগকে দেও। এবং যেমত

Neo-Aryan: Indic. Bengali alphabet. Spoken by about 50,000,000 people in Bengal. The Bengali script was developed in the 11th century from the Nagari character of northern India. It is the vernacular of the most thickly settled province of India. Spoken in Calcutta, formerly the capital of British India.

KASHMIRI

[illegible]
[illegible]
[illegible]
[illegible]

Aryan: Indic. Devanagari, Sarada, Gurmukhi. Lundi or Thakuri characters. Spoken by about 1,000,000 people in Kashmir, Northern Indian. The three styles of Kashmiri script are: 1. Brahmin. 2. Mohammedan. 3. Vulgar.

NEPALI

किनभन्ये ईश्वर्ले संसार् सङ येस्तो प्रेम् गर्‍यो उस्ले
आफ्नु एक्ले पुत्रलाइ दियो उस् मांथि बिश्वास् गर्ने जनंगे
नष्ट् न हवस् तर त्येस्लाइ अजम्मरे जीउंनि हवस् भन्ये
खातिर्ले। किनभन्ये ईश्वर्ले पुत्रलाइ संसार्मां उस्ले संसार्को

Neo-Aryan: Indic. Devanagari alphabet. Spoken by about 6,000,000 people in Nepal, chiefly the Gurkhas. Four Nepali scripts are: 1. Nevari. 2. Kaithi-nagari. 3. Randja. 4. Bandjin-Mola.

ORISSA

ଆମ୍ଭମାନଙ୍କର ଋଣ କ୍ଷମା କର ଅମ୍ଭମାନଙ୍କୁ ପରୀକ୍ଷାରେ ଘେନ ଯାଓ ନା ଦୁଷ୍ଟ
ଅମ୍ଭମାନଙ୍କୁ ଆପଦରୁ ରକ୍ଷା କର କିଆଁନା ସଦା ସର୍ବଦିନରେ ରାଜ୍ୟ ଓ ପରାକ୍ରମ ଓ
ଗୌରବ ତୁମ୍ଭର ଆମେନ।

Neo-Aryan: Semi-Tibeto-Burman. Uriya or Orya characters. Spoken by about 10,000,000 people in Orissa, North Madras region in India.

LEPCHA OR RONG

[illegible]

Tibeto-Burmese: Sikhim group. Lepcha characters. Spoken by several million people in Sikkhim and Darjeeling, North India.

KANARESE

ಏಕಾಂದರೆ, ದೇವರ ಚಿತ್ತದ ಪರಕಾರ ನಡೆವವಂ ಎಯು
ವೆಂಸೋ ಅವಂನೇ ಎನಗ ಅಣ್ಣತಮ್ಮನೂ ಅಕ್ಕತಂಗೆಯೂ, ಅವೆ
ಯೂ ಆಗಿದ್ದನೆಂ ಎನ್ನಂ. *Mk.* 1897

Dravidian. Kanarese or Tamil alphabet. Spoken by about 10,000,000 people in Mysore, southern India, Hyderabad and adjoining districts of Madras Presidency. Dialect: Badaga.

CAMBODIAN

១៣ គ្មាននាក់ណាដែលឡើងទៅស្ថានសួគ៌ឡើយ លើកតែព្រះ
អង្គដែលបានយាងចុះពីស្ថានសួគ៌មក គឺជាកូនមនុស្សដែលបានគង់នៅស្ថានសួគ៌ ១៤ហើយដូចជា
លោកម៉ូសេបានលើកពស់ឡើងនៅវាលស្ងាត់ នោះកូនមនុស្សនឹងត្រូវតែលើកទ្រង់ឡើងដូច្នោះដែរ

Mon-Khmer. Cambodian alphabet. Spoken by about 1,500,000 people in Cambodia, southern Indo-China. The Cambodian alphabets are called Nọmu and Kakha; the first seven syllabics of the Nomu alphabet were taken from a Buddhist ritual.

BURMESE

။ ၃၇ ။ ကောင်းကင်ဝပဉ် နေတော်မူသောကျွန်ုပ်တော်တို့အဘခ
မည်တော် ။ ကိုယ်တော်အမည်နာမတော် ရိုသေဖြတ်ခိုး သိည်
ဖြစ်စေ ။ ကိုယ်တော် နိုင်ငံတော်တည်သည်ဖြစ်စေ ။ ကိုယ်တော်
အလိုတော် ကောင်းကင်၌ ပြည့်စုံသကဲ့သို့ ပထဝီမြေကြီးအပေါ်

Tibeto-Burman. Burmese alphabet, derived from Pali. Spoken by about 10,000,000 people in Burma. Burmese is a monosyllabic and agglutinative language. Any single syllable may have a number of meanings depending upon the tones assigned to them. The tones are indicated by points. A single point written under the character denotes the soft or accute accent; two points, one above the character and one below, indicates the grave accent. The first tone, called the floating or natural tone, is sounded but not written. The second tone—an'myit (့) or accute. The third tone is sye'pak (း) grave.

SIAMESE

ເພາະວ່າພະເຈົ້າໄດ້ຮັກມະນຸດສະໂລກຍຸງປີຈົນ
ພໍໄດ້ປະທານໃຫ້ປາພະບຸດອົງດຽວເພື່ອວ່າຄົນ
ທຸກຄົນທີ່ໄດ້ເຊື່ອໃນທ່ານກໍ່ຈັກບໍ່ໄດ້ຈິບຫາງ ແຕ່
ວ່າຈັກມີຊີວິດອັນຕລອດເປັນເປັນນິດ ໑ 1910

Tibeto-Chinese: Thai. Siamese characters. Spoken by about 14,000,000 people in Thailand or Siam. Siamese is a monosyllabic language consisting of 44 consonants, 32 vowels and 5 tones.

TELUGU

ఓయి స్వర్గమందు ఉన్న మాయొక్క తండ్రీ। నీయొక్క నామము పవిత్రము
చెయ్యబడని నీయొక్క రాజ్యము రాని। నీయొక్క ఇష్టము యెలాగున స్వర్గమందా ఆలాగున
భూమియందున్న చెయ్యబడని। మాయొక్క జీవనానకు అహారమైన భక్ష్యమును ఈవేళ

Dravidian. Telugu characters. Spoken by about 25,000,000 people in the central and eastern parts of India, and Hyderabad.

TAMIL

பரமண்டலங்களிலிருக்கிற எங்கள் பிதாவே உம்முடைய
நாமம் பரிசுத்தமாவதாக உம்முடைய ராட்சியம் வருவதாக
உம்முடைய சித்தம் பரமண்டலத்திலே செய்யப்படுமோபோலே
பூமியிலேயுஞ்செய்யப்படுவதாக அன்றன்றுள்ள எங்கள் அப்பத்தை
எங்களுக்கின்று தாரும் எங்கள் கடன்காரருக்கு நாங்கள்
மன்னிக்குமாபோலே எங்கள் கடன்களை எங்களுக்கு மன்னியும்

Dravidian. Tamil characters. Spoken by about 18,000,000 people in southern India and Ceylon, Madras Presidency, Tanjore, Tinnevelly, Chittoor, Coimbatore and the Nilgris. The Tamil alphabet consists of 12 vowels: A, Ā, I, Ī, U, Ū, E, Ē, O, Ō, EI, AU, and 18 consonants: Hard–K, Ś, T, Ṭ, P, R. Soft (nasal) Ṅ, Ñ, Ṇ, N, M, N. Medium (semi-vowels) Y, Ṛ, L, U, R, L. The consonants are pronounced irregularly and K might be sounded KH, G and occasionally H; CH might be–S. The consonants K, CH, T, Ṭ, have slight nasal sounds. A point is written over the consonant when the inherent A is omitted. There are 4 semivowels: Ṛ, Ḷ, and liquid L. The vowels and consonants in various combinations consist of 216 syllabics.

MALAYALAM

എന്തെന്നാൽ ദൈവം തന്റെ ഏകജാതനാ
യപുത്രനിൽ വിശ്വസിക്കുന്ന ഒരുത്തനും നശി

Dravidian, Malayalam or Grantha characters. Spoken by about 6,000,000 people of the west coast of India.

SINHALESE

ස්වර්ගයෙහි වැඩසිටින අපගේ පියාණන්වහන්ස ඔබවහන්සේගේ
නාමය සුද්ධවේවා ඔබවහන්සේගේ රාජ්‍යය එවා ඔබවහන්සේගේ
කැමැත්ත ස්වර්ගයෙහිමෙන් භූමියෙහිද කරනුලැබේවා අපේ දවස්පතා
භෝජනය අපට අද දිවයිලමැනාව අපේ නයකාරයන්ට අපි
කමාවෙන්නාක්මෙන් අපේ නයත් අපට කමාවී වදාලමැනාව අප

Aryan: Semi-Tibeto-Burman. Sinhalese alphabet. Spoken by about 5,000,000 people in Ceylon. The Sinhalese alphabet consists of 18 medial vowels which when added to the 34 consonants in various combinations, may form about 612 syllabics. The short vowel is inherent in the written consonant, but when absent this is marked by *virama.*

EAST ASIATIC AND ORIENTAL LANGUAGES

TIBETAN

དེའི་ཚེ་དེའི་དུས་ན་ཡལ་བྲ་ར་ན་སེ་འདིར་དྲང་སྲོང་ལྔ་
བརྒྱ་ཞིག་གནས་ཏེ། དྲང་སྲོང་དེ་དག་གིས་སྟོན་པ་ཨུད་པ་
ལ་ཞེས་བྱ་བ་དམ་པའི་ཆོས་སློབ་ཅིང་བསྒོམ་པ་ལ་དགའ་
བས་ཀུན་ཏུ་རྒྱུ་ཞིང་། ས་ལ་དམ་པའི་ཆོས་ཡོད་པ་དེ་བདག་
ལ་སྨྲ་ན།

Foucaux, Gramm. sur la langue Tibét.

1	2	3		1	2	3		1	2	3	
ཨ			a	ཉ			ńa	ཝ			wa
ཨི			i	ཏ			ta	ཞ			ža
ཨུ			u	ཐ			tha	ཟ			sa
ཨེ			e	ད			ta	འ			’a
ཨོ			o	ན			na	ཡ			ya
ཀ			ka	པ			pa	ར			ra
ཁ			kha	ཕ			pha	ལ			la
ག			ka	བ			pa	ཤ			śa
ང			ṅa	མ			ma	ས			s̱a
ཙ			tša	ཙ			tsa	ཧ			hʻa
ཚ			tšha	ཚ			tsha				
ཛ			tša	ཛ			tsa				
ཨཱ			ā	ཨཽ			au	ཎ			ṇa
ཨཱི			ī	ཊ			ṭa	ཥ			स
ཨཱུ			ū	B			ṭha				
ཨཻ			ai	ཌ			ṭa				

1. Utshen. 2. Umin. 3. Khyugagi.

Sino-Tibetan. Tibetan characters. Spoken in Tibet and adjoining districts in India. The alphabet consists of 30 consonants including two letters used as bases for vowels. There are 5 vowels of which only 4 are written. The unwritten vowel is long A inherent in the consonant. Old Tibetan text is called *dbu-can*, later text is *dbu-med.* Tibetan characters were invented by Thon-mi-Sam-bhota (639 A.D.) of Lhasa, from characters of North India cursive Gupta. An offshoot of the Tibetan letters was Passepa, invented by Bashbah or Phags-pa-Lama, and introduced into Tibet to replace Uighur derived from Estrangelo-Nestorian.

Tibetan is allied to the Burmese languages and is sometimes called "Tibeto-Burman." The language is called *Bod-skad;* the vernacular is *P'al-skad.* There are several dialects: 1. Central dialect of Lhasa, etc. 2. Western dialects of Ladak, Lahul, Balistan, etc. 3. Eastern dialects of Chams, and others spoken in the Himalayan districts.

VOWELS

ི **Kiku, i**

ུ ུ **Sciapkiu, u**

ེ **Drengbu, e**

ོ **Naro, o**

MONGOLIAN

Altaic. Mongolian characters. Spoken in the regions beyond the Great Wall of China and by certain tribes and nomadic peoples in the Gobi Desert, in the eastern part of the Thian Shan area and east of the Kalmuck steppes. The Mongolian language was reduced to written form by the Lamas Saskya Pandiat, Phags-pa-Lama, and Thsoishoi Oder in the 13th century, from the Uighur letters of the Genghis Khan dynasty, which alphabet was in turn derived from old Syriac through Nestorian or Estrangelo. In the time of Kublai Khan (1259-1294) five additional letters from Tibetan were added, thus forming the Mongol Galik. Kalmuck, a simplified form of Galik was introduced by the Eleut Mongols in the 17th century.

In Mongolian some letters have different sounds depending upon their positions in words.

The Mongolian alphabet has seven vowels, with dipthongs derived from them, and seventeen consonants all of which are modified according to their position in a word as initials, medials or finals. Some letters have different sounds, depending upon their positions in words.

Mongolian is written in vertical columns and read from left to right, not right to left as in Chinese. Dialects are: Buriatic, Sharra, Kalmuck, Khalka, Galik.

3	2	1		3	2	1	
			a				k
			e				g
			i				m
			o				l
			u				r
			ö				t
			ü				d
			n				y
			b				ts
			χ				dz
			γ				s
							š
							w

1. Initials. 2. Medials. 3. Finals.

SYLLABLES

o	*ö*	*so*	*sö*	*ro*	*rö*	*yo*	*yö*
u	*ü*	*su*	*sü*	*ru*	*rü*	*yu*	*yü*
bo	*bö*	*no*	*nö*	*do*	*dö*	*zo*	*zö*
bu	*bü*	*nu*	*nü*	*du*	*dü*	*zu*	*zü*
go	*gö*	*χo*	*kö*	*to*	*tö*		
gu	*gü*	*χu*	*kü*	*tu*	*tü*		
lo	*lö*	*mo*	*mö*	*tso*	*tsö*		
lu	*lü*	*mu*	*mü*	*tsu*	*tsü*		

a	*ta*	*la*	*ba*	*tsa*	*sa*	*ga*	*wa*
ä	*tä*	*lä*	*bä*	*tsä*	*sä*	*gä*	*wä*
i	*ti*	*li*	*bi*	*tsi*	*si*	*gi*	∵
ma	*na*	*ra*	*dza*	*χa*	*yạ*	*da*	
mä	*nä*	*rä*	*dzä*	*kä*	*iah*	*dä*	
mi	*ni*	*ri*	*dzi*	*χi*	*yi*	*di*	

MONGOLIAN AND MANCHU

MANCHU

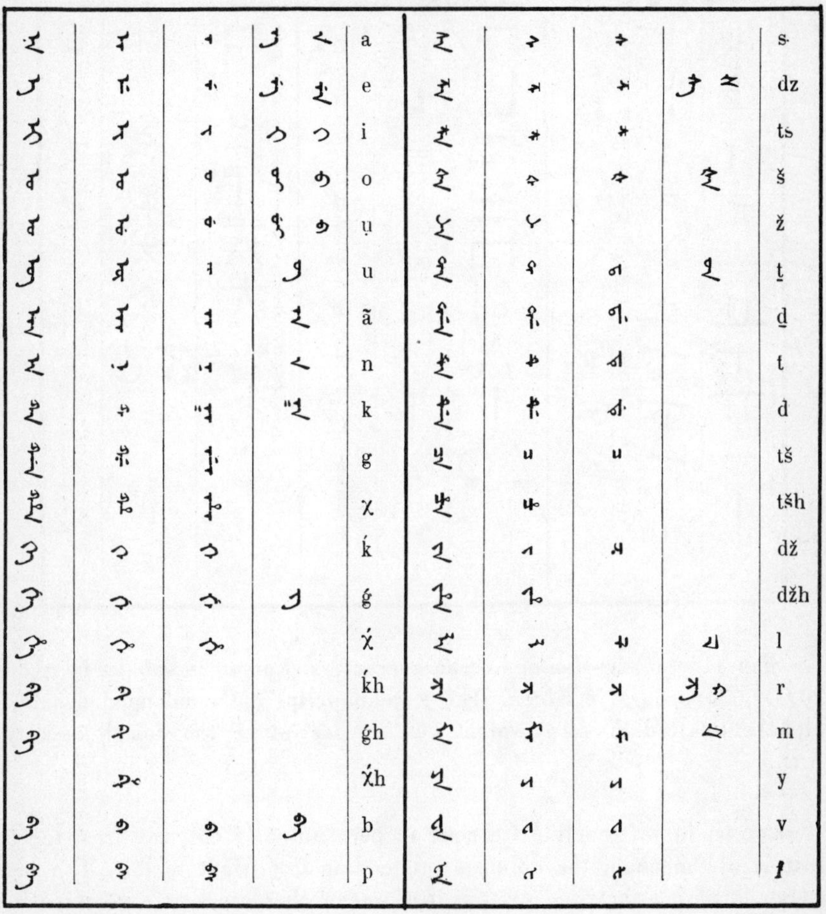

Vowels / consonants	Consonants
a	s·
e	dz
i	ts
o	š
ụ	ž
u	t̲
ã	d̲
n	t
k	d
g	tš
χ	tšh
ḱ	dž
ǵ	džh
χ́	l
ḱh	r
ǵh	m
χ́h	y
b	v
p	f

Tungus. Manchurian characters. Spoken in Manchuria north of the Chinese Republic by about 40,000 people. The Manchu alphabet is derived from Mongolian but contains a large number of additional characters. The present Manchu alphabet was established by order of the Emperor Tien Ming in 1599.

MONGOLIAN WRITTEN IN HORIZONTAL COLUMNS.

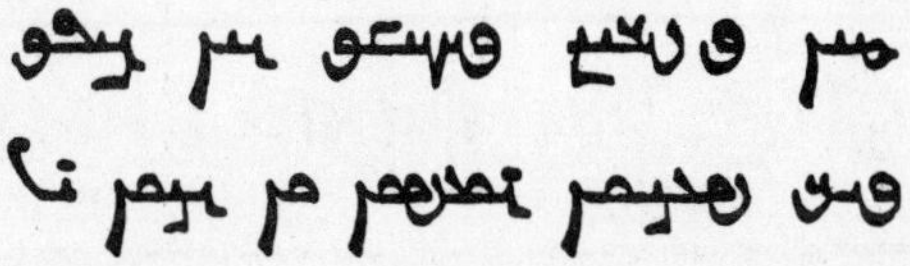

KOREAN

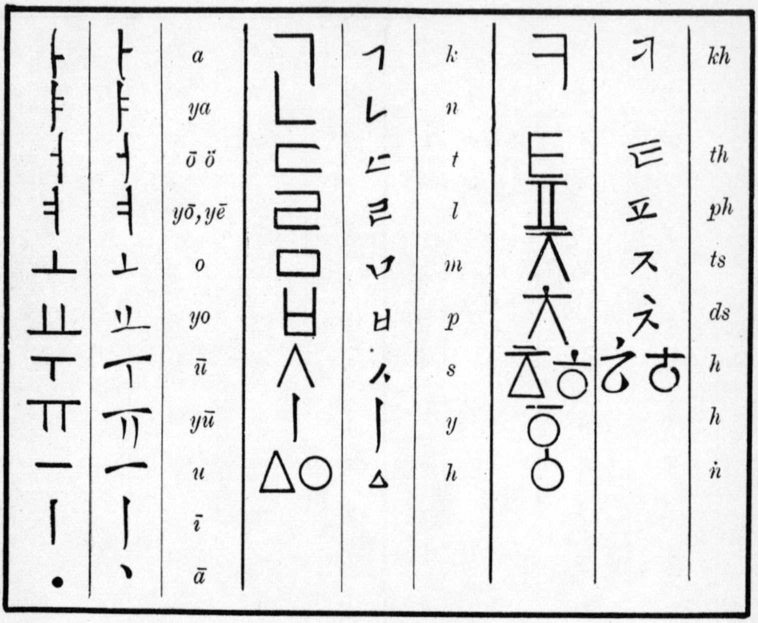

ㅏ	ㅏ	*a*	ㄱ	ㄱ	*k*	ㅋ	ㅋ	*kh*
ㅑ	ㅑ	*ya*	ㄴ	ㄴ	*n*			
ㅓ	ㅓ	*ŏ ö*	ㄷ	ㄷ	*t*	ㅌ	ㅌ	*th*
ㅕ	ㅕ	*yŏ, yē*	ㄹ	ㄹ	*l*	ㅍ	ㅍ	*ph*
ㅗ	ㅗ	*o*	ㅁ	ㅁ	*m*	ㅈ	ㅈ	*ts*
ㅛ	ㅛ	*yo*	ㅂ	ㅂ	*p*	ㅊ	ㅊ	*ds*
ㅜ	ㅜ	*ū*	ㅅ	ㅅ	*s*	ㅎ ㅎ	ㅎ ㅎ	*h*
ㅠ	ㅠ	*yū*	ㅣ	ㅣ	*y*	ㆆ		*h*
ㅡ	ㅡ	*u*	ㅿ ㅇ	ㅿ	*h*	ㅇ		*ṅ*
ㅣ	ㅣ	*ī*						
ㆍ	ㆍ	*ā*						

Sino-Tibetan. *En-Mun* or Korean characters. Korean is spoken by about 20,000,000 people in Korea. The Korean script is based upon a native alphabet called *En-Mun* which was in use since the fourth century. A.D.

Korean is written like Chinese in perpendicular columns from top to bottom of the page, the columns proceeding from right to left. The language is also sometimes written in Chinese characters or a combination of both Chinese and Korean characters.

VOWEL COMBINATIONS

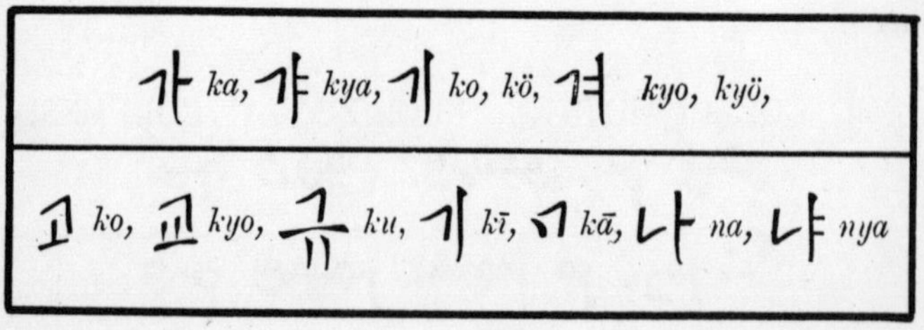

가 *ka,* 갸 *kya,* 거 *ko, kö,* 겨 *kyo, kyö,*
고 *ko,* 교 *kyo,* 규 *ku,* 기 *kī,* ᄀᆞ *kā,* 나 *na,* 냐 *nya*

하ᄂᆞ님이 셰샹ᄋᆞᆯ ᄉᆞ랑
ᄒᆞ샤 독싱ᄌᆞᄅᆞᆯ 주셧ᄉᆞ니
누구던지 뎌를 밋으면
멸망 ᄒᆞ지 안코 영싱을
잇으리라

YÜ INSCRIPTIONS OF CHINA

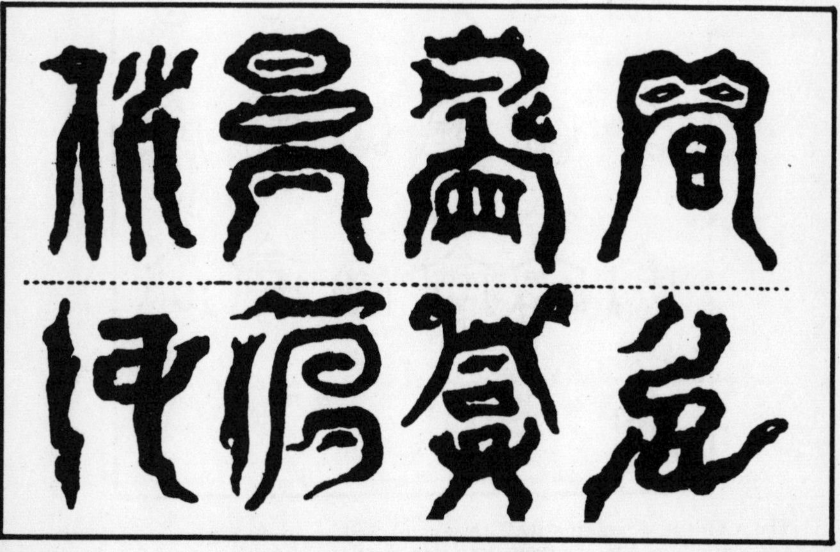

CHINESE: *FORTY-THREE STYLES*

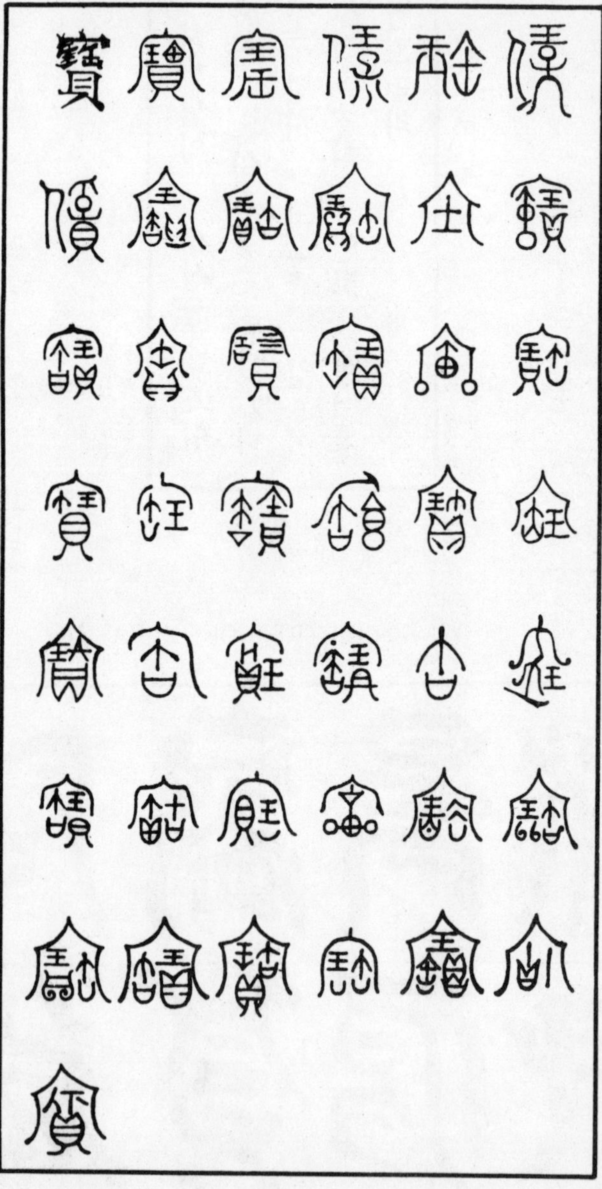

The Chinese character BAO (treasure) written in 43 styles, as inscribed on pottery, porcelain, etc. Source:—Heinrich Wuttke, in *Abbildungen Zur Geschichte der Schrift.* Leipzig, 1873, from Callery's *Systema phoneticum scripturae sinicae.* Macao, 1841

CHINESE

"SIX SCRIPTS"

1	2	3	4	5	6
上古結繩而治後世聖人易之	上古結繩而治後世聖人易之	上古結繩而治後世聖人易之	上古結繩而治後世聖人易之	上古結繩而治後世聖人易之	上古結繩而治後世聖人易之

Chinese, a monosyllabic language of eastern Asia, spoken by about 400,000,000 people in the Chinese Republic, is written in ideographic Chinese characters. The Chinese characters are arranged in native dictionaries under 214 radicals, each radical a Chinese character sometimes used as whole or in part to form parts of other characters. Under radicals arranged according to the number of strokes required in writing them are listed other characters of which the radical is part. This arrangement of classifying the Chinese characters dates from the *Shuo-Wen-Chieh-Tzu* of Hsu Shen, about 120 A.D.

The Chinese radical usually conveys some general idea of the meaning or ideographic group to which the whole radical belongs. The remaining portion of the character often serves as the phonetic, thus imparting its sound to the whole character. But this is not an unalterable rule, and some characters are used for their phonetic values alone.

The Chinese characters are modified pictographs since conventionalized and often bearing but little resemblance to their origin. Yet, in many of the characters evidence of their pictorial origin may be seen.

	Sun	Moon	Words	Mountain	Fish	Water	Eye	Horse
Pictographs								
Archaic Chinese								
Modern Chinese	日	月	言	山	魚	水	目	馬

This represents the first stage of picture writing. Now, other characters were invented to represent abstract ideas, and certain other characters conveniently called *indicators* were added to the pictograms or ideographs to form abstract meanings or ideas. Thus, the sun 日 and 月 *moon* 明 combined, means *clear* or *light.* Again, the character 人 –*man,* doubled means *woman*– 女 . Evidently, this was derived from the institution of marriage or union. Similarly, the word 子 *child,* originally written , and later but when added to the character for *woman,* seems to mean wife and child, and the Chinese word for the whole character 好 is *good.* This is probably derived from the institution of family and home–terms synonymous with goodness.

	To look	To fear	To sing	East
Pictographs				
Archaic Chinese				
Modern Chinese	看	瞿	鳴	東

1-A hand placed over the eye to shade the brow from the sun. 2-A timid bird with eyes searching the source of danger. 3-A mouth and a bird indicating song. 4-A tree and the sun–the sun in the east seen behind the tree at dawn.

The so called "Six Scripts" still widely used in Chinese writing are: 1-Ku-wen characters by Cheu (circa 800 B.C.) called Ta-chuan or great seal. 2-Hsiao-chuan by Li Szu (circa 200 B.C.) called small seal. 3-Li-shu court hand. 4-Kai-shu or square characters. 5-Hsing-shu or cursive characters. 6-Tsao-shu or grass writing—an abbreviated cursive hand. The most ancient scripts of China were: Chi'eh Sheng or knotted strings (circa 28th century B.C.); Hsu-chi of Ts'ang Chieh (circa 27th century B.C.); Chia-ku-wen or shell and bone, and Pa kwa.

PA-KWA

Chinese syllables may be arranged in three sections for convenience—the initial, the final, and the tone. In the Mandarin the initials are as follows: B, D, TZ, J, G, P, T, TS, CH, K, M, N, F, S, SH, H, L, R. The final forms are: A, E, Y, AI, EI, AU, OU, AN, EN, ANG, ENG, ONG, I, IA, IE, IAI, IAU, IOU, IAN, IN, IANG, ING, IONG, U, UA, UO, UAI, UEI, UAN, UEN, UANG, UENG, IU, IUE, IUAN, IUN, EL. The initial letters are pronounced about as in English. The letters CH, J, SH when not followed by I, IU or R, are pronounced with the tongue curled against the roof of the mouth, but when these letters are followed by I, IU, R, they are pronounced with the flat part of the tongue.

Final A is as in *father;* AI—*aisle;* EI—*eight;* AU-OW in *how;* OU—*soul;* ENG—nearly UNG; I—*machine;* IE—*yet;* OO—about as in *rude* but short UO-WA; IU—French U.

There are four tones in Mandarin. 1. *Inping sheng* (high level), *Yang-ping-sheng* (rising), *Shangsheng-sheng* (low), *Chiuh-sheng* (high falling) and the neutral tone. Marks indicating tone are sometimes shown by small numerals placed beside or following words or other marks.

Phonetic Table for Comparison

(initials)

Gwoyeu Romatzyh	Wade phonetics
B	P
P	P'
D	T
G	K
K	K'
TZ	TS, TZ
TS	TS'
J	CH
CH	CH'
R	J
SH	SH, HS
S	S, SS

In the Wade system of phonetics tones are indicated by the numerals written beside the word–1-4. *Gwoyeu Romatzyh* does not employ tone numerals.

The initial A Compounds

Gwoyeu Romatzyh	Wade phonetics
A, AR, AA, AH	A^1, A^2, A^3, A^4.
AI, AIR, AE, AY	AI^1, AI^2, AI^3, AI^4.
AN, ARN, AAN, ANN	AN^1, AN^2, AN^3, AN^4.
ANG, ARNG, AANG, ANQ	ANG^1, ANG^2, ANG^3, ANG^4.
AU, AUR, AO, AW	AO^1, AO^2, AO^3, AO^4.

The list of finals in the 4 tones consist of about 200 syllables.

Cantonese phonetics: A, E, I, O, U, AI, AU, EU, OI, UI, IU. Consonants–NG, CH, S, K, P, T. A–*father* as final otherwise nearly A in *fun;* E–*men* or as A in *date*; I–*pin* or as in *machine* as final; O–*no* or as in *pool* or as in *full*; AI–*aisle;* EU–E + U; OI–*toil;* UI–U + I; IU–I + U. NG as initial or final–NG in *sing*. This sound is often used as initial in the pronoun–'*Ngo* (I). CH–nearly J when unaspirated; S–between S in *sister* and SH in *shut;* K–nearly G in *get,* when unaspirated, otherwise K; P–*pet,* aspirated nearly B in *but;* T–*tent,* but nearly D when aspirated;

There are eight tones in Cantonese, four higher and four lower: 1. Even or monotone without rising or falling voice. 2. Rising tone like in the last word of a question. 3. Falling tone like the last word of a question to which an answer is not expected. 4. Entering tone. An abrupt termination as if the last letter of the word was clipped. In Cantonese this tone is indicated by the finals K, P, T.

<table>
<tr><th>MANDARIN</th><th>CANTONESE</th><th>CHU-YIN</th></tr>
<tr>
<td>用各樣寶石修飾的、第一根基、是金綠寶石、二十第五是紅瑪瑙、第六是黃寶璧璽、第十是翡翠、第十一是紅寶石、每門是一顆珍珠、城內的街道、都是殿、有 主全能的 神和 羔羊爲</td>
<td>遣佢嘅使者、將個的必要快成嘅事、預言嘅有福咯。〇呢的事、係我約翰示我嘅天使脚前俯伏、想敬拜佢、佢與及守此書言語嘅人、同埋做僕、你書嘅預言、因爲日期近咯。十一不義嘅等嘅、等佢仍然爲義、聖潔嘅、等佢仍然</td>
<td>[illegible]</td>
</tr>
</table>

Mandarin is the dialect of Peiping and the most widely spoken speech in all China. The literary language called Wenli was long a cultural lingua franca in all China, but Wenli has no arbitrary sounds; the sounds were supplied by the reader in his own dialect. Much of the literature of China is written in Wenli. Notable among the efforts of native Chinese for adopting the colloquial as a standardized tongue was the Vernacular Literature Movement of Hu Shih in 1917. But in 1919 was devised a system towards unification of the national tongue and revised in 1932. This system based upon Mandarin and now known as *Gwoyeu* consists of 39 National Phonetic Letters based upon the Peiping dialect, which has been adopted by the Chinese Government as the official spelling of the public; still, foreigners in China and in practice, many government departments continue to use the phonetic system of Sir Thomas Wade.

The new National Romanization system does not employ marks of tone, but distinctive syllables are written for various tones instead. The new letters are called *Romatzyh.* Another system extensively used for romanization of the Chinese characters *Latinxua* devised by A. Dragunov of Russia, used by Chinese Communists. Among the earlier systems of romanization of the characters are those of Mateer and Williams, and the early interdialectical system of Fathers Lamasse and Jasmin.

There is no accurate estimate as to the number of Chinese characters: The *K'ang-hsi* Dictionary (1716) lists about 40,000 characters; the *Kuan-yün* (1007) lists about 26,000 characters, many of which, of course are obsolete. But recently the Mass Education Movement of China proposed 1200 *Basic Characters*, selected because of their frequency and utility to the Chinese masses. Some newspapers and books are published in *Basic*, serving most useful purposes, but a knowledge of *Basic* only based upon three months intensive study as outlined by the sponsors of this system, can only lead to but a superficial knowledge of the language at best.

CHU-YIN OR THE NEW CHINESE NATIONAL ALPHABET

INITIALS								MEDIALS	
G	ㄍ	T	ㄊ	DZ	ㄗ	H	ㄏ	I	ㄧ
K	ㄎ	N	ㄋ	TS	ㄘ	HS	ㄒ	U	ㄨ
O	ㄫ	B	ㄅ	SZ	ㄙ	L	ㄌ	Ü,YÜ	ㄩ
GI	ㄐ	P	ㄆ	DJ	ㄓ	R	ㄖ		
CHI	ㄑ	M	ㄇ	CH	ㄔ				
N	ㄬ	F	ㄈ	SH	ㄕ				
D	ㄉ	V	ㄪ						

FINALS

A	ㄚ	OU	ㄡ
O,Ê	ㄛ	AN	ㄢ
EH	ㄝ	ANG	ㄤ
EI	ㄟ	ÊN	ㄣ
AI	ㄞ	ÊNG	ㄥ
AO	ㄠ	ÊRH	ㄦ

There are nine main groups of dialects in China. The first groups are Cantonese, Amoy-Swatow, Foochow, Wu, Hsiang, Kan-Hakka and Hsiang. The second dialect zone includes three groups of Mandarin dialects, divided as northern, southern and southwestern. A list of some of the chief dialects spoken in China follows:

North Mandarin Colloquial-Peking Dialect or *Kuoyü* (Peiping pronunciation. Spoken by about 300,000,000 people); *North Mandarin-Chihli Dialect* (Chihli Province, south of Peiping); *North Mandarin-Kiaotung Dialect* (Shantung Province); *North Mandarin-Shantung Dialect* (Shantung Province); *South Mandarin-Nanking Dialect* (Nanking, Kiangsu Province); *Cantonese* (Canton and Kwangtung Province); *Amoy colloquial* (Amoy district, Fukien Province): *Foochow Colloquial* (Foochow, northern Fukien Province); *Hainan Dialect* (Island of Hainan); *Hakka Colloquial* (Kwangtung Province) *Hakka Colloquial-Wukingfu Dialect* (East and Northeast Kwangtung); *Hangchow Colloquial* (Hangchow Region, Chekiang Province); *Hinghua Colloquial* (Fukien Province); *Hankow Colloquial* (Hankow); *Kienning Colloquial* (Northern Fukien Province); *Kienyang Colloquial* (Northern Fukien Province); *Kinhwa Colloquial* (Near Kinwha, Chekiang Province); *Sankiang Colloquial* (Lienchow Prefecture, Northwest Kwangtung); *Ning Po Colloquial* (Ning Po region, Chekiang Province); *Shanghai Colloquial* (Spoken by about 18,000,000 people in south Kiangsu Province); *Shaowu*, Fukien Province); *Soochow Colloquial* (Soochow, Kiangsu Province); *Swatow Colloquial* (Spoken by about 5,000,000 people in Chaochowfu and near Swatow in Kwangtung; *Taichow Colloquial* (Taichow, Chekiang Province); *Tingchow* (Tingchow Prefecture, Fukien); *Wenchow Colloquial* (Wenchow, Chekiang Province).

CHINESE NUMERALS – 1 to 10

Simple	Documentary	Soochow
一	壹	〡
二	貳	〢
三	叁	〣
四	肆	〤
五	伍	〥
六	陸	〦
七	柒	〧
八	捌	〨
九	玖	〩
十	拾	十

HIGH WENLI

一二 三四 五六 七八 九十 十一十二 十三十四 十五十六 十七十八 十九二十 二十一二十二 二十三二十四二十五 二十六二十七 二十八二十九 三十三十一 三十二三十三三十四 三十五三十六 一二三

第三章　有[一]法利賽人尼哥底母者、猶太宰也、[二]夜詣耶穌曰、夫子、我儕知爾爲師、自上帝而來、蓋爾所
行之異蹟、非上帝與偕、無能行者、[三]耶穌曰、我誠語汝、人非更生、不能見上帝國也、[四]尼哥底母曰、人既老、奚
能生、能再入母胎而生耶、[五]耶穌曰、我誠語汝、人非由水與聖神而生、不能入上帝國、[六]由肉而生者肉也、由
神而生者神也、[七]我語爾必更生、勿以爲奇、[八]夫風任意而吹、爾聞其聲、不知其何來何往、凡由聖神生者亦
若是、[九]尼哥底母曰、安有此乎、[十]耶穌曰、爾爲以色列之師、猶未知此乎、[十一]我誠語汝、我儕言所知、證所見、而爾
曹不受我證焉、[十二]我言屬地者、爾尚弗信、若言屬天者、爾詎信乎、[十三]從未有升天者、惟自天而降、即在天之人
子耳、[十四]摩西舉蛇於野、人子亦必如是見舉、[十五]致凡信之者、於彼而有永生、○[十六]蓋上帝愛世、至賜其獨生子、俾
凡信之者、免淪亡而有永生、[十七]因上帝遣子入世、非以鞫世、乃令由之獲救、[十八]信之者不受鞫、不信者已鞫矣、
以其未信上帝獨生子之名也、[十九]是鞫也、因光臨世、而人愛暗愈於光、以其行惡也、[二十]蓋凡爲惡者、惡光、而不
就之、恐其所行見責、[二十一]惟行眞理者就光、以彰其行乃遵上帝而行焉、○[二十二]厥後、耶穌與其徒至猶太地、居而
施洗、[二十三]約翰亦施洗於近撒冷之哀嫩、以其地多水也、衆至而受洗焉、[二十四]蓋約翰尚未下獄也、[二十五]其徒與一猶太
人辯潔禮、[二十六]遂詣約翰曰、夫子、昔偕爾於約但外、爾所證者、今施洗、而人皆就之、[二十七]約翰曰、非由天授、人則無
所能受、[二十八]爾曹證之、我曾言我非基督、乃奉遣於其前耳、[二十九]娶新婦者、新郎也、新郎之友立而聽之、聞其聲則
喜甚、故我此喜滿盈矣、[三十]彼必興、我必衰、[三十一]自上來者在萬有上、自地者屬地、所言者亦屬地、自天來者在萬
有上、[三十二]其所證者、乃其所見所聞、而無人受其證、[三十三]受其證者、如已鈐印、證上帝爲眞矣、[三十四]上帝所遣者、言上帝
之言、蓋上帝賜聖神無限量也、[三十五]父愛子、以萬有付其手、[三十六]信子者有永生、不順子者弗得生、上帝之怒止其
上矣、

第四章　主[一]知法利賽人聞己招徒施洗、多於約翰、[二]實則耶穌非自施洗、乃其徒也、[三]遂去猶太、復往加

THE 214 RADICALS

(As used in Chinese dictionaries)

1 Stroke.

1. 一 Yih. One.
2. 丨 Kwen. Pass through.
3. 丶 Chu. A point.
4. 丿 P'ih. A left stroke.
5. 乙 Yih. One, curved.
6. 亅 Küih. Hooked.

2 Strokes.

7. 二 Er. Two.
8. 亠 T'eu. A cover.
9. 人 亻 Jin. A man.
10. 儿 Jin. A man.
11. 入 Juh. To enter.
12. 八 Pah. Eight.
13. 冂 Kiung. A limit.
14. 冖 Mi. To cover.
15. 冫 Ping. Ice.
16. 几 Ki. A bench.
17. 凵 K'ang. A receptacle.
18. 刀 刂 Tau. A Knife.
19. 力 Lih. Strength.
20. 勹 Pau. To infold.
21. 匕 Pi. A spoon.
22. 匚 Fang. A chest.
23. 匸 Hi. To conceal.
24. 十 Shih. Ten.
25. 卜 Poh. To divine.
26. 卩 㔾 Tsih. A seal.
27. 厂 Han. A shelter.
28. 厶 S. Deflected.
29. 又 Yiu. Moreover.

3 Strokes.

30. 口 K'eu. The Mouth.
31. 囗 We. To enclose.
32. 土 T'u. Ground, earth
33. 士 Sh. A scholar.
34. 夂 Ch. To follow.
35. 夊 Shŭai. Walk slowly.
36. 夕 Sih. Evening.
37. 大 Ta. Large.
38. 女 Nü. Female.
39. 子 Ts. A child.
40. 宀 Mien. A cover
41. 寸 Ts'un. An inch.
42. 小 Siau. Small.
43. 尢 尤 尣 Yiu. Distorted.

44. 尸 Sh. A corpse.
45. 屮 Ch'eh. A sprout.
46. 山 Shan. A hill.
47. 巛 川 巜 Ch'üan. A stream.
48. 工 Kung. Work.
49. 己 Ki. Self.
50. 巾 Kin. A napkin.
51. 干 Kan. A shield.
52. 幺 Yau. Small.
53. 广 Yien. A roof.
54. 廴 Ying. A journey.
55. 廾 Kung. To join hands.
56. 弋 Yih. An arrow.
57. 弓 Kung. A bow.
58. 彐 彑 Ki. A swine's head.
59. 彡 Shan. Feathers, hair.
60. 彳 Ch'ih. A short step.

4 Strokes.

61. 心 ⺗ 忄 Sin. The heart.
62. 戈 Ko. A spear.
63. 戶 Hu. A door.
64. 手 扌 Sheu. A hand.
65. 支 Ch. A branch.
66. 攴 攵 P'ah. A blow.
67. 文 Wen. Literature.
68. 斗 Teu. A measure.
69. 斤 Kin. A catty, a pound.
70. 方 Fang. A Square.
71. 无 Wu. Without.
72. 日 Jih. The sun, a day.
73. 曰 Yüih. To speak.
74. 月 Yüih. The moon.
75. 木 Muh. Wood, timber.
76. 欠 Ch'ien. To owe.
77. 止 Ch. To stop.
78. 歹 歺 Tai. Evil.
79. 殳 Ch'u. Weapons.
80. 毋 Wu. Do not.
81. 比 Pi. To compare.
82. 毛 Mau. Hair.
83. 氏 Sh. The family name.
84. 气 Ch'i. Breath.
85. 水 氵 氺 Shŭe. Water.
86. 火 灬 Ho. Fire.
87. 爪 爫 Chau. Claws.
88. 父 Fu. Father.
89. 爻 Hiau. To imitate.
90. 爿 Ch'üang. A bed.
91. 片 P'ien. A splinter.
92. 牙 Ya. Teeth.
93. 牛 Niu. A cow.
94. 犬 犭 K'üin. A dog.

5 Strokes.

95. 玄 Hüin. Dark, sombre.
96. 玉 王 Yuh. A gem.
97. 瓜 Kwa. A melon.
98. 瓦 Wa. A tile.
99. 甘 Kan. Sweet.

100. 生 Sheng. Life.
101. 用 Yung. To use.
102. 田 T‘ien. A field.
103. 疋 P‘ih. A piece of cloth.
104. 疒 Nih. Sick.
105. 癶 Poh. To separate.
106. 白 Peh. White.
107. 皮 P‘i. Skin.
108. 皿 Min. A vessel.
109. 目 罒 Muh. The eyes.
110. 矛 Meu. A spear.
111. 矢 Sh. An arrow.
112. 石 Shih. A stone.
113. 示 礻 Sh. To show.
114. 禸 Jeu. To creep.
115. 禾 Ho. Growing rice.
116. 穴 Huih. A cave.
117. 立 Lih. To stand.

6 Strokes.

118. 竹 Chuh. Bamboo.
119. 米 Mi. Hulled rice.
120. 糸 S. Silk.
121. 缶 Feu. Earthenware.
122. 网 罒 冗 Wang. A net.
123. 羊 Yang. A sheep.
124. 羽 Yü. Wings.
125. 老 Lau. Aged.
126. 而 Er. And, still.
127. 耒 Le. A plough.
128. 耳 Er. The ear.
129. 聿 Lüh. A pencil.
130. 肉 月 Juh. Flesh.
131. 臣 Ch‘eng. A minister.
132. 自 Ts. Self, from.
133. 至 Ch. To, most.
134. 臼 Kiu. A mortar.
135. 舌 Sheh. The tongue.
136. 舛 Ch‘üan. Error.
137. 舟 Cheu. A boat.
138. 艮 Ken. Perverse.
139. 色 Seh. Color.
140. 艸 艹 Ts‘au. Grass.
141. 虍 Hu. A tiger.
142. 虫 Ch‘ung. Reptiles.
143. 血 Hüih. Blood.
144. 行 Hing. Walk, work.
145. 衣 衤 I. Clothes.
146. 西 襾 Si. West.

7 Strokes.

147. 見 Kien. To see.
148. 角 Kioh. Horn.
149. 言 Yien. Words.
150. 谷 Kuh. A valley.
151. 豆 Teu. Beans.
152. 豕 Sh. Swine.
153. 豸 Hie. Reptiles, wild beasts.
154. 貝 Pe. Pearls.
155. 赤 Ch‘ih. Scarlet.
156. 走 Tseu. To walk.
157. 足 Tsuh. The foot.
158. 身 Shen. The body.
159. 車 Kü, ch‘e. A chariot.
160. 辛 Sin. Acrid.
161. 辰 Ch‘en. Hour.

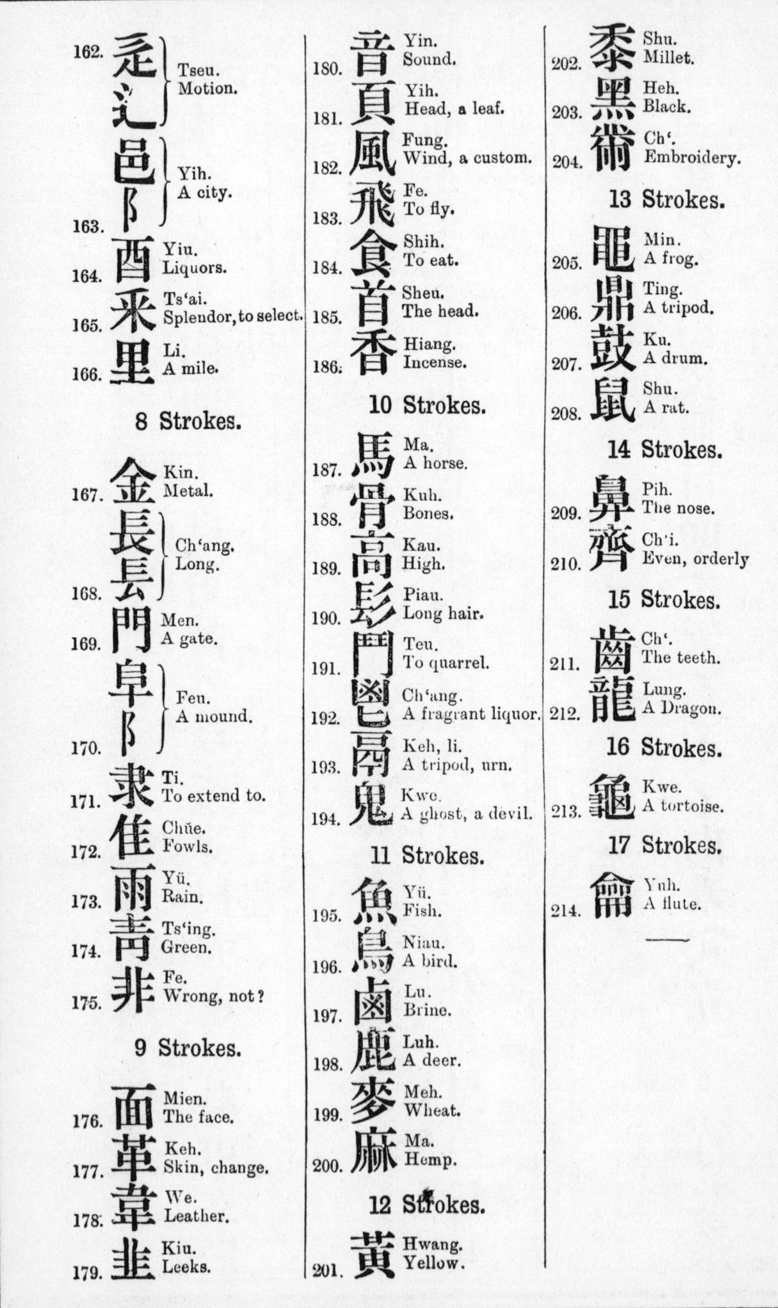

No.	Character	Sound	Meaning
162.	辵 辶	Tseu.	Motion.
163.	邑 阝	Yih.	A city.
164.	酉	Yiu.	Liquors.
165.	采	Ts‘ai.	Splendor, to select.
166.	里	Li.	A mile.
	8 Strokes.		
167.	金	Kin.	Metal.
168.	長 镸	Ch‘ang.	Long.
169.	門	Men.	A gate.
170.	阜 阝	Feu.	A mound.
171.	隶	Ti.	To extend to.
172.	隹	Chüe.	Fowls.
173.	雨	Yü.	Rain.
174.	靑	Ts‘ing.	Green.
175.	非	Fe.	Wrong, not?
	9 Strokes.		
176.	面	Mien.	The face.
177.	革	Keh.	Skin, change.
178.	韋	We.	Leather.
179.	韭	Kiu.	Leeks.
180.	音	Yin.	Sound.
181.	頁	Yih.	Head, a leaf.
182.	風	Fung.	Wind, a custom.
183.	飛	Fe.	To fly.
184.	食	Shih.	To eat.
185.	首	Sheu.	The head.
186.	香	Hiang.	Incense.
	10 Strokes.		
187.	馬	Ma.	A horse.
188.	骨	Kuh.	Bones.
189.	高	Kau.	High.
190.	髟	Piau.	Long hair.
191.	鬥	Teu.	To quarrel.
192.	鬯	Ch‘ang.	A fragrant liquor.
193.	鬲	Keh, li.	A tripod, urn.
194.	鬼	Kwe.	A ghost, a devil.
	11 Strokes.		
195.	魚	Yü.	Fish.
196.	鳥	Niau.	A bird.
197.	鹵	Lu.	Brine.
198.	鹿	Luh.	A deer.
199.	麥	Meh.	Wheat.
200.	麻	Ma.	Hemp.
	12 Strokes.		
201.	黃	Hwang.	Yellow.
202.	黍	Shu.	Millet.
203.	黑	Heh.	Black.
204.	黹	Ch‘.	Embroidery.
	13 Strokes.		
205.	黽	Min.	A frog.
206.	鼎	Ting.	A tripod.
207.	鼓	Ku.	A drum.
208.	鼠	Shu.	A rat.
	14 Strokes.		
209.	鼻	Pih.	The nose.
210.	齊	Ch‘i.	Even, orderly
	15 Strokes.		
211.	齒	Ch‘.	The teeth.
212.	龍	Lung.	A Dragon.
	16 Strokes.		
213.	龜	Kwe.	A tortoise.
	17 Strokes.		
214.	龠	Yuh.	A flute.

A LIST OF PHONETIC CHINESE CHARACTERS

—Baller-Mandarin Primer.

Initials

ch	摺	*hs*	吸	*m*	麥	*r*	熱	*t'*	特
ch'	撤	*k*	格	*n*	助	*s*	色	*ts*	則
f	法	*k'*	客	*p*	白	*sh*	舌	*ts'*	側
h	黑	*l*	勒	*p'*	珀	*t*	得		

Finals

a	呵	*ai*	愛	*uei*	爲	*o*	我	*ueh*	或
ia	亞	*iai*	挨	*ie*	也	*ong*	甕	*ieh*	葉
ua	瓦	*uai*	外	*üe*	靴	*iong*	用	*üeh*	月
an	安	*æ*	遮	*ien*	言	*u*	五	*ïh*	直
uan	完	*en*	恩	*üen*	遠	*iu*	憂	*ih*	一
ang	昂	*uen*	文	*ï*	之	*ü*	魚	*oh*	惡
iang	央	*eng*	硬	*i*	衣	*ah*	啊	*ioh*	約
uang	望	*eo*	偶	*in*	印	*iah*	押	*uh*	兀
ao	奧	*ui*	追	*üin*	允	*uah*	襪	*iuh*	鬱
iao	要	*ei*	貝	*ing*	影	*eh*	額	*üh*	余

COMBINATIONS OF INITIALS AND FINALS IN REGULAR ORDER.

cha	渣	*chuen*	准	*ch‘ïh*	尺	*hai*	孩	*hsüen*	喧
ch‘a	茶	*ch‘uen*	春	*choh*	捉	*huai*	懷	*hsi*	希
chua	抓	*cheng*	正	*ch‘oh*	戳	*hen*	恨	*hsin*	欣
chan	暫	*ch‘eng*	成	*chuh*	竹	*huen*	昏	*hsüin*	薰
ch‘an	産	*cheo*	周	*ch‘uh*	出	*heng*	恒	*hsing*	興
chuan	專	*ch‘eo*	丑	*fan*	凡	*heo*	侯	*hsiong*	凶
ch‘uan	川	*chui*	追	*fang*	方	*huei*	灰	*hsiu*	休
chang	張	*ch‘ui*	吹	*fen*	分	*ho*	火	*hsü*	虛
ch‘ang	唱	*chï*	紙	*feng*	風	*hong*	烘	*hsiah*	瞎
chuang	莊	*ch‘ï*	痴	*feo*	否	*hu*	呼	*hsieh*	歇
ch‘uang	牀	*chong*	中	*fei*	非	*huah*	豁	*hsüeh*	血
chao	招	*ch‘ong*	寵	*fu*	夫	*heh*	黑	*hsih*	吸
ch‘ao	潮	*chu*	註	*fah*	罰	*hueh*	或	*hsioh*	學
chai	齋	*ch‘u*	除	*fuh*	福	*hoh*	合	*hsiuh*	畜
ch‘ai	柴	*chah*	閘	*ha*	哈	*huh*	忽	*kia*	加
chuai	跩	*ch‘ah*	插	*hua*	化	*hsia*	下	*k‘ia*	卡
ch‘uai	揣	*cheh*	折	*han*	汗	*hsiang*	香	*kua*	瓜
chæ	這	*ch‘eh*	屮	*huan*	渙	*hsiao*	孝	*k‘ua*	跨
ch‘æ	扯	*chueh*	拙	*hang*	杭	*hsiai*	鞋	*kan*	甘
chen	眞	*ch‘ueh*	輟	*huang*	皇	*hsüe*	靴	*k‘an*	看
ch‘en	臣	*chïh*	直	*hao*	好	*hsien*	顯	*kuan*	關

liu	溜	kuh	骨	ku	姑	keo	狗	k'uan	寬
lü	呂	k'uh	哭	k'u	枯	k'eo	口	kang	扛
lah	辣	küh	局	kiu	臼	kuei	跪	k'ang	康
leh	勒	k'üh	曲	k'iu	求	k'uei	葵	kiang	江
lieh	獵	la	拉	kü	居	k'üe	茄	k'iang	強
lih	力	lan	濫	k'ü	去	kien	件	kuang	光
loh	落	luan	亂	kiah	甲	k'ien	遣	k'uang	狂
lioh	略	lang	浪	k'iah	恰	küen	倦	kao	羔
luh	鹿	liang	涼	kuah	适	k'üen	拳	k'ao	靠
lüh	律	lao	勞	keh	格	ki	計	kiao	轎
ma	麻	liao	了	k'eh	客	k'i	其	k'iao	橋
man	慢	lai	來	kueh	國	kin	近	kai	該
mang	忙	luen	輪	k'ueh	闊	k'in	禽	k'ai	開
mao	毛	leng	稜	kieh	結	küin	郡	kiai	界
miao	苗	leo	樓	k'ieh	怯	k'üin	群	k'iai	楷
mai	買	lui	雷	küeh	掘	king	經	kuai	怪
men	門	lien	連	k'üeh	缺	k'ing	輕	k'uai	快
meng	蒙	li	利	kih	極	ko	戈	ken	根
meo	謀	lin	臨	k'ih	泣	k'o	科	k'en	肯
mei	美	ling	靈	koh	割	kong	共	kuen	棍
mien	眠	lo	羅	k'oh	渴	k'ong	孔	k'uen	困
mi	迷	long	弄	kioh	脚	kiong	迥	keng	梗
min	民	lu	盧	k'ioh	却	k'iong	窮	k'eng	鏗

日	*rïh*	坩	*p'eh*	排	*p'ai*	你	*ni*	明	*ming*
若	*roh*	別	*pieh*	本	*pen*	賃	*nin*	模	*mo*
肉	*ruh*	撇	*p'ieh*	盆	*p'en*	佞	*ning*	母	*mu*
洒	*sa*	筆	*pih*	崩	*peng*	懦	*no*	繆	*miu*
傘	*san*	匹	*p'ih*	朋	*p'eng*	農	*nong*	帓	*mah*
算	*suan*	撥	*poh*	裒	*p'eo*	奴	*nu*	麥	*meh*
喪	*sang*	潑	*p'oh*	貝	*pei*	牛	*niu*	滅	*mieh*
箱	*siang*	不	*puh*	配	*p'ei*	女	*nü*	蜜	*mih*
騷	*sao*	僕	*p'uh*	邊	*pien*	納	*nah*	末	*moh*
小	*siao*	染	*ran*	翩	*p'ien*	揑	*nieh*	目	*muh*
腮	*sai*	軟	*ruan*	避	*pi*	匿	*nih*	那	*na*
森	*sen*	讓	*rang*	皮	*p'i*	虐	*nioh*	難	*nan*
孫	*suen*	饒	*rao*	殯	*pin*	巴	*pa*	暖	*nuan*
生	*seng*	惹	*ræ*	貧	*p'in*	怕	*p'a*	囊	*nang*
叟	*seo*	人	*ren*	兵	*ping*	半	*pan*	娘	*niang*
隨	*sui*	閏	*ruen*	平	*p'ing*	伴	*p'an*	鬧	*nao*
謝	*sie*	仍	*reng*	波	*po*	幇	*pang*	鳥	*niao*
先	*sien*	柔	*reo*	婆	*p'o*	旁	*p'ang*	乃	*nai*
選	*süen*	蕊	*rui*	步	*pu*	報	*pao*	嫩	*nuen*
四	*sï*	兒	*rï*	普	*p'u*	跑	*p'ao*	能	*neng*
西	*si*	戎	*rong*	拔	*pah*	標	*piao*	耨	*neo*
心	*sin*	如	*ru*	拍	*p'ah*	瓢	*p'iao*	內	*nui*
巡	*süin*	熱	*reh*	白	*peh*	拜	*pai*	年	*nien*

sing	性	*shuai*	帥	*tao*	道	*tong*	洞	*ts'ang*	倉
so	所	*shœ*	舍	*t'ao*	桃	*t'ong*	同	*tsiang*	匠
song	送	*shen*	身	*tiao*	掉	*tu*	都	*ts'iang*	詳
su	蘇	*shuen*	瞬	*t'iao*	挑	*t'u*	屠	*tsao*	早
siu	脩	*sheng*	聖	*tai*	歹	*tiu*	丟	*ts'ao*	曹
sü	須	*sheo*	收	*t'ai*	臺	*tah*	達	*tsiao*	焦
sah	撒	*shui*	水	*tuen*	遁	*t'ah*	塔	*ts'iao*	樵
seh	色	*shï*	詩	*t'uen*	臀	*teh*	得	*tsai*	在
sieh	褻	*shu*	暑	*teng*	等	*t'eh*	特	*ts'ai*	菜
süeh	雪	*shah*	殺	*t'eng*	騰	*tieh*	疊	*tsen*	怎
sih	息	*shuah*	刷	*teo*	豆	*t'ieh*	帖	*ts'en*	參
soh	索	*sheh*	舌	*t'eo*	頭	*tih*	的	*tsuen*	尊
sioh	削	*shïh*	失	*tui*	兌	*t'ih*	踢	*ts'uen*	存
suh	速	*shoh*	勺	*t'ui*	頹	*toh*	奪	*tseng*	爭
süh	戌	*shuh*	叔	*tie*	爹	*t'oh*	脫	*ts'eng*	層
sha	沙	*ta*	大	*tien*	電	*tuh*	獨	*tseo*	走
shua	耍	*t'a*	他	*t'ien*	田	*t'uh*	禿	*ts'eo*	愁
shan	山	*tan*	單	*ti*	地	*tsa*	咱	*tsui*	罪
shuan	拴	*t'an*	談	*t'i*	題	*tsan*	簪	*ts'ui*	催
shang	上	*tuan*	短	*ting*	丁	*ts'an*	蠶	*tsie*	姐
shuang	爽	*t'uan*	團	*t'ing*	聽	*tsuan*	揝	*ts'ie*	且
shao	燒	*tang*	當	*to*	惰	*ts'uan*	篡	*tsien*	賤
shai	篩	*t'ang*	堂	*t'o*	陀	*tsang*	葬	*ts'ien*	千

七 *ts‘ih*	鑿 *tsoh*	撮 *ts‘oh*	爵 *tsioh*	雀 *ts‘ioh*	卒 *tsuh*	促 *ts‘uh*
擦 *ts‘ah*	則 *tseh*	側 *ts‘eh*	節 *tsieh*	切 *ts‘ieh*	絕 *tsüeh*	疾 *tsih*
助 *tsu*	鋤 *ts‘u*	揪 *tsiu*	囚 *ts‘iu*	聚 *tsü*	取 *ts‘ü*	雜 *tsah*
俊 *tsüin*	井 *tsing*	清 *ts‘ing*	做 *tso*	錯 *ts‘o*	宗 *tsong*	從 *ts‘ong*
全 *ts‘üen*	子 *tsï*	慈 *ts‘ï*	祭 *tsi*	齊 *ts‘i*	盡 *tsin*	親 *ts‘in*

THE RADICALS: WRITTEN STYLE

		2	3	4	5	6	7	8	9	10		
1	一	丨	丶	丿	乙	亅	二	亠	人	儿	入	11
12	八	冂	冖	冫	几	凵	刀	力	勹	匕	匚	22
23	匸	十	卜	卩	厂	厶	又	口	囗	土	士	33
34	夂	夊	夕	大	女	子	宀	寸	小	尢	尸	44
45	屮	山	巛	工	己	巾	干	幺	广	廴	廾	55
56	弋	弓	彐	彡	彳	心	戈	戶	手	支	攴	66
67	文	斗	斤	方	无	日	曰	月	木	欠	止	77
78	歹	殳	毋	比	毛	氏	气	水	火	爪	父	88
89	爻	爿	片	牙	牛	犬	玄	玉	瓜	瓦	甘	99
100	生	用	田	疋	疒	癶	白	皮	皿	目	矛	110
111	矢	石	示	禸	禾	穴	立	竹	米	糸	缶	121
122	网	羊	羽	老	而	耒	耳	聿	肉	臣	自	132
133	至	臼	舌	舛	舟	艮	色	艸	虍	虫	血	143
144	行	衣	襾	見	角	言	谷	豆	豕	豸	貝	154
155	赤	走	足	身	車	辛	辰	辵	邑	酉	釆	165
166	里	金	長	門	阜	隶	隹	雨	青	非	面	176
177	革	韋	韭	音	頁	風	飛	食	首	香	馬	187
188	骨	高	髟	鬥	鬯	鬲	鬼	魚	鳥	鹵	鹿	198
199	麥	麻	黃	黍	黑	黹	黽	鼎	鼓	鼠	鼻	209
				齊	齒	龍	龜	龠				
				210	211	212	213	214				

JAPANESE

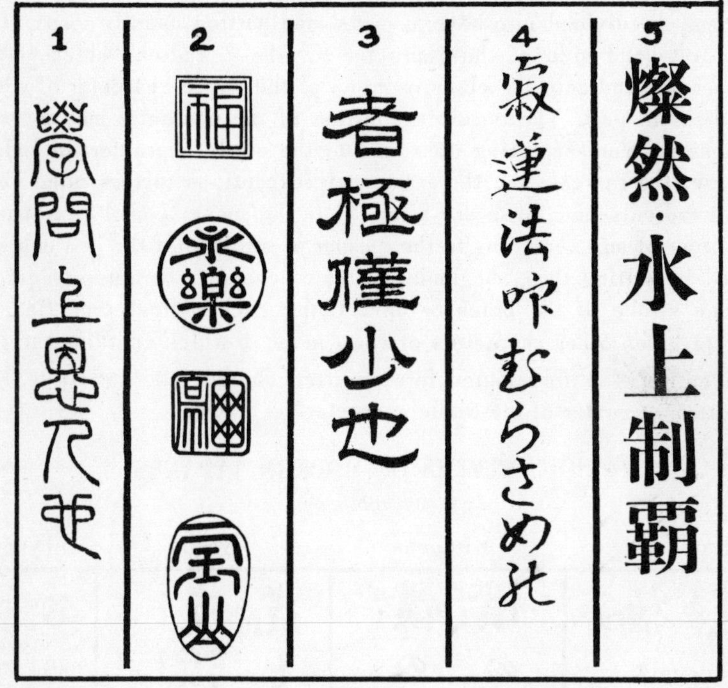

1. Tensho. 2. Old Seal. 3. Reisho. 4. Manyogana. 5. Kanji.

Oriental. Spoken by about 90,000,000 people in Japan. Japanese is a polysyllabic language and is written in phonetic symbols called *kana* of which there are two syllabaries in common use, and *kanji* or Chinese characters. The *kana* syllabaries are: 1–*Katakana*–square characters derived from Chinese characters or portions of Chinese characters. 2–*Hiragana*–cursive *kana* derived from Chinese cursive characters. Older *kana* (now rarely used) are: *Hentaigana* or other syllabaries such as *Yamato-Kana, Manyogana,* all of which were taken from Chinese characters for their phonetic values.

The kana syllabaries are commonly arranged in native dictionaries in the order of the syllables in a verse called *iroha,* an ancient Japanese poem which contains all of the syllables of the language (see *Hiragana* table); or *go-ju-on,* or "fifty sounds" (see *Katakana* table).

The Chinese characters or *kanji* which were borrowed from China remain for the most part unchanged and are identical with characters in modern Chinese, but the sense or meaning of a character in Japanese does not necessarily obtain in Chinese; however, in many instances the characters have the same values in both languages. Japanese-Chinese characters may be divided into several parts—one portion usually to be found on the left hand side of the character may be a radical which may in some measure indicate the class or group of the whole character of which the radical is part. The remaining portion of the character may serve as the phonetic, thus imparting its sound to the whole character—including, of course, the radical. But there are many exceptions to this rule. There are 214 radicals and these are arranged in Japanese (*kanji*) dictionaries in the order of and according to the number of strokes (of the pen or brush) required in writing them, beginning with, of course, characters requiring only one stroke of the brush or pen. Under each radical then (in word lists) are given other characters of *kanji*, each of which contains the radical in entirety or abbreviated form, written on the left (usually), right, top, bottom or center of the whole character.

VARIOUS STYLES OF MODERN JAPANESE

(Kanji with Kana)

Katakana	Hiragana	Gyōsho	Types
橋ノ近クニ交番所ガアリマス 道ノ側ニ郵便箱ガアリマス	僕の父は役所へ行きました 僕の兄は學校へ行きました	支流は東京灣に注ぎます 虎も獅子の様に強くあります	世界の若人六千を集めて勇しく正しく技 術大障碍を最後に二週余にわたる全競技

THE JAPANESE SYLLABARIES

1. KATAKANA (GOJUON)

ア a	イ i	ウ u	エ e	オ o
カ ka	キ ki	ク ku	ケ ke	コ ko
サ sa	シ shi	ス su	セ se	ソ so
タ ta	チ chi	ツ tsu	テ te	ト to
ナ na	ニ ni	ヌ nu	ネ ne	ノ no
ハ ha	ヒ hi	フ fu	ヘ he	ホ ho
マ ma	ミ mi	ム mu	メ me	モ mo
ヤ ya	イ (y)i	ユ yu	エ ye	ヨ yo
ラ ra	リ ri	ル ru	レ re	ロ ro
ワ wa	ヰ (w)i	ウ (w)u	ヱ (w)e	ヲ (w)o

2. HIRAGANA (IROHA)

い i	ろ ro	は ha	に ni	ほ ho
へ he	と to	ち chi	り ri	ぬ nu
る ru	を wo	わ wa	か ka	よ yo
た ta	れ re	そ so	つ tsu	ね ne
な na	ら ra	む mu	う u	ゐ i
の no	お o	く ku	や ya	ま ma
け ke	ふ fu	こ ko	え ye	て te
あ a	さ sa	き ki	ゆ yu	め me
み mi	し shi	ゑ e	ひ hi	も mo
せ se	す su	ん n		

ン —n (katakana)

In Japanese a Chinese character, depending upon its use may have several sounds or *on* as they are called, such as *Kan-on* of north China of the Han Dynasty (circa 206-250 B.C.O.), *Go-on* of South Shanghai Province (circa 300 A.D.), or *To-on* of the Tang Dynasty (circa 700-900 A.D.). These, of course, derive their names from the periods during which times the characters were introduced into Japan from China. Further, most Chinese characters possess native Japanese sounds which generally obtain when the character is isolated or is compounded with other Chinese characters with native Japanese sounds. But Japanese-Chinese characters usually possess one or other *on* sounds when part of a compound of two or more consecutive Chinese characters.

THE EPISTOLARY STYLE
(Sorobun)

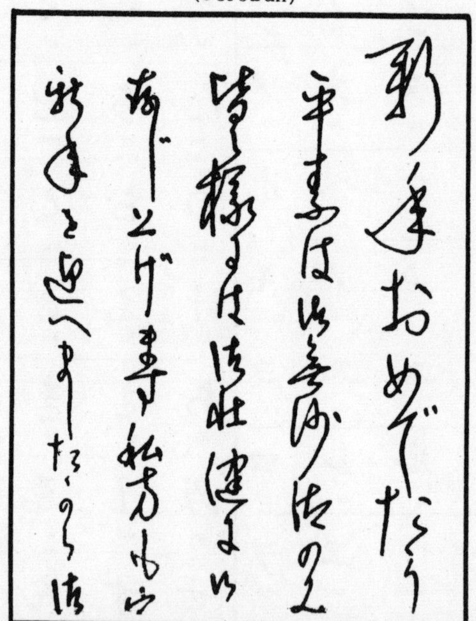

Japanese texts are usually written or printed in *kanji* with *kana* added for verbal terminations, etc. Such text is called *kana-majiri* (kana mixed in). Often additional *kana* characters are written on the right side of the *kanji* characters to simplify the text for those who cannot read *kanji*. Japanese books for adults and newspapers are usually printed in *kanji* and *hiragana*, telegrams and children's books are frequently printed or written in *katakana* with perhaps a few Chinese characters. Japanese written in Roman characters is called *Romaji;* the letters are *Romajiki*.

Common styles of writing *kanji* are: 1-*Kaisho*—square Chinese characters. 2-*Mincho*—standard *kanji* types. 3-*Gyōsho*—a semi-cursive style called "running hand." 4-*Sōsho*—Chinese characters abbreviated, written in cursive hand, called "grass writing." 5-*Reisho*—archaic Chinese characters in use about 1000 years ago. Mainly employed in inscriptions on monuments, tablets, etc. 6-*Tensho*—archaic Chinese characters of about 2000 years ago, used in book titles, seals and stamps (*Inban*-signature stamp) pottery, porcelain, kakemono markings, etc. Common Japanese styles, each with peculiarities of construction and grammar are: 1-*Bungotai*—the written language so-called. 2-*Kogobun*—the colloquial. 3-*Sōrōbun* or epistolary style. 4-*Kanbun*—old *kanji*. The standard dialect of Japanese is the so-called Tokyō dialect spoken in the capital.

Changes in consonantal compounds in some syllabics are shown thus: Two dots (゛) written on the upper right side of the character causes the changes—HA to BA, HO to BO, TE to DE, CHI to JI, TA to DA, SO to ZO, TSU to ZU, FU to BU, KO to GO, TO to DO, SA to ZA, KI to GI, SHI to JI, HI to BI, SE to ZE. The mark (゜) written on the upper right side of a kana syllabic causes the following sound changes: HA to PA, HO to PO, FU to PU, HI to PI.

ga	za	da	ba	pa
ガ が	ザ ざ	ダ だ	バ ば	パ ぱ
gi	ji	ji	bi	pi
ギ ぎ	ジ じ	ヂ ぢ	ビ び	ピ ぴ
gu	zu	zu	bu	pu
グ ぐ	ズ ず	ヅ づ	ブ ぶ	プ ぷ
ge	ze	de	be	pe
ゲ げ	ゼ ぜ	デ で	ベ べ	ペ ぺ
go	zo	do	bo	po
ゴ ご	ゾ ぞ	ド ど	ボ ぼ	ポ ぽ

The letters B, D, J, K, M, P, S, T, are pronounced as in English. A–*father* but slightly shorter; Ā–*father;* I–*pig;* U–*pull;* Ū–OO in *pool;* E–*red* or nearly A in *day;* O–*bone* but shorter; Ō–*bone.* The long vowels are prolonged or pronounced nearly as if doubled, thus O in Tokyo is pronounced nearly oh-oh. The vowel U commonly is elided when it precedes MA. The vowel E, when initial, is pronounced YE as in *yet.* Long E is written II and pronounced like EE in *beer;* long E is written EI and pronounced like A in *day.* In diphthongs AI, AU, EO, OU, each vowel retains its own sound but the first vowel is pronounced a little stronger.

F–about like F in *far* but pronounced with rounded lips; G–*get;* H–*hat;* L is not used in Japanese. This sound is replaced by R in transliterating foreign names; N–*not,* but about like NG or NK, G and K, but before M, B, P, N–M; R–*red* but nearly D in Satsuma; SH–*shut;* TS–*sets;* Y–*yet;* Z–*zest.* Double consonants:–KK, MM, NN, SS, TT, SSH–both consonants have about equal stress.

Some consonants undergo change when the word which begins with one of them is the second component of a compound. This change is called *nigori,* meaning "muddling": F and H become B; K becomes G; S and TS become Z; SH and CH become J; T becomes D. The letters Y or W are sometimes inserted between two vowels. The vowels I, U, in syllables are commonly elided in the colloquial:–SHI, SU, FU, KI, HI, SH', S', F', K', H', SH'. W is often changed to H (wa to ha); Wo is often changed to O (wo to o); W when initial usually becomes O except in the common particles wo. H followed by a vowel becomes WA or is silent.

Accent: Stress is usually upon the first syllable in words of two syllables except when this syllable is short I or U followed by a long vowel. In words of three syllables stress is usually upon the penultimate.

NENGO CHARACTERS

An	安	Ho	鳳	Ko	康	Ro	老	Tai	大
Chi	治	Ji	字	Ko	護	Roku	祿	Tai	泰
Chi	雉	Jiu	壽	Ko	衡	Roku	錄	Tei	貞
Chiu	中	Ka	嘉	K'wa	化	Sei	齊	Tei	禎
Cho	長	Kei	景	K'wan	觀	Shi	至	Ten	天
Do	同	Kei	慶	K'wan	寬	Shin	神	Toku	德
Do	銅	Ken	建	Kyo	亨	Sho	勝	U	烏
F'ku	福	Ken	乾	Man	萬	Sho	承	Un	雲
Gen	元	Ki	亀	Mei	明	Sho	昌	Wa	和
Hak	白	Ki	喜	Mon*	文	Sho	正	Wo	應
Hei	平	Ki	龜	Nin	仁	Sho	祥	Yei	永
Ho	寶	Kiu	久	Rei	靈	Shiu	朱	Yen	廷
Ho	保	Kits'	吉	Reki	曆	So	祚	Yo	養

OLD JAPANESE KANA

1	2	3a	3b	4	5	6	
伊	イ	以	以	い	以	い	*i*
呂	ロ	呂	呂	ろ	呂	ろ	*ro*
八	ハ	波	波	は	波	は	*ha*
仁	ニ	仁	尓	に	仁	に	*ni*
保	ホ	保	本	ほ	保	ほ	*ho*
乀	ヘ	皿	弊	へ	皿	へ	*he*
止	ト	登	登	と	登	止	*to*
千	チ	知	知	ち	知	ち	*chi*
利	リ	利	里	り	利	り	*ri*
奴	ヌ	奴	奴	ぬ	奴	ぬ	*nu*
流	ル	留	留	る	留	る	*ru*
乎	ヲ	遠	越	を	越	を	*wo*
和	ワ	和	和	わ	和	わ	*wa*
加	カ	迦	加	か	加	か	*ka*
與	ヨ	與	与	よ	與	よ	*yo*
多	タ	大	多	た	多	た	*ta*
礼	レ	禮	禮	れ	禮	れ	*re*
曽	ソ	曾	曾	そ	曾	そ	*so*
州	ツ	津	津	つ	津	つ	*tsu*
子	ネ	禰	禰	ね	禰	ね	*ne*
奈	ナ	奈	那	な	奈	な	*na*
良	ラ	良	良	ら	良	ら	*ra*
牟	ム	武	武	む	武	む	*mu*
宇	ウ	宇	宇	う	宇	う	*u*

1	2	3a	3b	4	5	6	
井	井	爲	為	ゐ	為	ゐ	*wi*
乃	ノ	乃	廼	の	乃	の	*no*
於	オ	於	於	お	於	お	*o*
久	ク	久	久	く	久	具	*ku*
也	ヤ	也	夜	や	也	也	*ya*
末	マ	萬	萬	ま	万	ま	*ma*
介	ケ	計	計	け	計	け	*ke*
不	フ	不	婦	ふ	不	不	*fu*
己	コ	己	古	こ	古	己	*ko*
江	エ	江	江	え	衣	江	*e*
天	テ	天	天	て	天	て	*te*
阿	ア	安	安	あ	阿	あ	*a*
薩	サ	佐	佐	さ	佐	さ	*sa*
幾	キ	幾	幾	き	幾	き	*ki*
弓	ユ	由	遊	ゆ	由	ゆ	*yu*
女	メ	女	免	め	免	め	*me*
三	ミ	美	美	み	美	み	*mi*
之	シ	之	之	し	志	し	*shi*
慧	ヱ	恵	恵	ゑ	恵	ゑ	*ye*
比	ヒ	飛	飛	ひ	比	ひ	*hi*
毛	モ	毛	毛	も	毛	も	*mo*
世	セ	世	世	せ	世	せ	*se*
須	ス	寸	寸	す	寸	す	*su*
	ン						*n*

LANGUAGES OF THE PACIFIC

UMA OKA (Nukahiva-Marquesas)

Most of the languages spoken in the south Pacific Islands belong to the Malayo-Polynesian group of the Austric language Family. The chief language groups of the Pacific Islands are:

I. INDONESIAN or MALAYAN: Malay, Javanese, Balinese, Madurese, Philippine Islands group, Malagasy (Madagascar).

II. MELANESIAN: Fijian, Solomon Islands and other islands of the south Pacific.

III. MICRONESIAN: Caroline Islands, Marshall Islands, Gilbert Islands, Marianas, Yap.

IV. POLYNESIAN: Hawaiian, Samoan, Tahitian, Maori (New Zealand)

V. PAPUAN: New Guinea, etc.

Very few of the south seas languages have native alphabets but are usually written in the Roman alphabet or Arabic characters with certain additional diacritical marks for transliterations of native sounds.

ALPHABETS OF THE PACIFIC

	1	2	3	4	5	6	7	8	9	10
a	[illegible]	[illegible]				[illegible]			[illegible]	[illegible]
i	[illegible]	[illegible]				[illegible]			[illegible]	[illegible]
u	[illegible]	[illegible]				[illegible]			[illegible]	[illegible]
e	[illegible]	[illegible]								
o	[illegible]	[illegible]								
ka	[illegible]	[illegible]	[illegible]	[illegible]	[illegible]	[illegible]	[illegible]	[illegible]	[illegible]	[illegible]
kha	[illegible]									
ga	[illegible]	[illegible]	[illegible]	[illegible]	[illegible]	[illegible]	[illegible]	[illegible]	[illegible]	[illegible]
gha	[illegible]									
ṅa	[illegible]	[illegible]	[illegible]	[illegible]	[illegible]	[illegible]	[illegible]	[illegible]	[illegible]	
ča	[illegible]	[illegible]	[illegible]	[illegible]	[illegible]	[illegible]	[illegible]	[illegible]		
čha	[illegible]									
ǧa	[illegible]	[illegible]	[illegible]	[illegible]	[illegible]	[illegible]	[illegible]	[illegible]		
ǧha	[illegible]			[illegible]	[illegible]					
ña	[illegible]	[illegible]	[illegible]	[illegible]	[illegible]	[illegible]	[illegible]	[illegible]		
ṭa	[illegible]	[illegible]	[illegible]							
ṭha	[illegible]									
ḍa	[illegible]	[illegible]	[illegible]							
ḍha	[illegible]									
ṇa	[illegible]									
ta	[illegible]	[illegible]	[illegible]	[illegible]		[illegible]	[illegible]	[illegible]	[illegible]	[illegible]
tha	[illegible]									
da	[illegible]	[illegible]	[illegible]	[illegible]	[illegible]	[illegible]	[illegible]	[illegible]	[illegible]	[illegible]
dha	[illegible]									
na	[illegible]	[illegible]	[illegible]	[illegible]	[illegible]	[illegible]	[illegible]	[illegible]	[illegible]	[illegible]
pa	[illegible]	[illegible]	[illegible]		[illegible]	[illegible]	[illegible]	[illegible]	[illegible]	[illegible]
pha	[illegible]									
ba	[illegible]	[illegible]	[illegible]		[illegible]	[illegible]	[illegible]	[illegible]	[illegible]	[illegible]
bha	[illegible]									
ma	[illegible]	[illegible]	[illegible]	[illegible]	[illegible]	[illegible]	[illegible]	[illegible]	[illegible]	[illegible]
ya	[illegible]	[illegible]	[illegible]	[illegible]	[illegible]	[illegible]	[illegible]	[illegible]	[illegible]	
ra	[illegible]	[illegible]	[illegible]	[illegible]	[illegible]	[illegible]	[illegible]	[illegible]		
la	[illegible]	[illegible]	[illegible]	[illegible]	[illegible]	[illegible]	[illegible]	[illegible]	[illegible]	[illegible]
va	[illegible]	[illegible]	[illegible]	[illegible]	[illegible]	[illegible]	[illegible]	[illegible]	[illegible]	
sa	[illegible]	[illegible]	[illegible]	[illegible]	[illegible]	[illegible]	[illegible]	[illegible]	[illegible]	[illegible]
śa	[illegible]									
ṣa	[illegible]									
ha	[illegible]	[illegible]	[illegible]	[illegible]	[illegible]	[illegible]	[illegible]	[illegible]	[illegible]	[illegible]

1. Sinhalese; 2. and 3. Javanese; 4. Rejang; 5. Lampung; 6. Batta; 7. Macassar; 8. Bugis; 9. Tagalog; 10. Bisayan.

Languages spoken in the Philippines

Spanish	Bisayan
English	Moro
Bicol	Pampangan
Cebuan	Panayan
Ibanag	Pangasinan
Ifugao	Samareño
Bontoc Igorot	Tagalog
Ilocano	Zambal

Malayan is spoken in the Straits regions and in the eastern Pacific Islands; Dutch is the official language of the government of the Netherlands East Indies and English is spoken in Australia, New Zealand and other British possessions and the possessions of the United States in the South Seas.

Pidgin, a native vernacular, consisting of English or Malayan with native words, is spoken by many of the natives in Oceania when conversing with foreigners. Pidgin (the word is derived from "business") is a simplified form of a language.

Languages of Australia and New Zealand

Aranda	Central Australia
Awabakal	New South Wales
Dieri	South Australia
Maori	New Zealand
Narrinyeri	Murray River, South Australia
Worrora	Northwest Australia

Melanesian, Polynesian Languages and Dialects of the Pacific Islands

Aniwa	New Hebrides
Aranda	Cent. Australia
Bicol	Philippines
Binanderi	Papua
Cebuan	Philippines
Chamorro	Guam
Dyak	Borneo, Sarawak
Epi	New Hebrides
Eromanga	New Hebrides
Fiji	Fiji Islands
Gilbert Island	Gilbert Island
Guadalcanar	Guadalcanar
Houailou	New Caledonia
Ibanag	Philippines
Ifugao	Philippines
Igorot	Philippines
Ilocano	Philippines

Madurese	Dutch E. Indies
Malekula	New Hebrides
Maori	New Zealand
Marquesas	Marquesas
Marshall Islands	Marshall Islands
Moro	Sulu Archipelago
Mortlock	Caroline Islands
Mwala	Solomon Islands
Narrinyeri	Australia
New Britain	New Britain
Pampangan	Philippines
Panayan	Philippines
Pangasinan	Philippines
Patpatar	New Britain
Ponape	Caroline Islands
Rarotonga	Cook Islands
Rotuma	Rotuma Islands
Samareño	Philippines
San Cristoval	Solomon Islands
Samoan	Samoa
Sangir	Philippines
Santa Cruz	Santa Cruz Island
Santo	New Hebrides
Sarawak	No. Borneo
Sundanese	Dutch E. Indies
Tagalog	Philippines
Tahitian	Tahiti
Tanna	New Hebrides
Tonga	Tonga Islands
Torres Island	Torres, New Hebrides
Tubetube	New Guinea
Ulawa	Solomon Islands
Uvea	Loyalty Islands
Vella Lavella	Solomon Islands
Wedau	New Guinea
Windessi	Dutch New Guinea
Yabim	New Guinea
Zia	New Guinea

MALAY

Karena demikianlah Allah mengasihi isi doenia ini, sehingga diberinja Anaknja jang toenggal itoe, soepaja barang siapa jang pertjaja akan dia djangan ia binasa, melainkan beroléh hidoep jang kekal.

Malay. Malayo-Polynesian. Roman alphabet or Arabic alphabet. Spoken in the Straits Settlements, Java, Sumatra, Borneo, Timor, Celebes and other islands in the East Indies.

Consonants are pronounced about as in English. The letter K as final is barely pronounced. R is pronounced with a ringing sound.

A—*father;* E—*met* but shorter; I—*machine,* but short I as in *pin* before N except as initial; O—*whole* as initial, otherwise O—*horse;* U—OO in *boot;* AI—*aisle;* AU—OW in *how.*

Arabic vowel points are: *Baris di-ates* (ـَ) A, E; *Baris di-bawah* (ـِ) I, E; *Baris di-hadapan* (ـُ) U, O; *Medda* (ـٓ) A;

Tashdid (ـّ) sign of doubling of the letter so marked; *Wasl* (ٱ) *Hamza* (ء) indicates guttural H sound before the letter so marked; *Anka* (٢) indicates doubling of a word.

Arabic Characters

مك سورڠ ڤون بلوم نايك كشرڬ

ملينكن يڠ سده تورن دري شرڬ ايت ، يأيت انق مانسي يڠ اد دشرڬ .

اد ڤون سڤريت موسى سده منايقكن اولر دتانه بلنتارا ايت ، بڬيتو جوڬ

هاروسله انق مانسي ڤون دنايقكن ، سڤاي بارڠسياڤ يڠ ڤرچاي ايت براوله

There are many Malay dialects. The above specimen is High Malay. Some others are: Low Malay, Baba Malay, Samsan Malay, etc.

JAVANESE

[illegible] 1915

°	k g	ṅ	h ः	-	χ γ
a,a̤	č ǰ	ń	-	y	-
e o	ṭ ḍ	ṇ	ṣ	r	-
i u	t d	n	s	l	z
	p b	m	-	v	f

Lepsius

Malayo-Polynesian. Javanese characters. Spoken by about 20,000,000 people in the Island of Java. The Javanese alphabet consists of 20 consonants or *aksara,* and 5 vowels. These letters are called *Aksara Jawa.* There are also 20 auxiliary signs called *Aksara Pasang'un*, with similar phonetic values but used to suppress the inherent vowel sounds. Three of the *Pasang'un* are written after *Aksara* letters, others are written below. The *Sandag'an* or "clothes" letters are written in full form when used alone but are abbreviated when used with consonants. These are written sometimes above, sometimes below the consonants.

The vowel marks are: *pepet* (E̥) written above the consonant; *wulu* (I) written above the consonant; *suku* (U) written below the letter; *taling-tarung* (O) written before and after the letter; *pinkal* (Y) written after the letter; *shakra* (R) written after the letter; *keret* (R̥) written after the letter; *lagar* (R) written at the end; *wignan* (H̥) written at the end; *sheshak* (Ṅ) written over the letter, *taling* (E) written before the letter.

	NA		NĚ
	NI		NU
	NE		NO
	-N		NAH
	NANG		NAR

Other points are: *nga' a lalet,* pronounced LE, and *pacherak,* pronounced RE. The marks of *pangkun* after a consonant serves as a mark of elision destroying the final vowel. Some Javanese dialects are: Balinese, Madurese, and Sundanese.

DYAK

Krana kalotä kapaham Hatalla djari sinta kalunen, sampai iä djari manenga Anake idjä tonggal, nakara genegenep olo, idjä pertjaja huang iä, djaton banasa, tapi bara pambelom idjä katatahi.

Spoken in Sarawak and the Netherlands Borneo.

BUGIS

Malayo-Polynesian. Celebes. Bugis characters. Consonants are syllabics with inherent A' vowels. Coalescent vowels are: *Ana irate* ( )–I; *Ana irawa* ( )–U; *Ana ri-boko* ( )–E; *Ana ri-yolo* ( )–O.

BATAK

Malayo-Polynesian: Sumatra Malacca group. Batta characters. Consonants are syllabics with inherent A vowels. Vowel points are: Initial A ( ); I–( ); U–( ); Medial and final U–( ); O–( ); A–( ). E–( ) at beginning of a consonant. Dialects: Toba, Dairi, Mandailung.

MACASSAR

Malayo-Polynesian. Celebes. Macassar characters or Bugis letters. Spoken by about 300,000 people in the Celebes.

TAGALOG AND BISAYAN

17 Sapagka't hindi sinugo ng̃ Dios
[g]ang Anak sa sanglibutan upang ha-
tulan ang sanglibutan; [i]kundi upang
ang sanglibutan ay maligtas sa pa-
mamagitan niya.

Malayan: Philippines. Tagalog is the most important native tongue of the Philippine Islands. The Tagalog and Bisayan alphabets resemble Sindhi and Multani letters of India from which they were probably derived. When written in native characters the vowels E, I, are not written, the vowel O is indicated by a dot written under the consonant and sounded after the letter so marked.

FIJI

Ni sa lomani ira na kai vuravura vakaoqo na Kalou, me solia kina na Luvena e dua bauga sa vakatubura me kakua ni rusa ko ira yadua era sa vakabauti koya, me ra rawata ga na bula tawa mudu.

Melanesian. Roman alphabet. Spoken in the Fiji Islands.

MWALA

Uria na tha God e liothau una eri ana fanua nei iano, nia ka falea mai tee fa Kaluwane nia, fasia ni tei bana na kai fitoona ka ai si sui, ma kai to ana marukia tatha.

Melanesian. Roman alphabet. Spoken on Malayta Island in the Solomons Islands group. Dialects: Fiu, Lau, Saa, Malu, Kwara'ae.

GUADALCANAR

Matena God e veila koaza na maramana, me mololuani a Dalena na vasu pesehe, ti asei te tutunina ke tau mate, ma ti ke taho nina na maurisali tuhudani matena.

Melanesian. Roman alphabet. Spoken in Guadalcanar in the Solomon Islands group.

CHAMORRO

Sa taegüenao na jaguaeya si Yuus y tano, janae ni linilsja Lajiña y para todo ayo y jumonggue güe, ti siña malingo, ya guaja linâlâña na taejinecog.

Spoken by the Chamorros on the Island of Guam.

HOUAILOU

We, na do meari ve kauau boejë na Bao, na bori kayai mi o xiē ka do rhaxaro, ceki da mè na dexa kamo rai pai pa tanewei ē, ae nè ye ma wi na moru xere ka ye da tawai seri.

Spoken in New Caledonia.

TOARIPI

Ipi Ualare mearovaekala maeaforoe mōri leipe Aré Areve Atute farakeka hariala miarōpe, ipi Arero sukaerereaita lĕa karu foromaila levi saroroapai roi; a-, eré peeita makuri ōvai veia.

Papuan. Spoken in New Guinea.

RAROTONGA

I'aroa mai te Atua i to tei ao nei, kua tae rava ki te oronga anga mae i tana Tamaiti anau tai, kia kore e mate te akarongo iaia kia rauka ra te ora mutu kore.

Spoken in Cook Islands.

HAWAIIAN

No ke mea, ua aloha nui mai ke Akua i ko ke ao nei, nolaila ua haawi mai oia i kana Keiki hiwahiwa i ole e make ka mea manaoio ia ia, aka, e loaa ia ia ke ola mau loa.

A E I O U. H, K, L, M, N, P, W

Polynesian. Roman alphabet. Spoken in the Hawaiian Islands. The Hawaiian language has only 12 letters. Diphthongs are: AI, AO, AU,

EI, EU, OU. Every word ends with a vowel; every syllable ends with a vowel. No two consonants are properly written together but are usually divided by vowels. The guttural break (') indicates omission of the letter K.

The consonants are pronounced about as in English. A—*father;* E—*vein;* I long—*machine;* O—*over;* U—*rule;* W—*water* but like V in *vest* as initial. Stress is usually on the first syllable.

SAMOAN

Aua ua faapea lava ona alofa mai o le Atua i le lalolagi ua ia au mai ai lona Atalii e toatasi, ina ia le fano se tasi e faatuatua ia te ia a ia maua e ia le ola e faavavau.

A E I O U F G L M N P S T V

Malayan: Polynesian group. Spoken in the Samoan Islands. Samoan dipthongs are: AE, AI, AU, EI, OU. There is also a sound between H and K with consonantal value, called the break ('). Every letter is distinctly sounded. The letters K and R are used in foreign words and D in foreign words becomes T, PH—F, Ç or hard C—K. In some foreign names H is changed to S. Accent is generally on the penultimate syllable.

TAHITIAN

I aroha mai te Atua i to te ao, e ua tae roa i te horoa mai i ta'na Tamaiti fanau tahi, ia ore ia pohe te faaroo ia 'na ra, ia roaa ra te ora mure ore.

Polynesian. Roman alphabet. Spoken in the Tahitian Islands. Consonants are pronounced about as in English. The letters B and D are rarely used but P and T are sometimes used instead. A—*father;* E—A in *day;* I—*machine;* O—*lone;* U—OO on *boot;* AI—*aisle;* OU—OW in *how.* Generally all syllables have equal stress.

MAORI

Koia ano te aroha o te Atua ki te ao homai ana e ia tana Tama kotahi, kia kahore ai e ngaro e tangata e whakapono ana ki a ia ,engari kia whiwhi ai ki te ora tonu.

Polynesian. Roman alphabet. Spoken by the aborigines of New Zealand.

AWABAKAL

Yanti kiloa, wiyan baġ nurun unnuġ ta pitål kåtan mikan ta aġelo ka Eloi koba wakål lin ba yarakai-willuġ minki kånůn.

Spoken in New South Wales, Australia.

NARRINYERI

Lun ellin Jehovah an Pornun an Narrinyeri: pempir ile ityan kinauwe Brauwarate, ungunuk korn wurruwarrin ityan, nowaiy el itye moru kellangk, tumbewarrin itye kaldowamp.

Spoken in the lower Murray River region in South Australia.

AUSTRALIAN PICTURE WRITING

AMERICAN INDIAN LANGUAGES

PICTURE WRITING

Formerly North and South America was inhabited by Indians of many tribes and languages. In Central America about 20 language families are known. In South America about 80 language families are recorded. The earliest languages of Central America are the Mayan group and the Arawak and Carib groups in the West Indies and the Quichuan families of the Inca nations.

Chief Languages of Hispano-America

Argentina	Guarani	Honduras	Miskito
Bolivia	Aymara, Quechua	Mexico	Aztec, Otomi, Mayan, Zapotec
Brazil	Guarani, Tupi	Nicaragua	Miskito
Costa Rica	Bribri	Paraguay	Guarani
Ecuador	Quechua	Peru	Aguaruna, Quechua
Guatemala	Cakchiquel, Quiche	Surinam	Arawak
Guiana	Arawak		

Some Chief Languages of British America and the United States

1, ALGONQUIN: (eastern Canada and eastern United States) Penobscot, Massachusetts, Natick, Narraganset, Delaware, Mohican, Micmac,

Cree. (western tribes) Sac, Fox, Ojibwa, Peoria, Kickapoo, Illinois, Miami, Menominee, Pottawotomi (far west) Arapahoe Blackfoot, Cheyenne.

2. ATHAPASCAN (northwestern Canada, California): Hupa, Mattole, (southwest U. S.) Apache, Navaho.

3. IROQUOIAN: Iroquois, Mohawk, Oneida, Onandaga, Cayuga, Seneca, Wyandotte or Huron, Cherokee, Tuscarora.

4. MUSHKOGEAN: Chickasaw, Choctaw, Creek, Seminole.

5. SIOUAN or SIOUX: Assiniboin, Crow, Dakota, Iowa, Kansas, Missouri, Ogalala, Omaha, Osage, Mandan, Teton, Winnebago.

6. UTO-AZTECAN: Piman in Mexico and California, Shoshonean, consisting of Comanche, Hopi, Paiute, Shoshoni.

7. NAHUATLAN: Aztec.

8. ESKIMO: Greeland, Labrador, Aleut.

Before the introduction of letters and written characters, the North American Indians wrote simple pictographs on dressed deer or buffalo skin, stones or totem poles. Most of the Indian languages are now written in Roman characters with diacritical marks provided for transliterating peculiar native sounds. It is estimated that more than 1,500,000 Indians of more than 50 language families inhabited the United States and British America in the late 17th century—today the Indian population in these regions perhaps does not exceed 250,000. Still, about 15,000,000 Indians speak a number of native languages in Central and South America and the West Indies.

MAYA

American Indian: Mayance. The Mayas formerly inhabited Guatemala, Honduras, Chiapas and Yucatan (c. 370 B.C.?–540 A.D.?). Their writings consisted of ideographic symbols and phonetic characters commonly called glyphs. The Maya alphabet was discovered by Diego de Landa, Bishop of Yucatan (1524-79) who also published a list of the day and month signs.

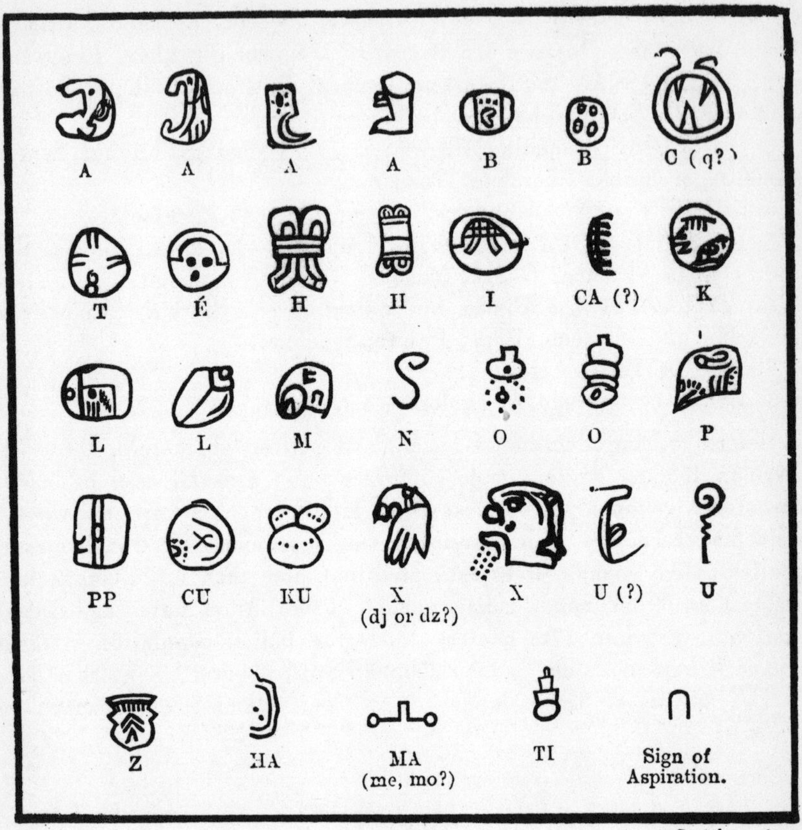

A A A A B B C (q?)

T É H H I CA (?) K

L L M N O O P

PP CU KU X (dj or dz?) X U (?) U

Z HA MA (me, mo?) TI Sign of Aspiration.

Smithsonian

The Maya calendar year had 365 days to which was added 5 "unlucky" days, or a short count year of 260 days, divided into 18 month periods, each with 20 days. Day and month names were used with numerals which were of 3 orders: 1. Glyphs 1-19, 2. Group symbols, 3. Normal count-bars and dots. Dots 1-4 bars-units of fives. These units were placed in groups. The first sign in such a group was *Kin* (1), the second was *Uinal* (20), the third—*Tun* (18 x 20), the fourth *Katun*—(18 x 20 x 20), and the fifth sign—*Baktun* or cycle equal to 20 *katun*. All numbers referred back to zero, at which time the world was created, according to Maya myth.

Mayance languages include at least 8 main dialects: Maya, Cholti, Pokonhi, Quiche, Mam, Tzeltal, Kekchi, Huastec.

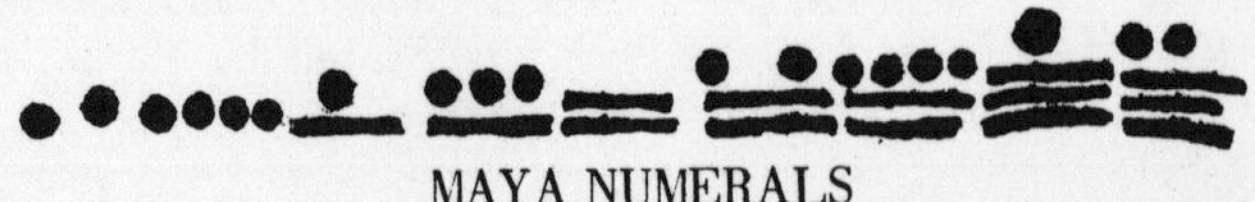

MAYA NUMERALS

MONTHS OF THE MAYA CALENDAR (LANDA).

DAYS OF THE MAYA CALENDAR (LANDA).

Smithsonian

AZTECAN

American Indian: Nahuatlan. The Aztecs or Nahuatl Indians of Anahuac founded the city *Tenochtitlan* (Mexico City) in the 14th century; they were the ruling nation in Mexico. The king of the Aztecs then was Montezuma II who was deposed by the Spaniards under Hernando Cortez (1519).

The consonants of the Aztecan language are pronounced about the same as in English, omitting, B, D, F, G, J, K, R, S, W. Other letters are pronounced about as in French. V is variously written U or HU, V. The letter O has about the same value as French EU. Consonants most frequently used are: L, T, X, Z, TL, TZ.

The Aztec calendar consisted of pictographs or ideographs, in which any fixed date could be established during any period of years. The year had 365 days or a short count of 260 days. The solar year was divided into 18 periods of 20 day-months with 5 additional days *(Nemontemi).* Each month or *Cempohualli* was divided into week periods. A period of 13 years was designated *Xiumalpilli.* Four years equalled one "sun year." Each period of 52 years of 2 cycles was called *Nexiuhilpilitzl* or binding of years.

The Aztec calendar stone, discovered in 1490, exhibits 20 figures arranged around central *Tonatiuh* and *Olin.* These surrounding figures are divided into 5 suns or ages: 1. *Oselotl,* 2. *Ehecatl,* 3. *Quiswitl,* 4. *Atl* which relate to the past and the last sun *Olin Tonatiuh* relating to the present or future, when according to Aztec myth the world will be destroyed by an earthquake.

AZTEC CALENDAR SIGNS

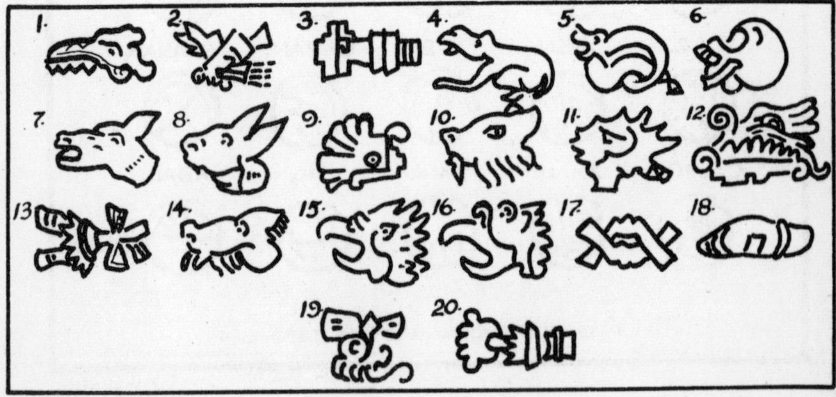

1-*Sikpatl* crocodile	11-*Ozomatl* monkey
2-*Ehekatl* wind	12-*Malanati* herb
3-*Kalli* house	13-*Akatl* reed
4-*Quetspalin* lizard	14-*Oselotl* jaguar
5-*Kohwatl* serpent	15-*Quahtli* eagle
6-*Mitstli* death	16-*Kozkaquahtli* vulture
7-*Mazatl* deer	17-*Olin* motion
8-*Rochtli* hare	18-*Tekpatl* stone
9-*Atl* water	19-*Quiswitl* rain
10-*Itsquiutl* dog	20-*Shotchitl* flower

Other Indian races of Mexico who had achieved a high state of culture before the coming of the Spaniards, were: Toltecs, Zapotecans, Chicemecas, Mextecas, Pipil tribes, Tecpanecs, Huicholes, Tlascalans, Otomis, etc.

CHEROKEE

Ꭰ	*a*	Ꭱ	*e*	Ꭲ	*i*	Ꭳ	*o*	Ꭴ	*u*	Ꭵ	*e̥*
Ꮖ	*gwa*	Ꮗ	*gwe*	Ꮘ	*gwi*	Ꮙ	*gwo*	Ꮚ	*gwu*	Ꮛ	*gwe̥*
Ꭽ	*ha*	Ꭾ	*he*	Ꭿ	*hi*	Ꮀ	*ho*	Ꮁ	*hu*	Ꮂ	*he̥*
Ꭷ	*ka*	-	-	-	-	-	-	-	-	-	-
Ꭶ	*ga*	Ꭸ	*ge*	Ꭹ	*gi*	Ꭺ	*go*	Ꭻ	*gu*	Ꭼ	*ge̥*
Ꮿ	*ya*	Ᏸ	*ye*	Ᏹ	*yi*	Ᏺ	*yo*	Ᏻ	*yu*	Ᏼ	*ye̥*
Ꮤ	*ta*	Ꮦ	*te*	Ꮨ	*ti*	-	-	-	-	-	-
Ꮣ	*da*	Ꮥ	*de*	Ꮧ	*di*	Ꮩ	*do*	Ꮪ	*du*	Ꮫ	*de̥*
Ꮎ	*na*	Ꮑ	*ne*	Ꮒ	*ni*	Ꮓ	*no*	Ꮔ	*nu*	Ꮕ	*ne̥*
Ꮜ	*sa*	Ꮞ	*se*	Ꮟ	*si*	Ꮠ	*so*	Ꮡ	*su*	Ꮢ	*se̥*
Ꮃ	*la*	Ꮄ	*le*	Ꮅ	*li*	Ꮆ	*lo*	Ꮇ	*lu*	Ꮈ	*le̥*
Ꮳ	*dsa*	Ꮴ	*dse*	Ꮵ	*dsi*	Ꮶ	*dso*	Ꮷ	*dsu*	Ꮸ	*dse̥*
Ꮭ	*tla*	-	-	-	-	-	-	-	-	-	-
Ꮬ	*dla*	Ꮮ	*dle*	Ꮯ	*dli*	Ꮰ	*dlo*	Ꮱ	*dlu*	Ꮲ	*dle̥*
Ꮉ	*ma*	Ꮊ	*me*	Ꮋ	*mi*	Ꮌ	*mo*	Ꮍ	*mu*	-	-
Ꮹ	*wa*	Ꮺ	*we*	Ꮻ	*wi*	Ꮼ	*wo*	Ꮽ	*wu*	Ꮾ	*we̥*
		Ꮏ	*hna*	Ꮐ	*nah*	Ꮝ	*s*				

North American Indian: Iroquoian. Southern. Cherokee characters. Cherokee is the only American Indian language in the United States with a syllabary invented by one of its own people—Sequoia or George Guess labored many years to devise an alphabet so that the Cherokee indians might be able to read and write their own language. The Cherokee syllabary consists of 86 symbols which renders all of the rounds of the language. It was invented about 1821. The Gospel of Saint Matthew in the Cherokee tongue and characters was published in New Echota, Georgia by S. A. Worcester in 1829. The Cherokee tribes lived in northern Georgia and North Carolina until the early part of the nineteenth century. The tribes were removed to the then Indian territory in 1838-9 and most of their descendants are now living in Oklahoma and other southwestern states.

IROQUOIS

Aseken ne Niio tsini sakohnoronk8ahon nonk8e, iah tatesakohnonhianiheki n'enskat ok ro8iraien, asakaon tosa aiahiheie tsini, iakon tiaka8etakon raonhake, ok eken tanon neh aiakoientake ne raonhake aietsenri atsennonniat.

Spoken by Indian tribes in Canada near Montreal.

ALGONQUIN

Ningota8asing8a saiakitosigok aking endagoni 8ak8ing daje okima8i8in o tibienndana8a.

Spoken by Indians in Quebec and Ontario.

CHOCTAW

Chihowa yvt yakni a̱ i̱ hullo fehna kvt, kvna hosh yvmma i̱ ymmikmvt ik illo hosh, amba ai okehayvt bilia yo pisa hi o̱. Ushi achvfa illa holitopa ya auet ima tok.

OJIBWA

Gaapij shauendy̱ sv Kishemanito iu aki ogionjimigiunenvn iniu baiezhigonijin Oguisvn aueguen dvsh getebueiienimaguen jibvnatizisig jiaiat dvsh iu kagige bimatiziuin.

Spoken by Indians near Lake Superior and Lake Huron in the United States and Canada.

MOHAWK

Iken ne Yehovah egh ne s'hakonoronghkwa n'ongwe, nene rodewendeghton nene raonhàon rodewedon rohhàwak, nene onghka kiok teyakaweghdaghkon raonhage yaghten a-onghtonde, ok denghnon aontehodiyendane ne eterna adonhèta.

Spoken by Indians in the Mohawk Valley in New York State and in Canada near eastern part of Lake Ontario.

DELAWARE

Nititechquo Getanittowit wtelgiqui ahowalap Pemhakamixit, wtelli miltinep nekti mehittachpit Quisall: wentschi wemi wulistawachtit mattatsch tawongellowiwak, schuk nachpauchsichtit hallemiwi Pommauchsowagan.

Spoken by Indians in Ohio along the Muskingum River.

NAVAHO

Hálah, God êi nihokā dineh t'ai'yisi ayoayo'nigo bańh Biye't'ała'i bayîżcîn'igiyenîłtńh, t'a-ħai-dah bodlan'igi ēi do á dodine dah ńidih hola'go inah hwê hodolėł.

SIOUX

Wakantanka oyate kin cantewicakiya, heon Cinhintku iśnana icage ein wicaqu, qa tuwe awacin kinhan owihankekte śni, tuka owihanke wanin wiconi yuhe kta.

Spoken by about 30,000 Indians in Minnesota, Dakota and Nebraska.

OTOMI

Matá ahe goguibyi àmahêtzi, dahnaen manhò ànimachâ thūthû, dabaêhe, amaxihè nuaningūnguepahà. Dadacha aninahnê nugua anximahay, teangūgadichá amahêtzi.

Spoken by about 350,000 Indians in Mexico.

ZAPOTEC

Pues de tanto gunàshihí Dios Guixhilayuh bìdh tubilucha Shînigana lessu cadi guinitiluh túh gacacreer lah; sino guibaní né Dios-para siempre.

Spoken by Indians in Southern Oaxaca, Mexico.

GUARANI

Oime Tûpâ Ñandeyára voi ojayjú tuvichaite gui umi ybypóra cuerape omeê Tayra peteî jaeñomívape. Icatu jaguâ opa oyerovidva guive Jesé anicheneocañŷ, ojupitýnte jaguâ pe Tecove ivapyraŷva.

Spoken by Indians in Paraguay and parts of Brazil and Argentina.

QUECHUA

Imaraicuchus Dios chai jinatapuni cai mundota munacurka c'ata Churinta korka tucuy jakai paipi creej ama huañanpaj, antes huiñay causayniyoj cananpaj.

Spoken by about 1,000,000 Indians in Bolivia.

AYMARA

Cunalaycutejga qhitisa Diosan manañapa lurijga, ucawa jilajgajga, cullacajgasa, raycajgasa.

Spoken by about 500,000 Indians around Lake Titicaca, Ecuador and in Bolivia.

CREE

		B	D,T	K	CH	L	M	N	R	S	Y
A	ᐊ	ᐸ	ᑕ	ᑲ	ᒐ	ᓚ	ᒪ	ᓇ	ᕋ	ᓴ	ᔭ
E	ᐁ	ᐯ	ᑌ	ᑫ	ᒉ	ᓓ	ᒣ	ᓀ	ᕃ	ᓭ	ᔦ
I	ᐃ	ᐱ	ᑎ	ᑭ	ᒋ	ᓕ	ᒥ	ᓂ	ᕆ	ᓯ	ᔨ
O	ᐅ	ᐳ	ᑐ	ᑯ	ᒍ	ᓗ	ᒧ	ᓄ	ᕈ	ᓱ	ᔪ

P	ᑊ	T	/	K	\	TS	—	CH	•	N	ↄ
M	c	S	∩	Y	+	R	z	W	o		

American Indian: Canadian and northwest tribes. The Cree character is employed in writing a number of the Indian tongues of Canada but with a few modifications and special characters for various tongues. Cree is spoken on the eastern shore of Hudson Bay, James Bay, near Lake Winnipeg and in lower Saskatchewan. Cree dialects are: Central, Eastern or Swampy Moose, and Western or Plains dialect. Slave is spoken along the Mackenzie River, Northwestern Canada, Ojibwa or Chippewa is spoken around Lake Superior and Lake Huron. Eskimo (Baffin dialect) is spoken around Hudson Bay and in Baffin Land, Ungava Bay in northern Quebec.

IDEOGRAPHS AND PICTOGRAPHS OF THE PLAINS INDIANS

IDEOGRAPHS AND PICTOGRAPHS OF THE PLAINS INDIANS

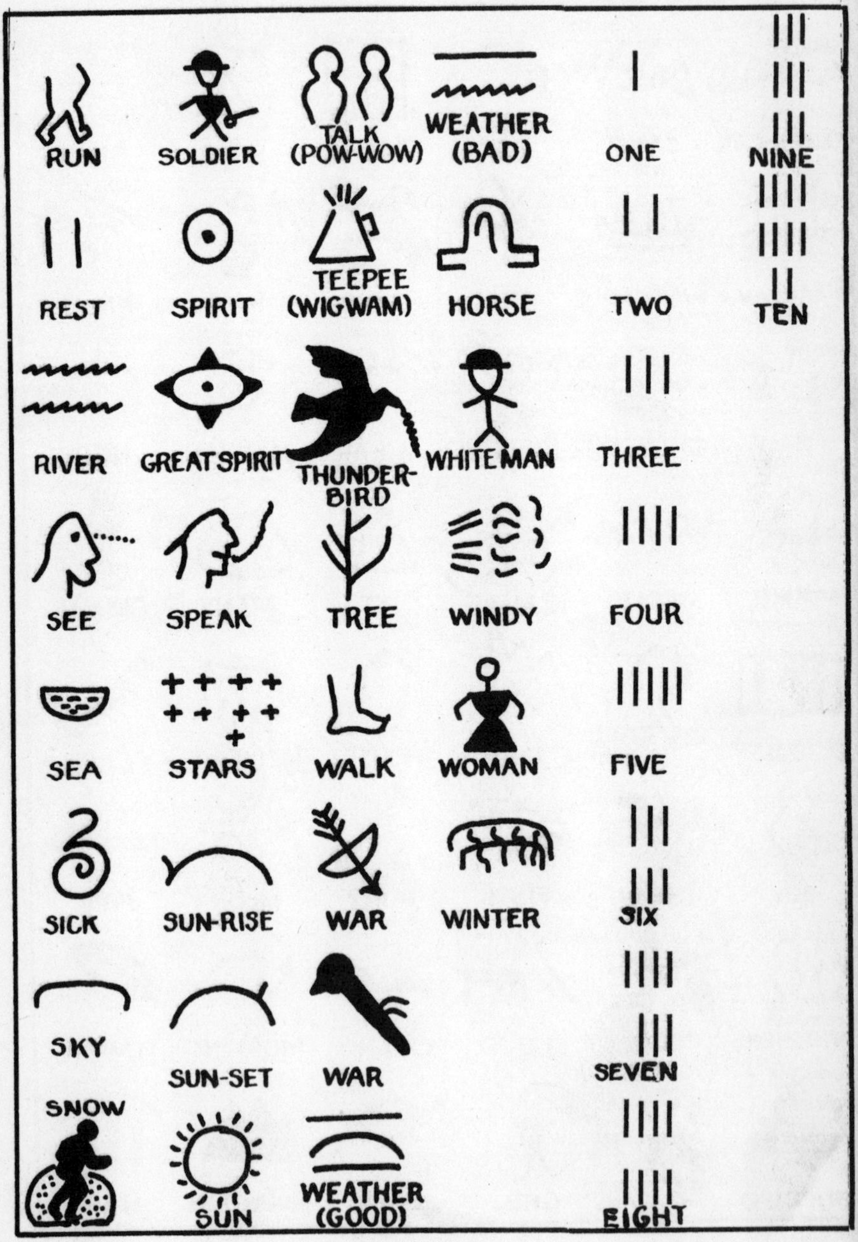

RUN SOLDIER TALK (POW-WOW) WEATHER (BAD) ONE NINE

REST SPIRIT TEEPEE (WIGWAM) HORSE TWO TEN

RIVER GREAT SPIRIT THUNDER-BIRD WHITE MAN THREE

SEE SPEAK TREE WINDY FOUR

SEA STARS WALK WOMAN FIVE

SICK SUN-RISE WAR WINTER SIX

SKY SUN-SET WAR SEVEN

SNOW SUN WEATHER (GOOD) EIGHT

Some American Indian Languages

Aguaruna	Peru
Algonquin	Quebec, Ontario
Arapahoe	Okla., Wyo., Montana
Arikara	North Dakota
Arawak	Brit. & Dutch Guiana
Aymara	Bolivia
Beaver	Peace River, Canada
Blackfoot	Alberta, Canada
Bororo	Matto Grosso, Brazil
Bribri	Costa Rica
Carib	Brit. Honduras
Cakchiquel	Guatemala
Cherokee	South U. S.
Cheyenne	Montana
Chinook	Alaska, Canada
Choctaw	So. U. S.
Chipewyan	N. W. Canada
Cree	Hudson Bay region
Dakota, Sioux	N. W., U. S.
Delaware	Ohio
Eskimo	Greenland, Aleutians
Guarani	Bolivia
Haida	British Columbia
Hidatsa	North Dakota
Hopi	Arizona
Iroquois	Canada
Kekchi	Guatemala
Keres	New Mexico
Kwagutl	Vancouver Isle
Maliseet	N.E. U.S. and Canada
Mam	Guatemala
Mandan	North Dakota
Mapudungu	Chile
Maya	Yucatan
Mexican or Aztec	Mexico
Micmac	N.E. Canada
Miskito	Nicaragua, Honduras
Mohawk	Northeast U. S.
Muskogee	S. W. U. S.
Navajo	Arizona, New Mexico
Nez Perces	Western U. S.
Nishga	Brit. Columbia
Ojibwa	Great Lakes region
Oneida	Wisconsin
Osage	Oklahoma
Otomi	Mexico
Ottawa	Kansas
Pottawotomi	Kansas
Quechua	Bolivia, Peru, Ecuador
Quiche	Guatemala
Seneca	New York
Shawnee	Oklahoma
Slave	Northwest Canada
Tukudh	Yukon
Tupi	Brazil
Winnebago	Western U. S.
Zapotec	Mexico

Variant Names of Languages

Abenaqui	Micmac
Acholi	Gang
Afghani	Pashto
Aleut	Eskimo
Aramaic	Chaldee
Araucanian	Mapudungu
Arctic	Eskimo
Astrakahn	Nogai Turkish
Aztec	Mexican
Bactrian	Zend
Bangala	Ngala
Batak	Batta
Benguella	Mbundu
Benguet	Igorot
Berber	Shilha
Bhojpuri	Bihari
Brezoneg	Breton
Carthaginian	Punic
Castilian	Spanish
Česky	Czech
Chippewa	Ojibwa
Creek	Muskogee
Cymraeg	Welsh
Czech	Bohemian
Damara	Herero
Dine	Navaho
Ebon	Marshall Islands
Enchorial	Demotic
Fanti	Ashanti
Folksmaal	Norwegian
Gabun	Fang
Gaura	Bengali
Ge'ez	Ethiopic
Gitano	Spanish Romany
Gruzinian	Georgian
Hai	Armenian
Hellenic	Greek
Hudson Bay	Eskimo
Illyrian	Serbian
Iranian	Persian
Kara	Falasha
Khoi-Khoi	Nama
Ki-Kongo	Kongo
Kingwana	Swahili
Kitchen Swahili	Shamba
Koine	Greek
Kuoyü	Chinese
Ladino	Judaeo-Spanish
Lao	Laos
Libyan	Nubian
Limosin	Catalan
Little Russian	Ukrainian
Luganda	Ganda
Magyar	Hungarian
Malabar	Tamil
Minoan	Cretan
Mohican	Massachusetts
Mon	Talaing
Mranma	Burmese
Multani	Lahnda
Ndadyu	Dyak
Ngonde	Konde
Oriya	Orissa
Panjabi	Sikh
Plattdeutsch	Low German
Pushto	Pashto
Riksmaal	Norwegian
Riffi	Shilha

Romansch	Rhaetic	Tai	Siamese
Rong	Lepcha	Thai	Siamese
Ruthenian	Ukrainian	Tamul	Tamil
		Telinga	Telugu
		Taureg	Tamachek
Sanis	Arikara		
Santee	Dakota	Urdu	Hindustani
Sechuana	Chuana		
Sheetswa	Tswa	Wallachian	Rumanian
Sikh	Panjabi		
Sioux	Dakota	Yiddish	Judaeo-German
Slave	Tinne	Yucatecan	Maya
Sorb	Wend		
Syriac	Syrian	Zanzibar	Swahili

Five Hundred Languages Written in the Roman Alphabet

Abor Miri
Accra
Acawoio
Addo
Adjukru
Agni
Aguaruna
Akunakuna
Aladian
ALBANIAN
Alfuor
Algonquin
Amele
Aneityum
Angas
Anglo-Saxon
Aniwa
Aranda
Arapahoe
Arawak
Arikara

Ashanti
Asu
Atche
Avikam
Aymara

Bachama
Bada
Bali
Bambatana
Bamum
Bankutu
Banu
Bare'e
Bari
Basa
Basque
Bassa
Baya
Beaver
Bemba

Bembe
Bena
Benga
Bentoeni
Bicol
Binandere
Bira
Blackfoot
Blas
Bobangi
Bobo
Bolaang Mongondo
Bolia
Bondei
Boran
Boroni
Bororo
Breton
Bribri
Bugotu
Bullum

Bulu
Bungili
Bura
Burum
Bwaidoga

Cakchiquel
Carib
Catalan
Cebuan
Chaga, Mochi
Chakma
Chamorro
Chawi
Chekiri
Cheyenne
Chikunda
Chin
Chinook
Choctaw
Chopi

Chippewayan
Chokwe
Chuana
Chungchia
Cornish
Creole
CZECH (Bohemian)

Dagbane
Dakkarkari
Dakota or Sioux
DANISH
Daui
Delaware
Dida
Dieri
Digo
Dimasa
Dinka
Dobu
Dioula
Duala
Duke of York Isle
DUTCH
–Afrikaans
Dyak
Dyerma

Efik
Ebrie
Egede
Eggon
Eleku
ENGLISH
Epi
Eromanga
Eskimo
Esperanto
ESTONIAN
Ewe

Falasha
Fang
Fanting
Faroese
Fernando Po
Fiji
FINNISH
FLEMISH
Florida Isle
Fon
Formosan
FRENCH
Frisian
Fula
Fuliro
Futuna

GAELIC
Galilla
Galla
Ganda
Gang or Acholi
Garhwali
Gbari
Gilbert Isles
Gimbunda
Giryama
Gisu or Masaba
Gogo
Grebo
Gu or Dahomey
Guadalcanar
Guarani

Habbe
Haida
Hanga
Hausa
Hawaiian
Haya
Herero
Heso
Hidatsa
Hmar
Ho
Hopi
Houailou
Hunde
Hungana
HUNGARIAN

Ibo
Ibanag
ICELANDIC
Ido
Idoma
Ifugao
Igabo
Igbira
Igala
Igorot
Ijo
Ikota
Ila
Ilocano
Iregwe
Iroquois
Isubu
ITALIAN

Jaba
Jatsi
Jita
Jolof
Jukun

Kabyle
Kachin
Kaguru
Kakwa
Kalana
Kamba
Kamberri
Kanakuru
Karamojong
Karanga
Karre
Kate
Keapara
Kekchi
Kele
Keres
Kimbundu
Kipsigis
Kikuyu
Kiriwina
Kisii Kenya
Kissi
Kituba
Kiwai
Kololo
Konde
Kongo
Konjo
Kono
Kpelle
Krongo
Kroo
Kuanyama
Kuba
Kunama
Kuranko
Kunini
Kusaien
Kwagutl
Kwese

Laewomba
Lakona
Lamba
Lapp
Latgalian
LATIN

Lega
Lendu
Lengua
Lenje
LETTISH
Lifu
Limba
LITHUANIAN
Livonian
Loda
Logo
Lomwe
Lualaba Ngwana
Luba
Luchazi
Lugbara
Luimbi
Lumbu
Lunda
Luo
Lur
Lushai
Lwena

Mabuiag
Madi
Maewo
Mafur
Mailu
Makua
Makushi
Malagasy
Malekula
Maliseet
Malo
Maltese
Malto
Malvi
Mam
Mamvu
Mambwe
Manda
Mandan
Manus Isle
Manx
Manyan
Maori
Mapudungu
Mare
Marovo
Marquesas
Marshall Isles
Masai
Masana
Masarete
Massachusetts
Mawken
Maya
Mbai
Mbum
Mbunda
Mbundu
Mende
Mbuti
Meninka
Mentawei
Mer
Meru
Mexican
Micmac
Mikir
Miskito
Mohawk
Mongo
Mongwande
More
Mori
Moro
Moru
Mortlock
Mota
Mpama
Mpoto
Mro
Mukawa
Munchi
Mundang
Muskogee
Mwala
Mwamba

Naga
Nama
Namau
Namwanga
Nandi
Napu
Narrinyeri
Nauru
Navaho
Ndandi
Ndau
Ndonga
New Britain
Ngala
Nez Perces
Ngambi
Ngandu
Ngbaka
Ngombe
Ngoni
Ngumba
Nguna
Nicobarese
Nias
Nishga
Nkole
Nobonob
Niule
Nkoya
NORWEGIAN
Nosu
Notu
Nsenga
Ntumba
Nubian
Nuer
Nuguor
Nupe
Nyamwezi
Nyanja
Nyemba
Nyika
Nyore
Nyoro
Nyungwi

Ogoni
Ojibwa
Omo
Omyene
Oneida
Ono
Opa
Ora
Orokolo
Osage
Oto
Otomi
Ottawa

Paama
Palityan
Pampangan
Panaieti
Panayan
Pangasinan
Patpatar
Pedi
Pende
Pero
Petats
Pokomo
POLISH

Ponerihouen
Popo
Ponape
PORTUGUESE
Poto
Pottawotomi

Quechua
Quiche

Raga
Ragetta
Ragoli
Rarotonga
Romansch
Romany-Gypsy
Ronga
Roro
Rotti
Rotuma
Roviana
Ruanda
Rukuba
Ruk or Truk
RUMANIAN
Rundi

Sakata
Salampasu
Samareño
San Cristoval
Samoan
Sangir
Sangos
Santa Cruz
Santo
Sarawak
Sebei Suk
Sena
Seneca
Sengele
Sengoi
Senji
SERBO-CROATIAN
Shamba
Shambala
Shanga
Shawnee
Silha
Shilluk
Shona
Sihong
SLOVAK
SLOVENIAN
Sobo
Soga
Sokotri
Somali
Songo
Songoi
SPANISH
Suk
Sukuma
Sundanese
Sura
Susu
Suto
Swahili
SWEDISH

Tabaru
Tae
Tabele
Tagalog
Tahitian
Taita
Tangale
Tanna
Tavara
Taveta
Teke
Tera
Teso
Tetela
Tharaka
Thonga
Toaripi
Toba
Tobelor
Tombulu
Tonga
Torres Isles
Tsamba
Tswa
Tubetube
Tukudh
Tula
Tumbuka
Tupi
Turkish, Modern

Ubir
Udin
Ulawa
Umon
Uvea

Valiente
Vejoz
Vella Lavella
Venda
Volapük

Waja
Warau
Wedau
WELSH
Windessi
Winnebago
Wiza
Wiza-Lala
Wongo
Worrora
Wurkum

Xosa

Yabim
Yahgan
Yaka
Yalunka
Yao
Yaunde
Yergum
Yoruba

Zande
Zapotec
Zia
Zigula
Zimshian
Zinza
Zulu

Index of Characters in which the Languages of the World Are Written

Abyssinian
Allahabad
Anglo-Saxon
Anaichi
Annamite
Arabic
–Neskhi
–Cufic
–Karmathic
–Mogreb
–Carshuni
–Saracenic
–Mauretanian
–Rika'a
–Ta'alik
–Diwanny
–Sulus
–Aljemi
Aramaic
Armenian
Assamese
Aztec

Balbodh
Balinese
Balti
Bamum
Banya
Barmani
Batta
Bengali
Berber
Brahmi
Boromat
Bugis
Burmese
Buthakükye

Cambodian
Chaldee
Chandra Gupta
Cherokee
Chinese
–Kai Shu
–Hsing Shu
–Tsao Shu
–Li Shu
–Ta Chuan
–Hsiao Chuan
–Chu Yin
–Wang Chow
Coptic
Cree
Cretan or Minoan
Cypriotic
Cyrillic
Cuneiform
–Sumerian
–Babylonian
–Assyrian
–New Babylonian
–Persian
–Mede

Demotic
Devanagari
Dogri

Elbassan
En Mun
Erse or Irish
Eskimo
Estrangelo
Ethiopic
Etruscan

Georgian
–Khutsuri
–Mkhedruli
Glagolitic
–Bulgarian
–Illyrian
Gothic
German Gothic
Grantha
Greek
–Archaic
–Classical
Gupta
Gujarati
Gurmukhi

Haurantic
Hebrew
Hentaigana
Hieratic
Hieroglyphics (Egypt)
Hiragana
Himyaritic
Hittite

Iyo

Jacobite
Jaunsari
Javanese
–Kawi
–Aksara
Japanese
–Mincho
–Kaisho
–Gyōsho
–Sōsho
–Katakana
–Hiragana
–Reisho
–Tensho
–Inban
–Kanbun
–Kana Majiri
Jirnar
Jou-Chen

Kaithi
Kanarese
Kharosthi
Khudawadi
Khutsuri
Kistna
Kutila

Lampung
Landa
Laos
Laotian
Lepcha
Libyan or Nubian
Lo-Lo

Maghada
Malayalam
Manchu
Mandaic
Manipuri
Manyōgana
Mayan
Mende
Miao-Tse
Minoan or Cretan
Mkhedruli

Modi
Moeso-Gothic
Mohajun
Mongolian
Moritsune
Multani

Nerbadda
Nestorian
Nsibidi
Niu-Chih
Numidian

Ojibwa
Oriya or Orissa
Oscan

Pali
Palmyrenian
Passepa
Peguan or Mon
Pehlevi
Peshito
Persian
Photimakkha
Phoenician
Phrygian

Quôc-Ngū

Rabbinical
Rejang
Roman
Runes
–Gothic
–Anglo-Saxon
–Markomanian
–Bardic
–Ogam
–Northern
Russian
Ruthenian

Samaritan
Sarada
Shan
Siamese
Siddhamatrka
Sinaitic Scripts
Sinhalese
Slave
Slavonic
Soghida
Surafa

Tagalog
Tai Lu
Tamil
Tankri
Tatar
Telugu
Thamudic
Tibetan
Tifinagh
Tinne
Tocharian

Uigurish

Vai or Vei
Veso Bei
Visayan

Yamato Kana
Yao
Yunnanese Shan

Zend

Index of Languages and Dialects

(Excepting English Dialects)

Note: Several dialects and vernaculars, particularly of the languages of India, are referred to languages such as Marathi, Hindi, etc., but are not mentioned in text because of uncertainty, interdialectical peculiarities and the vast complexity of the languages of India.

How Spanish Grew
Robert K Spalding 1962
Universit of Calif. Press, Berkly